"Professor Marienberg here offers us his deep gaze into the religiously ╌╌╌╌╌ lyrics of one of the world's most literate rock stars. It is a rich and rewarding *tour de force* that casts a fascinating light on Sting himself, as well as giving appropriate consideration to him as a modern metaphysical poet. More than this it moves into the formative context of his life and goes on to shine its searchlight on a lost age, telling how a blue-collar largely Irish immigrant church worked out an agenda of lifting up its cleverest folk into positions of leadership in wider post War society. A splendid achievement."

—JOHN A. MCGUCKIN
University of Oxford; author of *The Orthodox Church: An Introduction
to Its History, Doctrine, and Spiritual Culture*

"Marienberg compellingly demonstrates the enduring centrality of Christian theological concepts pivoting on sin, salvation, (sacred) love, spiritual longing, and celestial beings within the artistic output of (lapsed) English Catholic Sting. Those interested in Catholic Studies will find within a case study of prayer, parochial life, and the power of the 'Catholic imagination' before and after Vatican II and the profound religious transformations which have occurred in the Anglo-American cultural scene since the 1960s."

—ALANA HARRIS
King's College London; author of *Faith in the Family: A Lived Religious History
of English Catholicism, 1945–1982*

"Based on detailed historical research and an extended interview with Sting himself, this book offers new understandings into how the Catholicism of Sting's youth fueled his creativity. Marienberg offers a fascinating analysis of how the juxtaposition of Christian Scripture and Sting's problematic relationship with the religiosity of his upbringing are embedded in his songwriting, offering the reader detailed insights into his worldview on not only Christianity, but also spirituality and religion more broadly. A must-read for Sting fans interested in understanding the underpinning creative impulses of this iconic artist and how his past continues to shape his future."

—PAUL CARR
University of South Wales; author of *Sting: From Northern Skies to Fields of Gold*

STING AND RELIGION

STING AND RELIGION

The Catholic-Shaped Imagination of a Rock Icon

EVYATAR MARIENBERG

CASCADE *Books* • Eugene, Oregon

STING AND RELIGION
The Catholic-Shaped Imagination of a Rock Icon

Cascade Books
An Imprint of Wipf and Stock Publishers
199 W. 8th Ave., Suite 3
Eugene, OR 97401

www.wipfandstock.com

PAPERBACK ISBN: 978-1-7252-7226-2
HARDCOVER ISBN: 978-1-7252-7225-5
EBOOK ISBN: 978-1-7252-7227-9

Cataloguing-in-Publication data:

Names: Marienberg, Evyatar, author.
Title: Sting and religion : the Catholic-shaped imagination of a rock icon / Evyatar Marienberg.
Description: Eugene, OR: Cascade Books, 2021 | Includes bibliographical references.
Identifiers: ISBN 978-1-7252-7226-2 (paperback) | ISBN 978-1-7252-7225-5 (hardcover) | ISBN 978-1-7252-7227-9 (ebook)
Subjects: LCSH: Sting (Musician) | Popular music—Religion | Rock music—Religion | Rock musicians—England—Biography | Christianity and culture | Popular culture—Religious aspects—Catholic church | Catholic Church—England—History—20th century | Catholics—England—Social conditions—20th century
Classification: ML3921.8 M37 2021 (print) | ML3921.8 (ebook)

JANUARY 8, 2021

On the cover: Sting by Brian Aris (copyright www.brianaris.com, used with permission), Montserrat, 1987.

For Arthur and Lenny, my very own rock stars.

CONTENTS

Introduction

I'VE BEEN THINKING
'BOUT RELIGION

I've been thinking 'bout religion
I've been thinking 'bout the things that we believe
I've been thinking 'bout the Bible
I've been thinking 'bout Adam and Eve
I've been thinking 'bout the garden
I've been thinking 'bout the tree of knowledge, and the tree of life
I've been thinking 'bout forbidden fruit
I've been thinking 'bout a man and his wife
I been thinking 'bout, thinking 'bout
Sacred love, sacred love.[1]

You don't need to read no books on my history
I'm a simple man, it's no big mystery.[2]

---

1. "Sacred Love" (2003). Unless otherwise noted, all references using the format "Name" (year) are titles of Sting's (or Last Exit's/The Police's) songs. All references using the format *Name* (year) are titles of Sting's (or The Police's) albums. The lyrics of Sting's songs are available online through multiple sources, including at his official site, http://www.sting.com. They are quoted in this book with permission.
2. "Nothing 'Bout Me" (1993).

> My given name was Gordon, I was born Gordon. . . . When I was eighteen, I was in a band with much older people than myself, and I used to wear a black-and-yellow sweater. I looked like a bee, or a wasp. And then the trombone player on the band said, "We're going to call you Sting." And I thought that was a really ridiculous name, and of course it is, but the name stuck with me, and I have had it for most of my life, and you get used to it.[3]

Many artists use religious references, whether sayings, images, sounds, stories, or cultural motifs, in their work. In many cases, encounters with religious cultures are easily discernible in the biographies of these artists. This book is based on several assumptions, which are likely to be shared by many readers. That, on the one hand, there is a relationship between these artists' exposure to religious ideas and their use of them in their art, and, on the other hand, that it is often impossible to draw the direct line that connects an artist's exposure to a motif and its use later in art. Humans, religions, and art are simply too complicated. Nevertheless, this book assumes that studying in great detail both the religious culture surrounding an artist, with a special emphasis on the religious culture she or he was exposed to during childhood, and the religious motifs in that artist's work, can be enriching and enlightening, and can help us to understand both the artist's background (and that of countless others who have a similar background) and the artist's output. This book suggests one possible model for doing this. It is hoped that this model will offer others a way in which to think about the correlation between religion in biography and religion in art, as well as a possible structure that might be useful for the study of other artists and their art. The artist studied in this book is the musician Sting.

Sting, christened as Gordon Matthew Sumner, is arguably one of the most successful and respected rock writers-composers-performers active today.[4] He insists that he is first a singer:

> If I couldn't sing, I wouldn't be a songwriter. I'm a singer. I'm a singer. It all comes from having a voice. . . . My job is a singer.[5]

---

3. Sting explaining on December 2014 the origin of his "unusual name" to a six-year-old boy, Iain Armitage: http://links.stingandreligion.com/ia14.

4. In this book, I will generally use the names "Gordon" or "Sumner" when referring to Sting as a child, before he adopted his famous nickname, and "Sting" when referring to him as an adult.

5. Sting, interview by Charlie Rose, 8:40.

And yet, except for a few unique and noteworthy cases, he sings almost only his own, often complex, texts. Therefore, he is also very much a song-writer—something he says he has been doing since he was seven years old.[6]

As of now (2020), he has released thirteen solo studio albums, six solo live albums, and many compilations.[7] These do not include the five studio albums and two live albums of The Police—the band that he was a part of from 1977 to 1984—nor the demo cassette he recorded with his first band, Last Exit, in 1975. He has also had roles in many films and theatrical pro-ductions, written a best-selling memoir,[8] cooperated with other artists on various albums, and composed the music and lyrics for a musical. Unsur-prisingly, he has been honored with some of the most prestigious awards in the fields of performing arts, including many Grammy Awards (seventeen at the time of writing), the Kennedy Center Honor in 2014, and the Polar Music Prize in 2017. Earlier, in 2003, Queen Elizabeth II awarded him the title of "Commander of the Most Excellent Order of the British Empire" (CBE).

Sumner was born in 1951 and grew up in Wallsend, a small town near Newcastle upon Tyne, in North East England. In generational terms, he is a "baby-boomer": one of those born during the great increase in the birth-rate that followed the end of the Second World War. He studied in Catholic schools, had his first communion and confession when he was seven, and received the sacrament of confirmation at the age of fourteen. His first mar-riage, at the age of twenty-five, was also celebrated in a Catholic church.

He was born into a church ruled by Pope Pius XII. It was a church in which a mix of old conservatism and new ideas was boiling. When Gordon had his first communion in 1959, the pope was already John XXIII, a rather progressive pope, a very different figure from his predecessor. Gordon was a teenager when the drama of the Second Council of the Vatican was taking place. He had been confirmed in 1965 when the council's participants were preparing for its final session. The council's output (and some would add, "spirit") was having more and more of an impact on Catholic life during his last years in grammar school. Those who supported changes, the "pro-gressives," felt they were in control, while the "conservatives" were on the defensive. In 1968, however, one year before his graduation from grammar school, the church was shaken again by the publication of Pope Paul VI's encyclical *Humanae Vitae*, which prohibited the use of most contraceptive

---

6. Sting, interview by Charlie Rose, 11:10.

7. I do not include one of his most recent albums, *44/876*, as a "solo album," simply because it was done with another singer, Shaggy. If added, the number of Sting's "solo" albums at the time of this book's writing is fourteen.

8. Sting, *Broken Music*.

methods. If the council and the changes following it were traumatic for many conservatives in the church, *Humane Vitae* left the liberals dumbstruck. Sumner was still in school when the voices for and against the pope's position were roaring and when the image of the popes, as infallible authorities, began to crack in the eyes of many. When decades later he said in one of his songs that "A Pope claimed that he'd been wrong in the past; This was a big surprise,"[9] he expressed well the shaky ground on which Catholics walked in recent decades.

Sting no longer considers himself a Catholic. Is he a "lapsed Catholic"? An "ex-Catholic"? A "cultural Catholic"? It is hard to decide, and I preferred when speaking to him to refrain from asking whether he believes any of these (or other) terms is appropriate for him. Yet, as should be apparent to any person who pays attention to his lyrics, the importance of religion in general—and of the Bible and Catholicism in particular—is evident in his songs. Thus, in this book, Sting's texts—and not so much his music or style of performance—are among the primary sources for understanding his thoughts about the Bible, Catholicism, and religion in general. Materials taken from about twenty semi-structured interviews of, among others, people from his town and parish of origin, several of whom were his classmates and who are still in touch with him,[10] and other sources, such as documents found in local archives, newspaper articles, books popular during his childhood, interviews with him (including a lengthy meeting I had with him), and scholarly studies were used as well.

Religious topics are probably not the most central subjects of Sting's work (love and passions are arguably more central), but they are nonetheless extremely common. Religious feelings appear in one of his very first recorded songs, "O My God" (1975): "Everyone I know is lonely, and God's so far away; and my heart belongs to no one, so now sometimes I pray." Religious texts and practices have appeared in almost every album since then. Even though he left Catholicism a long time ago, Catholic concepts and ideas have never left him. He is not unique in this. Speaking about George Harrison and Bob Dylan, Michael Gilmour says the following:

> The decision of many to leave organized religion during the 1960s does not indicate a corresponding decrease in meaningful spirituality or engagement with religious questions and texts. Harrison and Dylan and a host of others present rich, insightful,

---

9. "Jeremiah Blues (Part 1)" (1991).

10. IRB Exemption #14–1638, issued by The University of North Carolina at Chapel Hill's Office of Human Research Ethics (July 14, 2014).

often humorous, often critical, often ironic dialogues with religious subjects in their music.[11]

At the same time, Gilmour continues, one should not expect a coherent religious worldview in the lyrics of artists who left behind, at least partially, their religious backgrounds:

> Whereas a great deal of discussion about religious questions—in religious studies departments, theological writings, houses of worship, creeds—strives toward a measure of consistency and clear definition, much of the music we hear is comfortable with ambiguity, paradox, and mystery.

Three chapters in this book mostly comprise of analysis of lyrics. Some might think such texts do not deserve serious attention. Obviously I disagree. In 2016, the Swedish Academy disagreed as well with those who treat popular song lyrics lightly, and awarded Bob Dylan (b. 1941), admired by Sting himself,[12] the Nobel Prize for Literature. Dylan, in his banquet speech of December 10, 2016, read out by the American ambassador to Sweden, Azita Raji, referred to the question whether lyrics are literature worthy of investigation:

> I was out on the road when I received this surprising news, and it took me more than a few minutes to properly process it. I began to think about William Shakespeare, the great literary figure. I would reckon he thought of himself as a dramatist. The thought that he was writing literature couldn't have entered his head. His words were written for the stage. Meant to be spoken not read. When he was writing Hamlet, I'm sure he was thinking about a lot of different things: "Who're the right actors for these roles?" "How should this be staged?" "Do I really want to set this in Denmark?" His creative vision and ambitions were no doubt at the forefront of his mind, but there were also more mundane matters to consider and deal with. "Is the financing in place?" "Are there enough good seats for my patrons?" "Where am I going to get a human skull?" I would bet that the farthest thing from Shakespeare's mind was the question "Is this literature?" . . . Not once have I ever had the time to ask myself, "Are my songs *literature*?" So, I do thank the Swedish Academy, both for

---

11. Gilmour, *Gods and Guitars*, xiii.

12. In some places Sting compares Dylan to Shakespeare, a compliment that in Sting's world cannot be surpassed. See for example in Sting, *All This Time CD-ROM*, at https://links.stingandreligion.com/cdr9.

taking the time to consider that very question, and, ultimately, for providing such a wonderful answer.[13]

These three chapters are intercut by two others which deal with the "micro-history" of the religious aspects of roughly the first two decades of our subject's life. The advantages and disadvantages of a microhistory are rather clear. On the one hand, a microhistory that is done carefully can be fascinating: it often exposes us to a more "intimate," "human" level of the story. On the other hand, a microhistory can also lead readers to assume that the perspectives or experiences of the person or community studied are representative of the larger community/place/time, even when this is not the case. The many interviews mentioned above were extremely beneficial for these "micro-history" sections. At the same time, they introduced problems specific to oral history, mostly regarding memory, the retelling of narratives, and the choices of the interviewees on what to speak about, things that the interviewer cannot always predict or control. Such information is, by its very nature, influenced by the fact that it is told many decades after the relevant events, by people who have experienced much since. It was also probably influenced by the fact that it was told to a foreigner: a younger, non-English, non-Catholic, non-local person. Interestingly, it is possible that my foreignness was an advantage, as the interviewees knew that they cannot assume prior knowledge (even if, certainly in the advanced stages of the research, I already had much knowledge on that matter), and thus felt the need to tell their memories in a clear and detailed way. In many cases I believe I was able to deal with the problems inherent to oral histories by comparing the accounts to written materials, by conducting some of the interviews in groups (thus allowing people to correct one another or to show a variety of remembered experiences), and by including various testimonies on similar topics. Still, as with any oral history, one should remember the advantages of the genre as well as its limitations.

Some of the other problems with microhistory are related to written sources: some aspects of daily life, or in this case, of ecclesiastical life, are better documented than others. Thus the choice of topics discussed, and the length of the discussions, are often influenced by the availability of documents, no less than by the intention and interests of the researcher.

For fans of Sting, this book is about him. Other readers who are mostly interested in religious or Catholic studies, however, can read it in an entirely different way. For them, it is not only about Sting, but about the hundreds of thousands of children who grew up in English Catholic families in the

---

13. Banquet speech by Bob Dylan, Stockholm, December 10, 2016. Copyright the Nobel Foundation, 2016. See https://links.stingandreligion.com/dyln.

1950s, and who benefitted from what was then considered a good education. There might also be readers who are interested in the way Catholicism and art intersect. For them, this book is much about the "Catholic Imagination," a term that possibly became most popular with the publication of one of the books of the late sociologist and priest Andrew Greeley (1928–2013), *The Catholic Imagination*, of 2000. Greely's book "attempt(s) to demonstrate the power of the Catholic imagination, even for Catholics who may have officially left the church—what we might call 'cultural Catholics,'" something that I will attempt as well here. In contrast, however, to Greeley's book, here I am not interested in how, to quote Greeley, "Catholic high culture continues to influence Catholic popular culture and artists who are not known for their explicit piety," but rather in how a relatively mundane, low-to-middle-class Catholic upbringing, not one that necessarily exposes children to "Catholic high culture," may have an impact on the later life of children raised in such an environment.[14] At the same time, like Greeley, "my effort is to explain to Catholics and others how these experiences, images, rituals, and stories so tenaciously cling to Catholics and bind most of them to their heritage regardless of how far away from the church they may move."[15] This can be true with regard to millions of not-so-famous people with a Catholic upbringing, as well as to countless major artists who were raised Catholic, people as varied as Salvador Dalí (1904–89), Graham Greene (1904–91), Andy Warhol (1927–87), Martin Scorsese (b. 1942), Bruce Springsteen (b. 1949), Madonna (b. 1958), or Lady Gaga (b. 1986).[16]

Does Sting's music not only express, among many other things, his thoughts about religion and the divine, but also influence his audience's thinking about these subjects? Greeley says in another place, with regard to Bruce Springsteen, that "Troubadours always have more impact than theologians or bishops, storytellers more influence than homilists."[17] I have no opinion on the matter.

Parts of my work on Sting and religion were previously published in three articles;[18] they are reused here with permission. This project could

14. Greeley, *The Catholic Imagination*, 10.

15. Greeley, *The Catholic Imagination*, 19.

16. When Bruce Springsteen received the Kennedy Award in 2009, Sting was among those playing in his honor. When Sting received the same award in 2014, Springsteen and Lady Gaga did the same for him. All songs played by the three had significant Catholic imagery, and I believe the Catholic connection played a part in those invitations to play. See https://links.stingandreligion.com/ken1, https://links.stingandreligion.com/ken2, https://links.stingandreligion.com/ken3.

17. Greeley, "The Catholic Imagination of Bruce Springsteen."

18. Marienberg, "Death, Resurrection," 167–85; Marienberg, "Bible, Religion,"

not have been completed without help from people whom I met and interviewed, and from those who helped in different other ways. Among them I would like to particularly mention Maurice Aherne, Yaakov Ariel, Barbara Ambros, Brian Aris (who very kindly allowed me to use his magnificent photo of Sting for the cover), Leonora Bergsjø, Ray Bruce, Steve Butler, Tracey Cave, Stewart Copeland, Ian Creeger, Alex Croom, Luke Drake, Malcolm Dunn, Tony Durkin, Bart Ehrman, Ian Ferguson, Steven Fine, Colin and Margaret Finlay (who generously hosted me twice at their home in Wallsend), Gad Freudenthal, Julie Galetar, Leo Gooch, Mark Hearn, Michael Heatherington, Michael Huscroft, Ken Hutchinson, Lawrence Kaplan, Paul Kennedy, Marc Larin, Margaret Lavery, Diane Leggett, Cary Levine, Thomas Long, Hugo Lundhaug, John McGuckin, Ethan McQuinn, Shari Molstad, Domenica Newell-Amato, Robin Parry, Zlatko Pleše, Marie Rice, Marraine and Roy Rix, Lena Roos, Kees van der Steege, Randall Styers, Mike Surber, Amanda Sweet, Nicole van Giesen, Bob Watson, the staff at the Tyne & Wear Archives in Newcastle, the staff at North Shields Library, the staff at the archive of the Catholic Diocese of Hexham and Newcastle, and others. Father Anthony Donaghue, the priest of Our Lady & St Columba's parish in Wallsend since 2003, was very helpful and kind, helping me getting much needed information. Sadly, he passed away in September of 2017, some months before the completion of a first draft of this book. I will remember him with fondness. Peter Kaufman encouraged me to take upon me this project: the book would not have existed without his help and support. My own Department of Religious Studies at the University of North Carolina at Chapel Hill generously assisted covering the costs of some of the expenses related to this project. Sting was kind enough to read and comment on drafts of most chapters, as well as to provide information that I had no other way of getting. We also met for more than two hours in Germany in July of 2017 and talked, among many other things, about religion in his life in the past and present. I am extremely grateful for this unique opportunity that he gave me. It should be noted that his involvement did not, in my opinion, have any impact on the academic, and hopefully relatively objective nature of this book. His memories of events from his childhood were always compared, if possible, to recollections from his peers, and many of his other statements are valuable to this study, which in any case, as any reader would see, does not try to either glorify or denigrate him, but rather to understand his background and thinking. Like many artists, he did not, other than in exceptional cases, comment on my interpretations of his work. Of course, I bear sole responsibility for the final shape of this project.

319–35; Marienberg, "O My God," 223–35.

Writing a book about the religious history surrounding Sting is a betrayal of one of the first songs of his that I knew and learned by heart as a teenager: "History Will Teach Us Nothing."[19] Despite his warning, I became a historian, and here I try to explicitly make his own history teach us something. I hope he will forgive me that one.

* * * *

The book is accompanied by a website: http://www.stingandreligion.com. Beyond providing links to online sources, this website includes additional sections discussing various related topics that were not included here, and may include possible updates in the future. Some material on the website is protected by a password, and is accessible using the access code "1951."

When texts quoted in this book were written in British English, I kept the original spelling and vocabulary. Biblical texts are generally quoted following the "Jerusalem Bible" (JB), an English translation of the Bible commonly used by British Catholics.

Real names of people interviewed, other than in the case of Sting and a few other rare exceptions, were replaced with a coded system, created by the author, of two or three letters. The code "A.N." followed by a number refers to interlocutors whose identity I was unable to discern while listening to the recordings. This pertains especially to cases in which the interviews were of a group of people. The information provided in the format RECXX:YYY refers to the interview recording number (XX), and the minute since its beginning, during which the quote appears (YYY). These recording are kept by the author. The two-and-a-half-hour interview with Sting that is often quoted throughout the book was fully transcribed by the author, and this transcription was meticulously read and confirmed by Sting.

During the research for this book I consulted various private, public, and ecclesiastical archives. Because some of the documents discovered are of possible value as collector's items and would be at risk of being stolen if their location were revealed, I decided in some rare cases to not provide this information, but to provide instead a coded reference in the format of "Archival material, XXX." Scholars who would like to consult these documents are welcome to contact me.

HND stands for the archive of Hexham & Newcastle Diocese; TWA stands for Tyne & Wear Archives.

19. "History Will Teach Us Nothing" (1987).

Chapter 1

THE BIBLE IN STING'S WORK

We were taught the Old Testament, and it was a resource
for my songwriting, for stories. I love those stories.[1]

DOES STING USE THE Bible in his work, and if he does, how? The Christian
Bible (and to simplify, we will imagine there is one type of "Christian Bible"
and not more) consists, as many know, of two main parts: The Old Testament and the New Testament. The Old Testament is a collection of texts, or
may better be said to be a library of books, which were originally written
almost entirely in Hebrew, between more or less the eighth and the second
centuries BCE. Almost all of them are included in the Jewish Bible (known
in English also as the "Hebrew Bible"). They cover the period from the creation of the world (according to the biblical view) around the fourth millennium BCE, to the second century BCE. The New Testament is a library
of books that were originally written in Greek, between the middle of the
first century CE to the middle of the second century CE. They concern the
life and ministry of Jesus of Nazareth (b. circa 4 BCE) and the early history
of the faith that developed in the generations that followed him. For Jews,
of course, they are of no importance, have no sacred status, and are not part
of the Bible. For Catholics, seven additional books, all by Jewish authors but
not defined in the Jewish tradition as part of the Holy Scriptures, are also
considered part of the Old Testament, along with a few additional chapters
in other books.

1. Sting, interview by author, July 23, 2017, Künzelsau, REC22:043.

If for Christians both parts of the Bible are of importance, in practice the books of the New Testament, as texts considered in many ways as the keys to the understanding of the Old Testament, are often better known and more often referred to.

Sting, as we will soon see, is fond of both parts. The use of biblical motifs in his lyrics is evident already in the very first recordings of his work that we have, with Last Exit, a band that formed in Newcastle in 1974, and included also Ronnie Pearson (on drums), John Hedley and later Terry Ellis (on guitar), and Gerry Richardson (on keyboard). The group's name came from the title of a controversial book from a decade earlier, *The Last Exit to Brooklyn*, which described in harsh and (according to some) vulgar terms the plight of the working-class in Brooklyn in the 1950s. It is likely that the members of the new group were able to identify with the world described in this literary piece, even though their working-class childhood happened in England, not in the United States. Last Exit was mostly playing "gigs" in clubs of various kinds, and its repertoire was mainly made of cover versions of known pieces. Unlike many groups, it also played original material, thus providing Sting and the others in the group with the possibility of playing and singing their own original creations.[2]

In some of the songs of Last Exit written by Sting (but not included in the group's only official recording, a cassette from 1975), one finds references that only a person with a knowledge of the New Testament can write or understand. Thus, for example, the phrase "though my flesh is willing, my spirit is weak," in the song "Don't You Look at Me" is an obvious play on an expression attributed to Jesus in Matthew 26:41, where he warns his disciples that in their case, "The spirit is willing, but the flesh is weak."[3]

In Last Exit's cassette of 1975 there are two songs, both written by Sting, with strong religious references. In "Carrion Prince" (referred to in some places as "Carrion Prince [O Ye of Little Faith]" or "...of Little Hope"), the song addresses one of the most (in)famous figures of the New Testament, the Roman prefect Pontius Pilate, who sentenced Jesus to death.

Shortly after Jesus allegedly declares that the spirit of his disciples is willing but that their flesh is weak, he is brought to Pilate. Pilate asks him if he is "the king of the Jews," and Jesus gives his famous and somewhat cryptic answer: "It is you who say it."[4] We are told that the crowd wanted Jesus

---

2. According to Paul Carr, Sting recorded twenty-nine songs with Last Exit; he wrote fifteen of them. See Carr, *Sting*, 58 and 83.

3. See also the words "My flesh was all too willing, my spirit guide was weak" in Sting's song "Saint Augustine in Hell" (1993).

4. Matthew 27:11; Mark 15:2; Luke 23:3. The quotations used here are from Matthew 27 (JB).

crucified, but Pilate was not able to find a crime justifying such a verdict. Jesus kept silent. Finally, "When Pilate saw that he was getting nowhere" in his discussion with those Jews who wanted Jesus's execution,

> but that instead an uproar was starting, he took water and washed his hands in front of the crowd. "I am innocent of this man's blood," he said. "It is your responsibility!"[5]

Like Jesus, Pilate was unquestionably a historical figure. What each of them actually did, or did not do, say, or did not say, we do not know with any certainty. In the Christian tradition, Pilate became a complex figure. Some saw him as responsible for the death of the Son of God; some saw him as a weak person forced by others to do evil. Others yet considered him a hypocrite: a powerful person who sent someone to his death even though he could have avoided it, yet pretending that this was done against his will. There were also those who saw him as a sinner who repented and became (together with his wife, often named "Claudia" or "Procula") a good Christian: this is the case in some noncanonical Christian writings; this tradition is particularly known in some Orthodox churches.

In reality, it is likely that the story of Pilate's handwashing is a rather clumsy attempt—invented several decades later and included in the Gospel according to Matthew—to partially absolve the Roman authorities (whom, by that time, early Christians needed on their side) from the guilt of the act, and to blame it on Jews (who, by that time, were probably mostly opposing the new group).[6] Sting addresses Pilate directly in "Carrion Prince," possibly in the person of Jesus himself:

> Oh Pilate, you speak to me so clear; Your voice of hell has filled my soul with fear; O ye of little blood; Your cloak lies [?][7] in the mud; Your hands are always washing them.

If these words are indeed supposed to be Jesus's, Sting provides a different understanding of the events compared to the traditional one. Hence, if Jesus's silence is traditionally seen as a sign of his superiority, self-assurance, and acceptance of his fate, Sting sees this behavior as a product of terror. The title of the song possibly refers to Pilate as a "prince" in charge of a dead body (of Jesus), and is perhaps inspired by the poem "King of Carrion"

5. Matthew 27:24.

6. On the various ways this is done in the New Testament, see Bond, *Pontius Pilate*. Bond's discussion on the verses from Matthew cited above can be found on pp. 136–37.

7. The lyrics here are unclear. As far as I know, there is no official transcription of the songs from this cassette, and all written lyrics are based on careful listening or, worse, the copying from one (online) source to another.

published by Ted Hughes in his book *Crow* a few years earlier, in 1970. If this is indeed the case, the entire song (and not just a handful of its lyrics) might be in reference to the story of Jesus's crucifixion. The parts that are not addressed to Pilate might be an imaginary view of Pilate's thoughts.

Why Sting chose to devote a song to Pontius Pilate in general, and in that stage of his own life in particular, is hard to tell, but the choice of subject is clearly related to his experience with and knowledge of the New Testament. As a child, he would have heard this story from the Gospel according to Matthew as part of a very long reading during Mass on Palm Sunday, a week before the major holiday of Easter. He may also have read about it in some religious books. In 1957, John Heenan, the Archbishop of Liverpool, published a booklet for British children called *My Lord and My God: A Book for First Communion Year*. The words in its title, "My Lord and My God," are attributed to Thomas in the New Testament (John 20:28), and were murmured at the time by Catholics during Mass when a bell signaled the consecration of the bread and wine. We will return to this book several times later. Sting, or Gordon as he was of course called then, was six years old when the book was published, and was to have his first communion two years later, in 1959. He was thus among those for whom the book was intended. Heenan describes the scene in a way that would probably be justly rejected today for containing anti-Jewish/anti-Semitic elements:

> The next day, [after a trial in a Jewish court,] Jesus was taken before Pontius Pilate the Roman Ruler. Pontius Pilate had heard a great deal about Jesus and he was glad to see Him. As soon as he talked to Jesus he knew that He could not be a wicked man as the Jews said. The Jews could not kill Our Lord themselves and that is why they had brought Him to the Roman ruler. Pontius Pilate had the power to put people to death. Pontius Pilate did not want to put Jesus to death but he did not know how to save Him. Suddenly he thought of a plan. In prison there was a man named Barabbas, a thief and a murderer. Pilate thought that nobody would want to set Barabbas free for he might kill other people. So Pilate said to them: "Here are two prisoners, Jesus and Barabbas. I wish to set one free. Which one shall it be?" He thought that they would all say "Jesus." But they all cried out: "Barabbas! Barabbas!" Pilate was very shocked. "What," he asked them, "shall I do with Jesus Who is called the Christ?" "Crucify Him!," they shouted, "Crucify Him!" Pontius Pilate was grieved. He asked for a bowl of water and washed his hands saying: "I am innocent of the blood of this just Man." And all the people called out: "His blood be upon us and upon our children." To please

the Jews, Pilate had Jesus scourged. . . . Then Jesus was led away
to Mount Calvary to be crucified.[8]

Sting believes that, already as a young person, he did not subscribe to some
elements in the story:

> I always thought [Pilate] was a fascinating character. I didn't
> believe the Jews killed [Jesus]. It was the Romans who killed
> him. It's obvious to me this was a political strategy by Saint Paul
> to sanitize Rome.[9]

Although it is not possible today to know exactly when Gordon/Sting noticed the flaws in this New Testament story, it is possible to imagine that an
intelligent young man growing up in an area where Roman presence and
history were an object of local pride—something we will return to later—
would ponder whether a Roman prefect was forced by the conquered locals
to execute a person he believed to be innocent.

In another song, which appears on the same tape of 1975, "O My God,"
Sting expresses a very heretical idea in the context of Christianity. If the core
of Christian theology is based on the assumption that something major, and
good, happened when Jesus, the Son of God, came, Sting does not buy it,
and explicitly says so to God: "The world don't seem no better since your
precious son was born." As this song is one of the most deeply religious
pieces of Sting's entire career, we will return to it in a later chapter devoted
to religion in Sting's work in general.[10]

At the beginning of 1977, Sting left the North East and moved with
his wife, actress Frances Tomelty, and their first child, Joseph, to London. A
rather complex chain of creating, breaking, and merging of various groups
(Last Exit, Curved Air, Strontium 90) took place, and a new group was created, The Police. From a very modest beginning, the group would become,
in about six years, what many considered then to be "the biggest band in
the world."[11]

After some changes in its composition, the group's members were
Stewart Copeland (drums), Andy Summers (guitar), and Sting (bass, vocals). The group's style was a merge of ("progressive") rock, punk, jazz, and

8. Heenan, *My Lord*, 109–10.

9. Sting, interview by author, July 23, 2017, Künzelsau, REC22:046. It was, in fact,
the Gospel writers rather than Paul who narrate the story of Jesus' trial before Pilate, but
that need not negate the wider point at issue.

10. See pp. 149–52.

11. The number of books written about The Police is very significant. To date, the
most important works of an academic nature on the band are probably these: Gable,
The Words and Music; Campion, *Walking on the Moon*; West, *Sting and The Police*.

reggae, and Sting rather quickly became its main songwriter. Only very few songs written by its two other members were included in the band's repertoire, and none of them has, as far as I can tell, religious themes. Whether this is related or not, it should be mentioned that Copeland and Summers had minimal, if any, religious background, although this, of course, does not necessarily mean they had no interest in the matter. Answering my question on his religious background and interests, Stewart Copeland, who passed much of his childhood in the Middle East, especially in Beirut, said this:

> I was raised in the Levant as Church of England, by atheists.
> Agnostic myself but fascinated by Mosaic religion and history.
> Not that any of this affected Sting in the slightest . . . . [12]

Andy Summers, who was born in Lancashire in the North of England, does not mention in his memoir much about religion. He says that classes in "Religious Instruction" during his childhood were useless due to the children's behavior and inability of the poor teacher to control them. For him, personally, as a child, "though the spiritual side of life slowly fills with music, the words of the Holy Bible fall on stony ground." Obviously, these words show by themselves a certain mastery of the Bible, as they allude to a parable in the New Testament.[13] He mentions in his memoir an "interest in Buddhism, and Zen in particular" later in life, but does not elaborate much about it.[14]

One of Sting's songs, "Visions of the Night," which was recorded at least twice (1977 and 1978), was originally supposed to be on the group's first record, *Outlandos d'Amour* (1978), but it was not included in the final version. It was instead released as the B-side of several singles but was never a part of any of The Police's official albums. Thus, other than among die-hard fans, it is almost unknown. Yet it seems to be the first time on record that Sting used a biblical motif that he would return to, more than once, later in his career, and thus it deserves our attention.

The song includes the phrase "They say the meek shall inherit the earth: How long will you keep it?" The first part of this line is based on a phrase in a famous New Testament text, the so-called "Sermon on the Mount." There, in Matthew 5:5, Jesus is reported to have said, "Blessed are the meek: for they shall inherit the earth." Sting uses it with minimal changes, other than turning a proclamation by Jesus to a general statement, a kind of a popular saying, using "they." The second half of the line, "How long will you keep it?" seems to be mocking the first, perhaps suggesting social and economic

---

12. Stewart Copeland, email exchange with author, September 23, 2017.

13. See Matthew 13:20 and Mark 4:5.

14. Summers, *One Train Later*, 15 and 143.

realities: inheriting is one thing; being able to keep an inherited property is quite another. Sting would return to the "Sermon on the Mount," and to the question of "inheriting the land," several times during his long career.

This interesting song aside, the first three albums of The Police include almost no discussion of religion. This should perhaps not surprise us: the band's members were three young rockers,[15] and religion was probably not on the top of their mind at the time. The band's fourth album, *Ghost in the Machine*, which was released on October 2, 1981, Sting's thirtieth birthday, has significantly more political, moral, and spiritual pronouncements than the band's previous albums, but it still hardly refers to the Bible.

In 1983, The Police released their fifth album, *Synchronicity*. The second song in the album, "Walking in Your Footsteps," ends with the same refrain taken from Matthew 5:5, "They say the meek shall inherit the earth," that we encountered in "Visions of the Night." Does Sting mean that those who came after the dinosaurs, mentioned in the song, are the meek who inherited the earth? Or is this an irony, saying the dinosaurs, "God's favorite creature,"[16] should have been those still in charge?

Synchronicity was the last album the trio released. When their tour to promote it ended at the peak of the band's success in 1984, Sting decided it was time to break up the group. Each of its members went in different directions. Sting himself immediately embarked on a solo career.

Three years later, Sting's mother Audrey died following a long battle with cancer. During her last months, Sting wrote the songs for his second solo album, . . . *Nothing Like the Sun*, and produced it. He admits that these circumstances strongly influenced his output:

> I ended up writing an album really, I think, about women. My relationship with not only my lovers, but my mother. My mother was dying. . . . I think that experience informed that record, as a shadow, over that record.[17]

It should be noted that in an earlier recording Sting said that he did not intend to have an album about women, even if this was perhaps the result:

> . . . *Nothing Like The Sun* didn't start out to be an album about anything. I came out with a bunch of songs, maybe 10–12 songs,

15. They were not, however, as young as the members of some other rock bands at the beginning of their existence: Summers was in his late thirties, Copeland and Sting in their late twenties. The Beatles, in comparison, were in their early twenties at the height of their success.

16. Compare to Psalm 104:26, where it is said that the fearsome sea-creature "Leviathan" was created by God "to play there/with."

17. *Behind the Music*, 44:20.

and [it] was only later that I realized that a lot of the songs were about women, but not just women as romantic objects: women as advisers, women as companions, as mothers, sisters. Very therapeutic record for me to make. . . . I mean my mother just died so I suppose I was obsessed by the idea of "a female" and how I'm gonna replace that.[18]

Appropriately, Sting says in the album's liner notes, "This album is dedicated to my mum and all those who loved her."

In the song that opens the album, "The Lazarus Heart," there are no obvious religious or spiritual themes, other than perhaps the line "Birds on a roof of a house," which may refer to the idea that birds flying into a home can be a sign that there is going to be a death in the house. And yet, it seems likely that the title refers to the most famous Lazarus in Christian culture: Lazarus of Bethany (not to be confused with another Lazarus in the New Testament, in Luke 16). In the New Testament story about Lazarus (John 11), Jesus resurrects him after he was dead for four days. The story is one of the longest descriptions of events related to Jesus, and also includes the famed shortest verse in the New Testament: "Jesus wept." In Sting's childhood region, the story existed not only as a text printed on paper, or a narrative in oral sermons, but also as an image carved in stone. According to some scholars' interpretation, a carving on the Rothbury Cross from Northumbria, made around 800 CE and visible in a local museum, shows the scene of the raising of Lazarus.[19]

Sting's classmate James Berryman recalls an incident that occurred in Grammar School, related to this biblical story. It is likely that Gordon/Sting was in the room also:

> F[ather] B. asked [in a Religious Instruction/Education lesson] why Lazarus had not been buried in a grave. I answered in flamboyant style, "Was it because he was not dead, Father?" It wasn't the wittiest retort I have ever given but I did not expect him to round on me in the way he did, almost frothing at the mouth in fury. But he calmed down as quickly as he had flared up and that was that.[20]

This event not only serves as a reminder that New Testament stories were frequently discussed in school during Sting's childhood, but also that some

18. Sting, *All This Time,* CD-ROM.

19. See Hawkes, "The Rothbury Cross," 77–94. It is also how the piece is presented where it is today, in The Great North Museum: Hancock in Newcastle upon Tyne.

20. Berryman, *Sting and I,* 71.

of the children had rather critical opinions of them, something their priest-teachers did not appreciate.

The idea of a life-giving wound is very much part of the Christian belief about Jesus's crucifixion. A common interpretation of a verse in the Gospel according to John (19:34), which states that water and blood poured from the wound in Jesus's side, is that these two liquids point to Christian baptism and Eucharist, both of which are sources of divine grace in Christian faith. During Sting's childhood, "devotion" to the "Sacred Heart of Jesus"—a practice with medieval origins, but which greatly expanded in the early twentieth century and focused on Jesus's love, as represented by his pierced heart—was extremely central. With all this, it is hard to imagine that the title, and the song that speaks about a wound from which "a lovely flower grew," do not, at least indirectly, relate to Christian and Catholic motifs. Throughout the song, a sentence that seems to describe the act of dying for the sake of others, which is how Jesus's death is explained in Christian theology, is repeated: "To sacrifice a life for yours."

Sting has said multiple times that the song is the result of a dream, or rather a nightmare, he had, and that "almost verbatim, the images were put down into verses."[21] It is quite reasonable that this dream/nightmare and the resulting song were also shaped by elements from Sting's religious background. Why he refers to "The Lazarus Heart," as if Lazarus is an object, not a person, is unclear. Sting would probably say he is not sure either.

Perhaps the clearest and most elaborate example of Sting's incorporation of biblical themes and images into his work up to that point is "Rock Steady," the ninth song in . . . Nothing Like the Sun, a song that is a modern rendition of the account of Noah's ark and the flood (Genesis 6–8). In the biblical account, God is unhappy with the humans he created only a few chapters earlier, and tells a man named Noah to build a boat (an "ark") that can hold his family and many animals. Noah obeys, and God sends a ferocious rain (the "flood") that covers the earth, killing all not aboard the ark. When the flood abates, Noah and those who are with him repopulate the emptied earth.

This summary of the story has been greatly simplified. In reality, the narrative as it appears in the Bible is full of additional details, as well as contradictions. For more than a century already, most scholars have agreed that what we have in the Bible is a complicated mix of at least two different versions of the same story.

Like any person wanting to tell this story in a more or less coherent way (the author of this book included, as regards the two previous paragraphs!)

21. Quote from Garbarini, "Invisible Son," 51.

Sting had to make specific choices regarding which biblical elements to include, and which to ignore. So, for instance, in Sting's version, Noah tells the narrator "I'll save two of every animal," following Genesis 6:19–20 and 7:7–9, and ignoring Genesis 7:2–3, which states that, for some species, seven of each were to be saved. Sting's version also says that "it rained for forty days and forty long nights" (following Genesis 7:4, 12, 17), although the biblical text—in the composite form that we have it—seems to say that the flood continued for much longer (even after the rain stopped), and that the boaters remained on their ark for almost a year. In Sting's version, the male narrator and his female companion, both assisting the unnamed "Noah" figure, want to leave the moment the rain ends, even if the earth is still covered with water. In the biblical account, Noah decides after a long period of time to send a dove to check if the earth is again habitable (assuming that if everything is still covered with water, the dove will return). The dove returns. When sent a second time, the dove returns with "a new olive branch" in its beak,[22] which apparently indicates to Noah that—although the land is not yet dry and all must stay on board—the water is receding and the end of their time on the ark is approaching. In Sting's version, the narrator and his female partner initiate the experiment with the dove, and recount it to Noah. Sting describes the object brought by the dove as a "manna from heaven," another biblical image about miraculous food that God provided to the Israelites during their wanderings in the desert.[23] Having found a steady rock to stay on, the couple seem to have left the boat, even though sailing in it felt, to the male narrator at least, like "sailing with the Lord."

Upon the release of the album, Sting began a major tour to promote it. Meanwhile, far away in Northumberland, his father died of cancer as well. Sting had thus lost both of his parents within a few months of each other.

In 1991, four years after his previous album and the loss of his parents, and nine months before turning forty, Sting released a new album: *The Soul Cages*. This time, he dedicated it to three people who had passed away shortly before: "John Dexter, Ethyl Eichelberger and my father."[24] In one interview, Sting said the following about the album:

> It is an album about trying to understand grief, and trying to come to terms and at the same time almost running away from it. I had no choice but to make that album as a fairly dark record.

22. Genesis 8:11 (JB).

23. See Exodus 16; Numbers 11; John 6:31; Hebrews 9:4.

24. Both Dexter, a theater director, and Eichelberger, a performer, died a year earlier in 1990. Sting worked with both of them the previous year, in 1989, in a Broadway production of *Threepenny Opera*. See also Sting, *Lyrics*, 139.

> And probably my most maligned record and my most misun-
> derstood record. . . . I think it has a resonance to it that it is about
> grief, and about trying to come to terms with grief, that strikes
> people. And I am proud of that. I'm proud of that.[25]

The album's second track, "All This Time," includes many religious references. Most of them are of a Catholic nature. One significant reference is
based on the previously mentioned "Sermon on the Mount," but due to its
inclusion among many Catholic images, it is discussed, with all other allusions, in a later chapter on Catholicism in Sting's work.[26]

The album's third track, "Mad about You" is, according to Sting, based
on the story of the biblical King David and a married woman he desired,
Bathsheba, the wife of Uriah the Hittite.[27] While his army is engaged in a
war against the Ammonites, David stays in his palace in Jerusalem. Seeing
Bathsheba bathing and desiring her, David "took her. . . [and] lay with her,"
an act that can be most probably described as rape, adultery, and an abuse
of power, all at the same time. When Bathsheba becomes pregnant, David
hatches a vile plan to make Bathsheba's pregnancy appear to be the result of
sexual relations with her husband Uriah. When this fails, David arranges for
Uriah to be sent to the front line to die there. David then marries Bathsheba,
but the child resulting from his adulterous rape dies. He and Bathsheba then
have another child. That child will later succeed David, becoming the famous and wise King Solomon.[28]

It is interesting to note that if Sting had not said that the song is based
on this biblical story, it would have been practically impossible to make such
a link. The only terms that might spark such a connection are quick mentions of Jerusalem, kingdoms, dominions, and an ancient nameless king.
Sting's decision to use this biblical text as inspiration for a song was probably largely affected by his interest in and knowledge of the Bible, but there
may have been a more personal reason as well, related to his thinking of
how his own marital relationships started and evolved.

The following song in the same album is entitled "Jeremiah Blues (Part
1)." If, by using the term "Blues," Sting meant to signal the song's rather
depressing content (as opposed to its genre, since the song does not share

25. *Behind the Music*, 49:11. See also Sting, *Lyrics*, 143.

26. See pp. 76–81.

27. See for example in Sting, *Lyrics*, 149. See also 2 Samuel 11:1—12:25. An extremely famous song dealing, among other things, with this same biblical story, is "Hal-
lelujah" by Leonard Cohen, released in 1984.

28. We know that there was an actual Judean dynasty known as "The House of David." We do not know, however, whether the details of this and other stories about its
members are historical.

the formal characteristics of blues), then the title is an appropriate one. The biblical prophet Jeremiah was not a joyful person. As the prophet of the up-coming destruction of Jerusalem in the sixth century BCE, he was rejected by many, yet was later proven to be right.

Some years later, in his 1996 album *Mercury Falling*, Sting made some passing references related to our study. When he speaks there in "The Hounds of Winter" of "A season for joy, a season for sorrow," it is difficult to imagine that these words are not related to the famous biblical chapter known as "A Time for Everything": "There is a season for everything, a time for every occupation under heaven: . . . A time for tears, a time for laughter; a time for mourning, a time for dancing" (Ecclesiastes 3:1, 4).

Several years and two studio albums passed, and Sting released a new album, important for our discussion, in 2003: *Sacred Love*. The album's title song has religious motifs in almost every line. It ends with a lengthy re-flection on faith, the Bible, and relationships, which was also quoted in the introduction of this very book:

> I've been thinking 'bout religion,
>   I've been thinking 'bout the things that we believe;
> I've been thinking 'bout the Bible,
>   I've been thinking 'bout Adam and Eve;
> I've been thinking 'bout the garden,
>   I've been thinking 'bout the tree of knowledge, and the tree of life;
> I've been thinking 'bout forbidden fruit,
>   I've been thinking 'bout a man and his wife;
> I been thinking 'bout, thinking 'bout, sacred love, sacred love.

Sting tells us, it seems, that "sacred love" is at the center of the story of the Garden of Eden from the second and third chapters of the book of Genesis. There, Adam and Eve, a man and his wife, eat a forbidden fruit from the "Tree of Knowledge." Sting seems to have in mind some personal interpreta-tion of this story, but at the end, he does not share it with us, keeping this passage enigmatic, and perhaps thus even more intriguing.

In 2010, Sting began to speak to the media about a new project: a musical about life in Wallsend, the town in North East England where he was raised in the 1950s. It was to concentrate on the local shipyard, the economic engine of the community, and the yard's painful decline, until its closure in 1993. The idea for the musical came to Sting via a 2009 *New York Times* article about a group of unemployed Polish men building a ship under the guidance of a Catholic priest.[29] Initially, the musical was supposed to be, according to Sting,

---

29. Kulish, "Homeless in Poland."

based upon an album I did many, many years ago, about my hometown Newcastle in the north of England, the death of my father, and the death of the industry, which is shipbuilding.[30]

The album Sting was referring to is *The Soul Cages* of 1991. Later, in 2011, journalists were informed that the musical would be based on new material. As promised, in 2013 Sting released a concept album entitled *The Last Ship*, which became the foundation for a musical of the same name, with a book written by John Logan and Brian Yorkey. The musical opened first in Chicago in the summer of 2014, and then traveled to New York in the fall. It played there until late January 2015, with Sting himself performing in it during its last seven weeks. In 2018, a revised version of the musical, based on a new book by the Scotland-born Lorne Campbell, played in Britain. Later, it went on tour in North America, and is likely to continue to be performed in different places in the coming years. This might mean that when I refer to the "British Version," the reference may have come to include many past and future performances throughout the world, all following mostly the later version of the musical, the one that was developed for British audience.[31]

The studio album of *The Last Ship* includes, in its longest version ("Super Deluxe"), twenty tracks. At least eleven of them have some religious or spiritual references. The title song, "The Last Ship," opens the studio album. The title reveals immediately that the story we are about to hear is a sad one: it is the story of the end of an era. Someone, or some place, is going to launch its last ship. The launching of a ship is generally done ceremonially. In many countries of dominant Christian culture, Britain included, the ceremony is sometimes called "christening": just like a human, the ship is "baptized" (generally, by smashing a bottle of champagne on its hull), named, and blessed. The person doing this, the "sponsor," is generally a dignitary and often, in many countries, a woman. In England, a female member of the royal family is the most sought-after sponsor of a new ship.

During the 1950s and 1960s, the vast majority of shipyard workers in the North East of England were, like the entire British population, of Christian background. Many of them were Catholics, often of Irish descent. They were used to having humans, dwellings, and objects blessed by a priest "in the Name of the Father, and of the Son, and of the Holy Spirit," and sprinkled with holy water. New ships were the object of a similar ritual. In this song, Sting decided to have the last ship, launched from his hometown of Wallsend, blessed not by a layperson, a priest, or even a queen, but by

---

30. Sting, interview by Charlie Rose, 19:30.

31. For a more thorough examination of the musical, in its two versions, see Marienberg, "Bible, Religion," 319–35. See also Browne, "The Last Ship," 377–85.

Christ himself. Jesus's first commitment following his resurrection is to rush to Newcastle for the launch of the last ship. In fact, according to Sting's lyrics, this was the actual reason God the Father resurrected him.[32] Indeed, "The Last Ship" includes one of Sting's most explicit and elaborate references to the Bible in many years. The song is about a modern event, yet within ten seconds from the first note, Sting tells us what happened according to Christian tradition on Calvary Hill in Jerusalem, almost two thousand years earlier, on what was to become Easter Sunday:

> It's all there in the gospels, the Magdalene girl,
>   comes to pay her respects, but her mind is awhirl.
> When she finds the tomb empty, the stone had been rolled,
>   not a sign of a corpse in the dark and the cold.
> When she reaches the door, sees an unholy sight,
>   there's this solitary figure in a halo of light.
> He just carries on floating past Calvary Hill,
>   in an almighty hurry, aye but she might catch him still.

It is not rare to depict the events around Jesus's crucifixion, burial, and resurrection, while relating them to contemporary issues. It is possible that while writing this text, Sting thought of the poem "At a Calvary near the Ancre" by Wilfred Owen, to which he was exposed as a child and in which the line "Near Golgotha strolls many a priest" appears.[33]

The "Magdalene girl" that Sting refers to is, of course, the woman known in the New Testament as Mary Magdalene, a name based on her being from the village of Magdala near the Sea of Galilee in today's northern Israel. In several of the accounts found in the Gospels, she comes to visit the tomb where the corpse of Jesus of Nazareth, whom she had followed just a few days earlier, was laid after he was executed on a cross. His death was on Friday, and because the Sabbath was approaching, a day on which many activities are forbidden by Jewish law, the Gospels tell us that his body was put temporarily in a rock-cut tomb. We are told by the Gospels that she was there for the entombment,[34] after which the cave was sealed with a large rock. When the Sabbath passed and Sunday morning came, she rushed back to the cave.[35] The rock had been rolled away.[36] Jesus's body, unexpectedly, was not there.

---

32. See a similar interpretation in Macpherson, "Heritage, Home and Heredity," 229.

33. See Sting, *Broken Music*, 19.

34. Matthew 27:61; Mark 15:47.

35. Matthew 28:1; Mark 16:1–2.

36. The stone placed at the tomb's entrance as described in the New Testament:

It is possible that one of the first times Sting read the story of the resurrection (and not only heard it) was in some pious book, perhaps the booklet mentioned earlier, *My Lord and My God: A Book for First Communion Year*, by the then Archbishop of Liverpool, John Heenan. This is how the beginning of the story of the resurrection is presented there:

> Early on Easter morning some holy women came to the tomb. But to their great surprise they found that the stone had been rolled back. They looked inside but the Body of Jesus was no longer there.[37]

Heenan chose to use the three Synoptic Gospels (Matthew, Mark, and Luke), according to which several women arrive at the grave.[38] Sting, on the other hand, chose the Gospel of John's version, in which only Mary Magdalene is present.[39] Heenan speaks of "some holy women," resolving quietly the issue of how many "holy women" came to the grave: one (according to John), two (according to Matthew), three (according to Mark), or at least five (Luke).

In Sting's version, similar to Mark and Luke, Mary stands inside the tomb. She then goes outside and sees Jesus. In this, Sting returns to the Gospel of John for inspiration. John does not explicitly state that Mary went inside the burial cave, but it seems that in his account Jesus was further outside of the cave than Mary:

> As she said this she turned round and saw Jesus standing there, though she did not recognise him. . . . Jesus said, "Mary!" She knew him then and said to him in Hebrew, "Rabbuni"—which means Master.[40]

In the Gospels, we are told that a mysterious man or an angel—perhaps two—was inside or near the cave, but Jesus's body was missing. Sting says Mary saw some "unholy sight" and, in some of his performances of the

---

Matthew 27:60, 66; Mark 15:46. The stone rolled away from the tomb's entrance: Matthew 28:2; Mark 16:3–4; Luke 24:2; John 20:1.

37. Heenan, *My Lord and My God*, 112.

38. Matthew 28:1; Mark 16:1; Luke 24:1, 10.

39. John 20:1. In Mark, later in the chapter (Mark 16:9), there is a sudden mention of a revelation of Jesus to Mary Magdalen alone. This contradiction, many other problems in the text, and its absence in early manuscripts led to a practically unanimous agreement among scholars of the New Testament that verses 9–20 were added to the final text at some point after it was completed. See Metzger, *A Textual Commentary*, 102–6.

40. John 20:14, 16 (JB). In Matthew, the women also see Jesus, but this seems to happen when they are already far away from the grave.

song, he has winked as if telling us some kind of unholy secret.[41] In some of the Gospels we are told that the cloth which covered Jesus's body was visible in the cave. Maybe Sting is hinting that Jesus was also there, but naked. Mary turns around, and she sees a mysterious figure rushing. Since it does not seem to be the angel(s) that she saw previously, it appears that Sting has chosen here to incorporate the story as it appears in the Gospel of John, with some amendments.[42] In Sting's version, Jesus is rushing, not standing, and he is "in a halo of light." Mary speaks to him: "Tell me where are ye going Lord, and why in such haste?" Sting's Jesus does not answer politely but rather chastises Mary: "Now don't hinder me woman, I've no time to waste!"

In presenting the event this way, Sting again follows John, where Jesus responds in a rather blunt way to the scared and excited Mary.[43] John, however, gives a different reason than the one Sting does. According to John, "Jesus said to her, 'Do not cling to me, because I have not yet ascended to the Father.'"[44] According to Sting, Jesus rebuffs Mary not because he must ascend to heaven, but because he needs to get to Newcastle. In fact, as mentioned above, he was resurrected not for some cosmic redemption, but rather so that he can attend a local event:

> For they're launching a boat on the morrow at noon,
>   and I have to be there before daybreak.
> Oh I canna be missing, the lads'll expect me,
>   why else would the good Lord himself resurrect me?
> For nothing will stop me, I have to prevail,
>   through the teeth of this tempest, in the mouth of a gale!
> May the angels protect me if all else should fail,
>   when the last ship sails.

Jesus is not the only one to attend the launch of the ship. Others arrive as well, and Sting continues to use biblical imagery when describing what brought them there. They went to England's (North) East because, just like the mysterious wise men in the New Testament who came to honor the baby Jesus after seeing a star,[45] or like King Belshazzar in the fifth chapter of the book of Daniel, they are led by special signs:

> Well the first to arrive saw these signs in the east,

41. See for example http://links.stingandreligion.com/wink.

42. John 20:14–16.

43. It should be noted that Jesus is said to have answered many questions in a way we might consider rather impolite. See for example Matthew 8:26; 16:8; 17:17; Mark 3:33; Luke 2:49; John 2:4.

44. John 20:17 (JB).

45. Matthew 2:2–12.

like that strange moving finger at Balthazar's Feast.[46]

Like other biblical characters, they ask for help from religious figures they meet on their way, and even speak with the dead:[47]

> Where they asked the advice of some wandering priest,
>   and the sad ghosts of men whom they'd thought long deceased.

A blessing based on the Trinitarian formula is then repeated several times. It seems this blessing is what Sting imagines Jesus to utter at the launch of the last ship:

> In the name of the Father, in the name of the Son,
>   and whatever the weave of this life that you've spun,
>   on the Earth or in Heaven or under the Sun.

A few other songs from the album/musical have biblical themes. In "What Say You Meg?" the classic Christian wedding vows are used several times. A statement attributed to Jesus in the New Testament,[48] which traditionally concludes the wedding ceremony, is rephrased in the song on the studio album "Jock the Singing Welder," in which Jock refers to his own work: "That no man puts asunder, what I've joined together here."

In 2016, Sting released his album *57th & 9th*. The title is a tribute to an intersection in New York City that Sting crossed often while working on the album. One song from the album, "Petrol Head," contains many somewhat disconnected, but definitely religious/biblical/Christian concepts and terms: "Where every gospel word is true," "I speak in tongues, in tongues of fire," "Like Moses driving to his promised land, left turn at the burning bush," "Bring me my Chariots of fire," "I fought my way from Hell to this," "two stone tablets, God's commandments in my hands." What all of this means together is not fully clear. The fact that the author of these lyrics is immersed in biblical references and finds them useful is, however, unquestionable.

One of Sting's most recent albums, *44/876*, released in 2018 and recorded in collaboration with the Jamaican reggae singer Shaggy, has three quick references that can be attributed to his, or his collaborators, knowledge

---

46. Sting most probably made an understandable mistake here, confusing Belshazzar, from the book of Daniel, with Balthazar, a name traditionally ascribed to one of the "wise men," or magi, or kings, who visited baby Jesus. It is also possible he made it intentionally, wanting to bring in the name of Balthazar, one of those who saw "these signs on the east," mentioned in the previous line of the song. Another song by Sting ("Shipyard" (2013)) also hints at the same story from the book of Daniel: "See's the writin' on the shipyard wall."

47. See 1 Samuel 28.

48. Matthew 19:6; Mark 10:9.

of the Bible: the mention of a "revelation day" ("Morning Is Coming"), of a wait for "another kingdom" ("Waiting for the Break of Day"), and of a "land of milk and honey" ("If You Can't Find Love"). The Bible, and religion in general, are definitely not a major topic in this relatively unusual album.

It is obvious that not all Sting's references to the Bible in his lyrics are created equal. In his analysis of the use of the Bible in popular music, Michael Gilmore organizes his findings into two useful categories. As we saw, examples of both types are found in Sting's work:

> The first contains examples of the Bible in popular music that are, in effect, *brief moments* in songs. Like the single kick of a bass drum, the sound of which is loud but momentary, these lyrical glances at Scripture are fleeting. The writer makes a point, and then moves on to something else. The second category is more like the sustained sound of a struck cymbal; it lingers for a time, depending on how hard the drummer hits it. In these cases, the writers introduce, build on, explore and repeat biblical content. To switch metaphors, they are analogous to a recurring motif in a symphony or a repeated guitar riff in a rock song. In these examples, biblical passages linger throughout a song or album, giving these works a particular character or shade of meaning.[49]

How did Sting acquire the knowledge of all these biblical motifs and an interest in them? The assumption of this book is that this had already happened during his childhood. Which is, therefore, the topic of the next chapter.

49. Gilmour, "The Bible," 67.

Chapter 2

RELIGION SURROUNDING
GORDON SUMNER: PART I

Teachers told us the Romans built this place
They built a wall and a temple on the edge of the Empire garrison town
They lived and they died, they prayed to their gods
But the stone gods did not make a sound.[1]

STING WAS NOT ALWAYS called by this name, nor was he always a global rock superstar. In his long and still ongoing career, he has used extensively, as the previous chapter has hopefully shown, religious images and notions, and among them many that are based on, or derive from, the Bible. Where was he exposed to this material? As this chapter will demonstrate, his dealings with religion began quite early in his life. The more-or-less first ten years of this encounter will be discussed in the following pages.

In 1950, Ernest Matthew Sumner (b. 1927 according to his eldest son, but 1926 according to one official document I found; d. 1987), from Gosforth, then an urban district to the north of Newcastle upon Tyne, in the North East of England, was preparing to marry Audrey Cowell (1931–1987), a nineteen-year-old resident of the nearby Wallsend. Because Audrey was under the age of twenty-one, she needed written consent from her parents—something we can assume she received. Ernest was twenty-four years old, and had been recently discharged as a soldier serving with the British

---

1. "All This Time" (1991).

Army's Corps of Royal Engineers in Germany in the years following the war. Audrey was working as a hairdresser.

England was just starting to recover from the devastation of World War II. Many parts of the country had suffered from bombardments by the Germans during the war. Soldiers and civilians had been killed or harmed physically or psychologically. And yet, attempts to find reasons to celebrate were not rare. Wallsend, the birthplace of Audrey, was preparing to mark in the following year the fiftieth anniversary of its becoming a borough. The entire country was preparing for the "Festival of Britain," a series of events and exhibitions that showed to the public its successes. King George VI reigned, and the prime minister was Clement Attlee from the Labour party. Attlee has been considered by many to be a very successful prime minister. It was under him that the welfare state was, in many ways, born. It was his government that created the British National Health Service, improved the working conditions of workers and the legal status of women, and helped people to acquire homes and enhance those they had.

Attlee was not a member of any religious denomination, and was considered by many to be agnostic. Ernest, on the other hand, was Catholic, even if, according to his eldest son, only nominally so:

> His mother was very religious, she was a priest's housekeeper, she went to Mass every day, and then her two younger boys went to Ushaw College to study to become priests,[2] [but] they did not become priests. His father was born Protestant, Plymouth Brethren. I imagine he converted [to Catholicism] prompted by my Irish Catholic grandmother, but didn't seem all that interested. . . . [He did not speak about religion at home]. He went to church, but I think in the 1950s and 1960s people still went to church [because] it was expected. They still were under the threat of mortal sin, [that] if they'd missed Mass on Sunday they go to hell. It's pretty severe. It's pretty severe. [laughing].[3]

Audrey was a member of the Church of England's parish of St Luke in Wallsend, and was apparently more committed to her denomination than her future husband was to his. According to her future famous son,

> As a teenager she taught Sunday school [at St Luke's]. I suppose Bible lessons, I don't know what they did there.[4]

---

2. On Ushaw College, see below, pp. 108 and 110.
3. Sting, interview by author, July 23, 2017, Künzelsau, REC22:015, 017.
4. Sting, interview by author, July 23, 2017, Künzelsau, REC22:014.

More than four centuries have passed since Henry VIII broke the ties that connected England with the Roman papacy, and created a separate "Church of England." The vast majority of British citizens, and Audrey among them, were by then members of this Anglican church.

On their "Notice of Marriage,"[5] both future spouses attested their religious background ("Catholic" and "Church of England" respectively), and answered "Yes" to the question, "Do you practice [your religion]?" By definition then, the marriage would have been what many called a "mixed marriage."[6]

They surely knew that they had, theoretically at least, three options. The first was to get married civilly, at the Registry Office. This would have possibly led to Ernest's excommunication from his church, created some unhappy relatives, and forced the couple to have a wedding without the decorum a church offers. Their second option was to get married in an Anglican church. This would have offered a nice atmosphere and would have made about half of the family and guests happy, but would have made it almost impossible for the other half to attend the ceremony; Ernest's ecclesiastical status as Catholic would have still been at serious risk. The third option was to get married in a Catholic church. Some Anglican relatives might, of course, not have been thrilled, but they would not have been discouraged by their own church from attending the ceremony. Both spouses would be able to keep their respective standing in their churches: the Church of England allowed its members to marry elsewhere without losing their status. Like many couples in such a situation, they chose this option.

Ernest still needed to get a permission, a "dispensation," from the local Catholic bishop, to marry a non-Catholic. Thus, in December 1950, he asked for the dispensation through the Catholic parish of St Aidan, in Benton, another district of Newcastle upon Tyne where he apparently resided. A priest of the Catholic parish of St Mary in Sunderland, a city to the southeast, was required to confirm that Mr. Sumner, born in the port of Sunderland, was properly baptized there as an infant in 1926, which he did. From the available documents, it seems Audrey was not asked to provide a proof of her own baptism in the Church of England. This was possibly due to the fact that even if she could prove that she was baptized—and she was— it would have been, from a Catholic perspective, a dubious baptism. She was "acatolica, dubie baptizata": The validity of baptisms by non-Catholics was

---

5. Archival material, 974.

6. In Catholic and Anglican parlance of the time, the terms "mixed religion," or "mixed faith," or "religion disparity," were also often used to describe unions when the non-Catholic/non-Anglican partner had a religious affiliation of some kind.

considered dubious by the Catholic church at the time.[7] It should be noted that dispensation for "mixed marriages" was given in cases when there was a so-called "positive doubt" about the baptism of the non-Catholic partner. If it was certain that a non-Catholic was not validly baptized—meaning, according to Catholic Canon Law, that she or he was not Christian—this would have been a "Disparity of Cult" marriage, requiring a different regulation. Thus, one can assume that even if this was not recorded, the priest assumed, perhaps after asking her or perhaps because this was the norm, that Audrey was baptized.

Audrey and Ernest were asked if Ernest would keep his Catholic faith, and if they would baptize and raise their future children in the Catholic church. In the "Notice of Marriage," which was filled out for Audrey and Ernest by a priest, both were said to have responded positively to the priest's questions: "After the promises have been fully and clearly explained, ask [the future spouses]: Do you understand the promises and give them willingly?" Many mixed couples from the diocese in general and Wallsend in particular also signed a document entitled "Declaration to Be Made before the Marriage." Even though I did not find one with Audrey's and Ernest's signatures, I suspect they signed one as well. This form had an opening declaration and then two statements to be signed by each of the spouses. In the case of our young couple, it went probably like this:

> We, the undersigned, do hereby each of us, solemnly promise and engage that all the children of both sexes, who may be born of our marriage, shall be baptized in the Catholic church, and shall be carefully brought up in the knowledge and practice of the Catholic religion.
>
> I, Audrey Cowell, do hereby solemnly promise and engage that I will not interfere with the religious belief of Ernest Sumner, my future husband, and that I will allow him full and perfect liberty to fulfil all his duties as a member of the Catholic religion.
>
> I, Ernest Sumner, am aware of my obligation to help Audrey Cowell, my future wife, to know and love the Catholic religion and of my duty to pray for her and give her good example.

The commitment of Ernest and Audrey to raise their children as Catholics was at least the second time the Catholic church won the children of a mixed

7. This remained the situation up until 1982, even though by 1967 it became more and more common for Catholic clergy to consider previous baptisms in some churches as valid, and in May 1971, baptisms performed in the Anglican Communion, and many other churches active in England and Wales, were declared officially valid by the Catholic church.

marriage in Ernest's family. Ernest had a Catholic mother, Agnes Wright, of Irish background. His father Tom (Thomas), on the other hand, was raised, as mentioned earlier, in a relatively small Protestant group, the "Plymouth Brethren." Most members of this group could be described as moderate Calvinists, following a theological line (parts of which were preached by the French theologian John Calvin of the sixteenth century) which supported, among other things, the idea of predestination, saying, with some simplification, that the spiritual destiny of each individual is already determined before that person's birth. Although the group's members had their own strong convictions, they could not be strictly described as a sect, since they kept multiple chains of communication and exchange with people outside their group. A subset of this group, the "Exclusive Brethren," founded by the famous translator of the Bible into English John Nelson Darby (1800–1882), had kept much higher barriers between themselves and outsiders.[8]

Apparently, Tom's parents were quite wealthy. When Tom decided to marry the Irish Catholic Agnes, his father disowned him. Tom converted to Catholicism, perhaps because of the break with his father's strict denomination, perhaps under the pressure of Agnes. As their future famous grandson would write many decades later,

> [Agnes was the] second-youngest child in a stereotypical Irish family of ten brothers and sisters, [was] fiercely intelligent, pretty and devout. . . . [Her] Catholicism was a major part not only of her spiritual life but also the outer life of the family.[9]

Penniless due to Tom's father objection to the union, Agnes and Tom ended up living in a Catholic Convent in Westmorland Road in Newcastle, "The Little Sisters of the Poor," looking after the resident priest, whose name was Father Jim Thompson. Their future grandson remembers that priest as a person with "an impossibly plummy accent and the distracted air of a disheveled, displaced intellectual, shuffling into the house in his clerical collar, soutane, and Biretta, Jesus-sandaled, black-socked, and bespectacled."[10] At some point, Tom became a shipwright. Later, he worked at the same convent where his wife looked after the priest. "[My grandfather Tom] was very remote in my memory. He didn't say very much, he was very taciturn," the

---

8. See Coad, *A History*.

9. Sting, *Broken Music*, 28. Sting said that it was from her that he heard the expression "broken music," describing his early attempts to play on a piano. Later, he used this as the title for his memoir. See in Sting, *Broken Music*, 69.

10. Some of the information here comes verbatim from Sting, in an email exchange with author, November 4, 2014, and some from his memoir Sting, *Broken Music*, 30.

subject of this study recalls.[11] Agnes and Tom raised their children, including their older child Ernest, as Catholics. Ernest was therefore a Catholic resulting from some kind of a "mixed marriage."

On January 5, 1951, after receiving the appropriate fee, a secretary of the Catholic Diocese of Hexham and Newcastle produced a form in Latin, in the name of the bishop, Joseph McCormack, allowing the union of Sumner and Cowell.[12] McCormack had about 250,000 Catholics (about 10 percent of the entire Catholic population of England and Wales), 420 priests, and 180 churches and chapels under his authority. Judging by the size of the Catholic population, it was the fifth largest among the eighteen Catholic dioceses of England and Wales. The planned marriage of Ernest and Audrey was one of about 2,500 Catholic marriages that took place every year in his diocese. This dispensation was one of forty-one "dispensations" given that year to members of St Columba's parish. Compared to other years, it was a relatively high number, possibly due to the high number of marriages celebrated in the immediate post-war years.[13]

The marriage, one of the seven sacraments according to Catholic tradition, was celebrated five days after the issuance of the "dispensation" in the bride's hometown, Wallsend, in St Columba's parish. The officiating priest was Father Timothy O'Brien, who had presided over the parish since 1941. One of my interlocutors remembers Father O'Brien as an older man, a grandfatherly figure: "People would smile at him a lot. He often touched my head the way I do with my grandchildren. A nice man."[14] The young couple settled in Wallsend, and St Columba's, about a minute walk from their residence, and almost visible from their windows, became the family's parish.[15]

At the time, St Columba's was one of two Catholic parishes in Wallsend: St Aidan's was the other one. It is important to remember that in the age before private cars were the norm, and in many places in England, Europe, Africa, and elsewhere, still today, people would walk to their parish. The parish has been a significant part of the fabric of the walkable unit known as

11. Sting, interview by author, July 23, 2017, Künzelsau, REC22:016.

12. Archival material, 974.

13. In general, there were significant fluctuations from year to year, but until the end of the 1960s or the beginning of the 1970s, the average number in the parish was about thirty dispensations a year. It then started to drop significantly, until it reached the single digits in the 1990s. My guess is that this drop was either because couples in general, and "mixed couples" in particular, chose to marry outside the church (if they got married at all), or that they were, in practice, allowed to skip this formality.

14. B.G., interview by author, December 16, 2014, Wallsend, REC20:13. See a picture of O'Brien, from *Wallsend News* edition of July 18, 1958, here: http://links.sting andreligion.com/tiob.

15. See a picture of Audrey and Ernest at https://links.stingandreligion.com/ausu.

the neighborhood. In the context of England, where Catholic and Anglican communities often share a very similar geographical space, the Catholic insistence that one should frequent the parish serving one's home, and not pick and choose a parish based on other preferences, is particularly apparent, because unlike Catholics, members of the Church of England have the possibility to regularly attend a parish of their choice (even if they might remain administratively associated with another).

There were many other religious groups active in the area at the time: most are still active today. Wallsend had an interesting nickname, one of my interlocutors, not Catholic himself, told me. Indeed, I later found the same nickname also in written accounts:

> It [was] nicknamed . . . "Wallsend the Holy City" because of so many churches it had in a small area. . . . Probably people about our age, maybe older than us, would know, but the young people [today] wouldn't know [about it].[16]

Some examples of churches built in Wallsend during the nineteenth and early twentieth centuries are a parish church for the Church of England in 1809, a Methodist church in 1812, a Presbyterian one in 1823, again a Methodist one in 1900, a Congregationalist church in 1902, and a Baptist church in 1911. In Sting's musical *The Last Ship* (2013–14), Gideon, a young man whose biography has strong similarities to Sting's, says that in Wallsend there are "just churches and pubs where ye drink or ye pray."[17] I am not sure how many churches were in Wallsend during the 1950s, but in a brochure published in 2001, the author gives the names and information of eighteen different churches and says this list includes "the majority of the churches in Wallsend today." Most if not all of them were well established by the 1950s.[18]

A survey of the marriage registers of St Columba's parish during the years 1941–60 reveals that mixed marriages were very common: about half of the marriages in every given year were mixed. In each record of a mixed marriage, the Latin words "Dispensatione mixtae religionis obtenta" ("dispensation of mixed religion approved") or some shorter form of it, and sometimes also the word "mixed" in English, appear above or under the last name of the spouses. One can also note the cases in which both spouses were Catholic, because it is then marked that there was a "Nuptial Mass," an honor reserved only for the marriage of two Catholics. In the marriage of a Catholic and a non-Catholic, the wedding was carried out without a

---

16. Q.L.S., interview by author, June 25, 2014, Newcastle upon Tyne, REC07:00.

17. Logan, *The Last Ship*, 12.

18. See Bolt, *800 Years of Service*, Appendix 1.

Mass. It was assumed, with reason, that many of those present, in addition
to one of the spouses, would not be Catholic, and thus would anyway not be
able to take communion. In addition to this and other theological and legal
considerations, this practice of course also expressed the reservation the
church has with such unions. At some point in 1945, the word "Catholic"
also appears above unions of two Catholics: marrying two Catholics became
almost an unusual event, worth marking. Obviously, because these records
were preserved in the parish, they only testify of marriages performed in a
fully Catholic context. One can assume the actual number was higher, since
some chose not to marry in the Catholic church. Mixed couples were thus,
among the local Catholics, unexceptional.

Did Audrey join the Catholic church? I was not able to find a document that confirms it, but her eldest son believes that the answer is yes: "I
think she did [convert to Catholicism]. I would imagine when I was very
tiny."[19] One of my other interlocutors remarked that "the people who converted [to Catholicism] were often the strongest Catholics in the parish."[20]
Even if she converted, it does not seem Audrey became one of these.

St Columba's parish was an active community, consisting of about
4,400 members. At the time, four priests served it.[21] Many groups and organizations, typical for the time in England, played an important part in
the parish: The Society of St Vincent de Paul (with its special aim of helping
the poor), The Legion of Mary (a group that was started in Ireland, and
works mostly as a missionary society among Catholics and non-Catholics),
The Children of Mary (comprising many of the girls in the parish and enabling them to participate in some public liturgical activities such as special
processions), The Catholic Women's League,[22] The Knights of St Columba
(founded in Scotland, promoting Catholic social doctrine), The Catholic
Young Men's Society, Boys' and Girls' clubs (including the "Scouts" for the
boys, and the "Guides," or "Brownies," for the girls), and more. Some of
these groups helped raising money for the parish, or supported members
in times of need. The existence of all of these associations not only kept the

19. Sting, interview by author, July 23, 2017, Künzelsau, REC22:034.

20. A.N.1., interview by author, December 13, 2014, Wallsend, REC12:54.

21. By 1964, about a decade later, the number of priests would go down to three.
Several years later, around 1970, it would go down to two. Later, up to today, it would
be served by one priest. It should be noted that, at the time of writing this book, prior
to the appointment of the priest currently serving the parish, the bishop apparently
considered providing the parish with only a part-time priest, one who serves another
parish at the same time.

22. On this association see Gilroy and Lawson, "The Catholic Women's League,"
63–69.

community cohesive, but also served as a sign that religious rituals or faith were not sufficient to keep a parish in good shape.

It should be remembered this was hardly a new phenomenon. As Eamon Duffy, in his famous work on the English Reformation, noticed, "three of the central, focal points of the late medieval Catholic sense of the sacred [were] the Mass, the holy communities of parish and gild, and the saints."[23] It seems this was true also during the period we explore. When these types of associations later dwindled, in part because there were many other ways to associate during one's leisure time, and when the centrality of saints was also questioned, church attendance likewise fell in general. Without making a correlation between all these, it is rather clear that even if some people were not very strong in their faith, social associations offered them an incentive to remain in the group. When these associations ended, the reality of their lack of belief and interest came to the foreground of their lives.

On October 2, 1951, the first child of Ernest and Audrey, Gordon, was born. He was baptized in St Columba's three weeks later, on October 21, a Sunday.[24] Four days later, general elections took place in Britain. Clement Attlee lost the majority of the seats his party had held in the House of Commons, and Winston Churchill, who had been prime minister previously, during the war, returned to power. For the next thirteen years, Britain would be ruled by the Conservative party, with four prime ministers leading it: Winston Churchill, Anthony Eden, Harold Macmillan, and Alec Douglas-Home.

Traditionally, some weeks after a child's birth, a celebration of "churching" took place: the mother's first appearance at church, and indeed, at times, her first outing away from home since giving birth. It is possible that Audrey was already Catholic at this early point in the marriage. If she was not, she could not be "churched"—that is, she could not receive a blessing—as a Catholic woman would. The rules were clear:

> Only a Catholic woman who has given birth to a child in legitimate wedlock, provided she has not allowed the child to be baptized outside the Catholic church, is entitled to it.[25]

23. Duffy, *The Stripping*, 7.

24. Archival material, 910. The Sumners later had three other children: Phillip, Angela and Anita.

25. Quote from the *Catholic Encyclopedia* of 1917. See http://links.stingandreligion. com/chrc. Outdated today, the *Catholic Encyclopedia* of 1917 still reflects well the traditions that were common in the Catholic church before the late 1960s. The rituals of "Churching of Women" disappeared from many parts of the Latin Catholic church since the Second Council of the Vatican.

The boy's name, Gordon, was chosen in honor of another Gordon in the family, Ernest's brother: "I was named Gordon after my uncle, my father's younger brother, who immigrated to Australia," Sting told me. "I never liked the name, nor did he. He changed his name to Tom!"[26] Gordon's second name was the rather Catholic name of Matthew, similar to his father's second name. The priest baptizing him was John White, who served in St Columba since 1945.

Do you think, I asked my interviewee, that your mother would have liked you and your siblings to have been baptized and raised in the Anglican tradition? "No, I think she was in love with my father, he came from a large family, I think she went along with it." So in some ways leaving the Anglican church was hard for her, but she came to another home, I asked? "Yes, for a while."[27]

This question about the children's upbringing would not have been much more than a theoretical discussion. In reality, the two were committed, like many thousands of couples, to the promises they made before the marriage. Even if Agnes was perhaps at peace with it, we know that many non-Catholics did not appreciate this reality, which was a by-product of a decree called *Ne Temere*, issued under the authority of Pope Pius X in 1907, regarding betrothals and marriages of Catholics. Many non-Catholics (and possibly some Catholics as well) felt that by enforcing such a condition upon mixed couples, the Catholic church was "kidnapping" children that should be raised in other denominations. Demographic statistics suggest they were right: this law caused a decline in the numbers of Protestants in some places, causing some to refer to it as a cultural genocide. A few decades later, an Irish foreign minister said that the Protestant population in Southern Ireland fell by about 1 percent per year between 1946 and 1961 due to this regulation.[28] Many Anglicans, and probably some Catholics as well, held the opinion that the decision on how to raise children should be left to the parents. For generations, the implications of *Ne Temere* for families caused a degree of anger among both Catholics and non-Catholics towards the church hierarchy that some consider to have been unmatched for decades. And yet the promises

26. Sting, interview by author, July 23, 2017, Künzelsau, REC22:066. See also Sting, *Broken Music*, 29. Many Catholics are named after a saint. Even if the primary inspiration for their name is, for example, a relative, a shared name with a saint tends to create a special relation with, or at least interest in, that saint. I did not find any significant saint named Gordon, so unless I missed something, the young Gordon probably did not have this experience.

27. Sting, interview by author, July 23, 2017, Künzelsau, REC22:043.

28. See also de Bhaldraithe, "Mixed Marriages," 295. See also the wonderful film of Macartney, *A Love Divided*, on the same issue.

made were generally considered serious. It would have been an extremely dishonorable act for a British person to break them. Moreover, it should be also noted that many of the Church of England parishes in the area under discussion here were (and still are) "high church," or "Anglo-Catholic." The theological, liturgical, and practical differences between those Anglo-Catholics and Catholics could have been considered by some as relatively minor (while, of course, others saw the differences in language, motions, and other aspects of the service as fundamental). For many members of such "high church" Anglican parishes, having their children or grandchildren raised as Catholics did not warrant a battle.

Shortly after Gordon was born, Britain had to deal with the surprising death of King George VI. His eldest daughter, Elizabeth, became the new queen. This also made her the Supreme Governor of the Church of England. A new chapter in the history of Britain began: The extremely long regency of Queen Elizabeth II was launched.

For centuries already, of course, British royals had not been Catholics. And yet, contrary to how it often was in the first centuries, or at least decades, of the English Reformation, there was a seemingly genuine respect between British members of the royal family and Catholic leaders. Elizabeth met Pope Pius XII a year before she was crowned. Upon the death of her father she received a telegram from him:

> We hasten to extend to Your Majesty, to the members of the royal family and to the entire nation our profound sympathy on the death of His Majesty, King George VI. We shall keep him in prayerful remembrance.

For Gordon and his friends, Catholicism was present not only in the church, but at home also. During his childhood, his family owned a Bible. Sting has mentioned this fact in many places. In his autobiography he wrote that other than some engineering texts of his father, the Bible was the only book they had at home.[29] In an interview in 2013, when asked "Did you grow up with a lot of books?" Sting gave a slightly different answer: "We only had two in the house, an illustrated Old Testament and Volume 1 of *Encyclopaedia Britannica*."[30] It is possible that the Sumners had a Bible because Audrey came from an Anglican background and most probably had her own Bible already before the wedding. Before the middle of the twentieth century, the

---

29. See Sting, *Broken Music*, 98.

30. See http://links.stingandreligion.com/sbok. It should of course be remembered that such discrepancies are natural, and are to be expected in recollections of past memories.

presence of a Bible in an English home was common almost exclusively among Anglicans and members of other Protestant denominations.

Encouraging people to buy and read the Bible was obviously important in the eyes of Protestant pastors. B. H. Mather was an assistant curate in the Anglican St Luke's church, which literally faced the Sumners' home. Gordon knew at least one of the clergy members of that church: perhaps he knew Mather as well. In the local *Wallsend News* in 1959, after saying that having a big, "old-fashioned family Bible . . . the kind which needed a table of its own" was obsolete, Mather wrote that

> To buy yourself a modern edition of the Bible and to read it will be an eye-opener and a treasure you will never want to forego. If you have a child who needs a present—buy a modern Bible and you will equip him or her with a guide for life.

The big Bible of the Sumners was perhaps what the curate meant by "old-fashioned," even though Sting remembers it as "modern." This is how he described it to me in 2017:

> [That] Bible was big, illustrated with color drawings. I have no idea if it was related to my mother's [Anglican] background. I used to go through it [both New Testament and Old Testament]. It was a pretty modern book, it wasn't an old book. I found it fascinating, with the pictures. David slaying Goliath. . . . I remembered a lot of these stories . . . .[31]

It is possible the Sumners also had a Bible because this was exactly the time when Catholics were beginning to acquire Bibles. In 1943, Pope Pius XII called on Catholic Bible scholars to produce new translations of the Bible. One of the first and most important translations made as a result was the French *La Bible de Jérusalem*, produced by a group of French Catholic scholars in Jerusalem, and published in 1956. English-speaking Catholics did not yet have access to an up-to-date translation based on the ancient languages, but they were nevertheless slowly starting to purchase copies of the Bible, most commonly the version known as the Douay-Rheims translation.

Besides having the (possibly somewhat unusual, compared to his peers) ability to read these texts alone at home, the young Gordon surely heard, like all his friends, readings from the Bible in church, where the segments integrated in the liturgy were often read twice: once in Latin during the core of the service, and again in English during the sermon.

Having a Bible or not, English Catholic homes often had a statue of the Virgin Mary, and a picture of the "Sacred Heart of Jesus," which was popular

---

31. Sting, interview by author, July 23, 2017, Künzelsau, REC22:043.

at the time.[32] When I asked Sting if his childhood home had such an image, he said this:

> No. It was true about my [paternal] grandmother's home. She had a picture of Pope Pius XII, the Sacred Heart, and the statue of the Virgin. All we had in our home was a metal crucifixion scene. Without any bodies on it. Just three crosses, and two places for candles. Jesus' cross and the thieves'. I don't remember the candles being lit.[33]

It is quite plausible that the "mixed" Catholic/Anglican nature of the household contributed to its being less materially Catholic than was usual, though formally the family's children were raised as Catholics. It is also possible that this was not the reason. According to one of Gordon's classmates, who grew up in a family with an apparently stronger Catholic identity, rituals that had once been central in many Catholic households were already becoming a rarity:

> By the time we get at my generation, [home rituals] began to drift away. . . . Most families didn't do that. Some families did. [Grace before meal, for example], we never did that. Some families did, but hardly anybody I know did.[34]

There was a picture that Anglican households often had, but Catholics did not: a picture of the current monarch. Catholics instead had an image of the pope. The many and complex layers of history, theology, and national feelings that this difference, explicitly or implicitly, signified are striking.

In very religious Catholic homes, a daily recitation of the prayer known as the Rosary, a complex meditative prayer cycle, often said using a special string of prayer beads, was common. Because, among other things, this prayer encourages reflection on "mysteries" related to the lives of Jesus and his mother Mary, Pope Pius XII said five years before Gordon was born that it is a "summary of the entire Gospel,"[35] a statement that became quite popular. The Rosary includes several other prayers integrated into it, the most prominent of which is the rather famous *Hail Mary*. Considered mostly as an act of devotion to Mary, many of those who say it believe that Mary has aided and continues to aid those who turn to her using this prayer.

32. See also above, p. 9.

33. Sting, interview by author, July 23, 2017, Künzelsau, REC22:044. It is possible that the candles were to be lit when a priest visited the home.

34. B.G., interview by author, December 16, 2014, Wallsend, REC20:25.

35. *Acta Apostolicae Sedis* 38 (1946), 419.

The Rosary was of course not the only popular prayer at the time. In some households, children were taught to recite a "prayer for a happy death" at night, composed about a century earlier by the Catholic English Cardinal, converted from Anglicanism, John Henry Newman. Indeed, prayers, recited either individually or in groups, were considered central to Catholic life: "A family that prays together stays together" was a well-known slogan at the time. Whether it reflected reality is another question.[36]

Audrey and Ernest Sumner's home in Wallsend was not only very close to their Catholic parish church, and even closer to an Anglican church, it was also near a site where a Roman fortress stood almost two millennia earlier. The fortress was related to a massive Roman structure, a wall, remains of which were visible during Gordon's childhood in multiple places, including in Wallsend itself and at a site close to the secondary school he would later attend.

That wall was the reason for Gordon's town's name. In what we call today 122 CE, during the reign of Emperor Hadrian, the Roman forces, which had intruded into the island with a significant army eighty years earlier (but which had conquered the North East only a few decades earlier), began to build a wall cutting through England from east to west. The eastern parts were built of stone, but the western ones, initially at least, were made of turf. The completed wall, accompanied by ditches and mounds on its southern side, stretched across the narrowest point of the island, from the River Tyne on the east coast, to Solway Firth on the west coast. The easternmost point of the wall was located in the place known today as "Wallsend." At the time, it was called "Segedunum," possibly meaning a "Strong Fort." There was no need to continue the wall further to the east, because at that point the River Tyne is wide enough to act as a natural barrier.

The wall came to be known, even if only in recent centuries, as "Hadrian's Wall." Why this astonishing project took place is not entirely clear. Was it to mark a northern edge of the Empire, even if Roman forces were active to the north of it? To better control the movements of people and goods, and to levy taxes? To protect the area south of the wall? To make a visual statement of Roman might? To provide work for thousands of soldiers? The answer is probably a mixture of all these suggestions.

The place where the Roman fortress stood had been known for some decades when Gordon was born, and was marked on the roads with white stones: the actual site was beneath modern houses. The Sumners lived, for about two years, when Gordon was very young (possibly between 1952–54, from the time Gordon was one to three years old), in a house on Gerald

---

36. See Sting's comment on this saying below, p. 128.

Street, just outside the fort's limit.[37] The fact that the location of the town had such a long history and was part of the actual border of a huge historical empire has been a source of local pride, even though, according to some of my interlocutors, many children and adults were not fully aware of the details. "Nobody had ever told us [at school] that it was actually a forted wall," said one of my interlocutors, while another replied, "I knew about it. . . . My dad told me."[38]

Between 1954 and 1974, with some gaps (for example, in late 1959), Wallsend had its own newspaper: *Wallsend News*. As a local newspaper, it was packed with petty crimes, local accidents, local celebrities, pictures of children winning prizes, stories about locals, job announcements, advertisements by local stores, flower festivals, advice for housewives, announcement of marriages with a detailed description of what the brides wore, stories of locals who "made it" elsewhere (preferably in faraway places: USA, Canada, Australia, or Zambia), and stories of natives who came back to visit after many years.[39] "A lot of it was done by contribution by people, residents," said one of my interlocutors, and continued:

> So, for example, if you look for the mid-sixties onwards, you'll find a column about Wallsend's Rugby club. Well, I wrote that! . . . It hasn't got my name in it. . . . [The paper] looks like it was written by reporters, but [much] was actually done by local residents. . . . The pictures were always very popular. . . . Everybody bought *Wallsend News*. Once a week, people bought it. It was a popular publication.

While it served as a popular, local source of information, the nature of its material required its readers to deal with it carefully: "It was 'a primitive Wikipedia' in the sense that it was written by contributors, so not necessarily the most accurate account of what went on," said the same interlocutor.[40]

37. "Number 35 Gerald Street stood just outside the southwest corner of the fort of Segedunum above one of the ditches build around the fort" (Ken Hutchinson, email exchange with author, January 2015). Later, in the late 1970s, these houses were demolished before an extensive excavation of the actual site took place. See a possible reconstruction of how a fort of this kind looked in a video on the neighboring fort of Pons Aelius in Newcastle at http://links.stingandreligion.com/pons. See a map showing the fort of Segedunum under Gerald Street at http://links.stingandreligion.com/gera.

38. A.N.2., interview by author, December 15, 2014, Wallsend, REC10:31.

39. For this project, I went over these years of *Wallsend News* in their entirety: The year Gordon entered Infants School (1956), the year he started Junior School (1959), the years in which the Second Council of the Vatican opened and closed (1962, 1965), and the crucial year of 1968 when Gordon was seventeen years old. Other than in some special cases, I did not review issues from other years.

40. B.G., interview by author, December 15, 2014, Wallsend, REC10:27.

The newspaper always dedicated some space to religion, though not without variation. In its first years, it had a section entitled "Church Notes," which was dedicated mostly to news regarding the various local religious denominations. Some churches were mentioned more than others, and news about Catholics appeared only sporadically. And yet, when Catholics were discussed in the news, it was not disrespectful in any way. A substantial article on Catholics was written, for example, in May 1956: Derek McCartney explored in *Wallsend News* the history of Catholics and Catholicism in the borough as part of a series on local churches.[41]

The newspaper also often had a section entitled, "Topic of the Week," which was written by different clergy members from the area. This section generally discussed politics, religion, culture, and local concerns. At times, it was a type of a written sermon or homily. The paper's interest in religion declined dramatically in the 1960s. A comparison between 1956 and 1962, for instance, shows how religion literally lost its place. The "Church Notes" section of the 1950s was replaced with a section entitled "District News by Churchman"; this new section appeared on page 6 (sometimes, on page 8), adjacent to letters to the editor, advice about gardening, crosswords, and advertisements of underwear. It was much shorter than its predecessor, and it was generally limited to small paragraphs. Unlike in the 1950s, readers in the 1960s only rarely had access to long articles related to religion. There was also a section of "Church Notices" at times, but it often only consisted of short notices about past and future events in local churches. One thing, however, remained consistent in the journal: relatively little was said about Catholics. That said, information from this journal can still tell us something about the religious issues that were of concern to Wallsend's residents.

The historian Hugh McLeod, summarizing nicely the work of another historian, Alan D. Gilbert, says this:

> [Gilbert] suggests that, although the British working class was thoroughly dechristianized in the nineteenth century, the full significance of this did not become apparent until the twentieth. . . . Right up to the 1960s the working class comprised the great majority of the British population. To stay in business, the mass media had to reflect the values of the largest part of their customers—including a lack of interest in religion, and (in the prosperous 1960s) an increasing hedonism. . . . Irreligion and hedonism have become characteristic features of this national culture.[42]

41. McCartney, "'How Many 'Papists.'"

42. McLeod, *The Religious Crisis*, 14. The work of Gilbert he refers to is Gilbert, *The Making*.

Wallsend News seems to be a perfect example of this trend.

There were also Catholic newspapers available, such as the *Universe* (whose name was modified slightly from time to time). It was read by the type of people I am mostly interested in this study: the working class. Another important Catholic publication, *The Tablet*, was mostly read by the middle/high class and clergy. One of my interlocutors, a retired priest, noticed that,

> Most of the people in this parish and the next forty other parishes in the area would not know what *The Tablet* was. . . . [Most of those Catholics who read a Catholic paper, which were anyway a minority] would read *Universe*. In every parish you would get twenty *Universe*, two *Catholic Times*, possibly one *Tablet*, which came above the pile when it arrived, but went into to the presbytery. Nobody in the parish would read the *Tablet* . . . .[43]

He and others added that if people felt they were active Catholics they would also read the *Northern Cross,* a monthly publication of the diocese of Hexham and Newcastle, which began to appear in 1956. From the non-religious newspapers, in addition to the weekly *Wallsend News*, people would attentively read the daily *Evening Chronicle,* which came from Newcastle.

In September 1956, shortly before his fifth birthday, Gordon and his peers began their formal education at the Catholic St Columba's Infant School, which was founded eighty years earlier, in 1876. It was one of countless Catholic schools that were built in Britain in the nineteenth century to accommodate the growing number of Catholic children. Until 1833, the state did not support schools for the working class. When the movement to educate the poor started, Catholics joined in, and in 1847 applied for state support. At the time, Catholics already had hundreds of schools, but the huge influx of Irish immigrants made it urgent for them to build many more.

Going to the family's parish school was the norm. It was even regulated by the state: if a child was baptized Catholic, the allocation for his or her tuition went directly to the parochial school, and he or she was expected to attend it. At that time, this meant that about 20 percent of the education budget in Wallsend went to these Catholic schools.

When I asked my interlocutors who went to Catholic schools whether they felt like they were a minority (because statistically, they were: Catholics made about 10–12 percent of the English and Welsh population at the time, and possibly around 20 percent of the local community), most answered in the negative. They felt "different" sometimes, but they were surrounded

43. A.N.3., interview by author, December 13, 2014, Wallsend, REC12:21.

by a strong community, with its own institutions, so they had no feeling of numerical inferiority. The 1950s were a time in which some members of the parish gained local prominence in Wallsend in business or in other fields; they thus indirectly raised the general standing of the Catholic community as a whole.

If we assume that a high rate of mixed marriages, as discussed a few pages earlier, applied to the children at school,[44] children like Gordon with a non-Catholic parent were by no means a rare phenomenon. It is reasonable to assume that their presence was often a factor, conscious or not, in reducing the heat in critics against other religious groups, as expressed by teachers or peers. As Sting himself wrote decades later, "So-called mixed marriages were still frowned upon by the church hierarchies, but not as much as they were in the previous generation."[45] It is also possible that, even if there were many of them around, this was not something that the students were aware of. Sting told me this:

> I am not sure how many people in my class were of a mixed re-
> ligion. I really don't know. It's not something that we discussed.
> It was kept quiet. Maybe [because of shame]. I don't think I've
> ever admitted it to my friends or my teachers that my mother
> was Protestant.[46]

Children from such families were in a position that was not extremely different from what was experienced by many people in the very first generations of the English Reformation: they considered themselves members of a group with a certain theology and practice, while some of their parents or grandparents were seen as part of another. It was not easy for many of them to believe that their living (grand)parents were heretics, or that their dead ancestors were burning in hell. Some compromises often had to be found.[47] A scholar of the English Reformation described in a chapter about tensions in families during the time what happened when people were supposed to believe that their living or dead Catholic family members are damned. Some could, many could not: "Humans, emotionally unable to live as theologians,

---

44. This necessitates two assumptions that I could not verify: that mixed couples did not have significantly fewer children than non-mixed couples, and that mixed couples, in fact, sent their children to Catholic schools at a similar rate to that of non-mixed couples.

45. Sting, *Broken Music*, 28.

46. Sting, interview by author, July 23, 2017, Künzelsau, REC22:122.

47. There was a prayer about "The Evil of Mixed Marriages" that at least one of my interlocutors remembers by heart. I do not know when teaching it to school children stopped.

tend towards compromise. In families, if nowhere else, people had to learn to accept a multi-denominational world . . . ."[48] Sting himself, in his memoir, expressed a similar idea:

> Implicit in all of this [Catholic teaching] was that God was a Catholic and that anyone who wasn't a Catholic would not be able to enter the Kingdom of Heaven and ought to be pitied or, if at all possible, converted to the true church. Luckily, being the child of a mixed marriage—my mother Church of England, my father nominally a Catholic—I didn't really swallow this idea whole. Consigning millions of lost souls to eternal hellfire just because they weren't members of the Catholic Women's League or the Knights of Saint Columba seemed hubristic long before I'd even heard the word.[49]

In the previously mentioned 1956 book for children written by John Heenan, later to be the leader of English Catholics as Archbishop of Westminster,[50] Heenan spends half a page saying that he is aware the reader might think that mixed marriages should not be condemned. He recognizes the fact that many of his readers are actually likely to be the result of such matches. I suspect he had access to real-time statistics and knew exactly how common such unions were. Perhaps this, among other things, explains why he tackles the issue with more tact than many others:

> If I say that mixed marriages are usually a failure you may not agree with me. You may be a child of a mixed marriage. Perhaps your mother is not a Catholic but she has always seen that you went to Mass on Sunday. When you were small she took you to the Catholic school each morning and was waiting at the school gate to take you home when school ended. She was just as pleased as your Catholic father when you made your First Holy Communion. . . . It is true that non-Catholic parents are sometimes better than Catholic parents. . . . But the story of mixed marriages is not usually as happy as this.[51]

As it was common then, the school Gordon went to, headed by Mr. A. R. Hutchinson, was divided in two parts: the "Infants School," which was located in a building on St Columba's church grounds (currently, having

---

48. See Jones, *The English Reformation*, 34.

49. Sting, *Broken Music*, 46–47.

50. Westminster, of course, had been the headquarter of English Catholics since the Restoration of the Catholic Hierarchy in 1850, after they lost Canterbury during the Reformation.

51. Heenan, *Our Faith*, 118–19.

been remodeled, the parish social hall), and the "Junior School" on the nearby (and no longer existing) Hedley Street. Gordon attended the first school until the summer of 1959, and then attended the second school for another three years. Both schools were mixed, in that boys and girls studied together, even though there were moments of separation, such as during recess on the playground. The children did not consider the two schools as forming one unit. The head of the Infants School was Miss E. Cosgrove. All teachers were laywomen and laymen: there were no nuns or priests among the permanent staff. And yet, the parish priests played a crucial role in the school, both behind the scene and on the public front. A study of St Aidan's, a nearby school, notes something that was likely true also of St Columba's as well as of other Catholic schools:

> Log books witness to the fact that each successive parish priest, as correspondent manager, was not only intimately concerned with financial responsibilities but was a regular visitor to the schools, at many periods on a daily basis.[52]

Catholic parents were strongly discouraged from sending their children to non-Catholic schools. A statement originating in 1905 as a "Declaration of the Bishops of the Province of Westminster on the Frequentation by Catholics of Non-Catholic Schools" was printed, it seems, in each edition of the *Northern Catholic Calendar* from 1915 until 1940. The statement warned Catholics that going to such schools will harm them, their children, and the spiritual and financial well-being of the entire church.

It is obvious that some parts of that statement targeted members of high social classes who were able to choose between Catholic and non-Catholic schools, had less fear of social pressure from their co-religionists, and were seen as a model by some. It is likely that the majority of Catholics in Wallsend and in the surrounding areas did not really consider other options. They were Catholics, thus they sent their children to Catholic school without much thought. And yet, even in such places, it seems there was a strong pressure to not even consider other educational options.

While Catholic children went almost without exception to the school of their parish, children from Anglican families would go either to the Church of England school (for example, to Wallsend's St Peter's Primary School) or to a "state school" (where children from other denominations, such as Methodists, Presbyterians, Congregationalists, and others, or the rare "non-affiliated" would go).[53] Unlike the circumstances of their Catholic

---

52. Conway, "An Investigation," 67.

53. In England, the term used to describe schools associated with a religious group is "Faith Schools" or "Confessional Schools."

neighbors, in which not going to the parish school would have been seen as unacceptable by the community and clergy, Anglicans did not generally view the situation in the same way. It was clear that parents could legitimately make the decision where to send their children based on practical issues such as distance to school or other non-religious considerations.[54] State schools had, after all, "Religious Education," which was generally taught by Anglicans.

Earlier that same year, in May 1956, the old church of St Columba, the one in which Gordon's parents got married (also known as the "Tin Chapel" or the "Iron Church" due to the materials it was made of in 1904) was demolished, in order to make place for a new one:

> After forty years,[55] there is a gap on the familiar landscape in Carville Road, Wallsend. Demolition has been completed on St. Columba's Roman Catholic church and workmen will soon be busy with the new church which is expected to be up within a year or 18 months. In the meantime, services are being held in part of the St. Columba's Infants' School and marriages and baptisms are also being performed there. The last service in the old corrugated iron building was to celebrate the Pope's 80th birthday[56] and now the members of the church are looking forward to what their parish priest, Father T. O'Brien, described as a "bigger and a very beautiful church."[57]

A "communion rail," where laypeople waited to receive the Eucharist during Mass, was placed in the children's classroom, and it became a temporary chapel.[58] The following year, as planned, the new church was completed:

> The Solemn Blessing and opening of the New church took place on 7th October, 1957 at 7:30 p.m. There was a great gathering

---

54. L.S., interview by author, June 25, 2014, Newcastle upon Tyne, REC04:14.

55. Unless I am missing something, this number is mistaken, and the article should have said "More than fifty years."

56. The pope in question was Pius XII, who was eighty on March 2, 1956. This celebration was not spontaneous in any way: it was requested by Bishop McCormack, in a letter he sent to all priests in the diocese on February 1, 1956. The letter gave rather precise instructions on how the day should be marked. It even encouraged parishes to send telegrams to the "Common Father." See HND, Ad Clerum Letters, February 1955–March 1966, MR8. According to McCormack, this was an initiative of the entire Catholic hierarchy of England and Wales.

57. "St. Columba's Church Demolished."

58. A.N.4., interview by author, December 15, 2014, Wallsend, REC10:02. See an image showing an example of a "communion rail" at http://links.stingandreligion.com/cora.

and queues formed in Carville Road and Hugh Street, directed by the police.[59]

In line with strong Marian devotions of the time, the parish changed its name. It became the parish of "Our Lady and St Columba": Mary was now one of its patrons. The *Newcastle Journal* also reported about the event, using the new name:

> More than 1,000 sang hymns in the street to the accompaniment of the church carillon before the opening and blessing of the new church of Our Lady and St. Columba at Wallsend last night. In the absence of the Bishop of Hexham and Newcastle, Dr. J. McCormack, the ceremony was performed by the Vicar General of the diocese, Monsignor Cunningham. . . . More than 150 priests from all over the diocese followed the Vicar General's party into the church for the blessing of the interior. Solemn High Mass, which followed, was attended by civic dignitaries, a party of 200 old age pensioners and the general public. There were about 1,700 people in the church. . . .[60]

A year later, another new Catholic church, St Bernadette, was erected in Wallsend as well. The name chosen for this new church is a good example of the great admiration English Catholics had of Bernadette of Lourdes, who had her supposed visions exactly one hundred years earlier. Fifteen years before the erection of this new church, in 1943, one of the bloodiest years of the war, the film *The Song of Bernadette* was released. It had a major impact on many Catholics, including British Catholics. It was based on a book by Franz Werfel, a Jewish refugee who had escaped from the Nazis, and who spent some part of the war close to Lourdes in France. Lourdes, it should be reminded, is the site where, according to Catholic tradition, in 1858, Mary the mother of Jesus appeared to a young woman named Bernadette Soubirous. The film won four Oscars (it was nominated for twelve in all) and was a phenomenal success for many years, especially among Catholics. It opens with a famous disclaimer, which is uttered later in the film by a priest: "For those who believe in God, no explanation is necessary. For those who do not believe in God, no explanation is possible." Lourdes was of course already

---

59. *Our Lady and Saint Columba Centenary, 1885–1985*, 27.

60. *Newcastle Journal*, October 8, 1957. According to an article published ten days earlier, on September 27, in the *Evening Chronicle*, the bishop was supposed to be present. Perhaps his absence was due to health concerns: he died several months later. One can imagine that his absence was a great disappointment for the community. Note that the person who replaced him in the ceremony was not the James Cunningham who later became the bishop. On Cunningham the Vicar General, and the local myth regarding the confusion of their names, see below, p. 55.

well-known before the film. Some people travelled to the major shrine built there, and theatrical productions about the event (such as *The Shepherdess of Lourdes*, which was performed in St Aidan parish of Wallsend in the early 1930s) were not uncommon. The film, however, brought public enthusiasm about Lourdes to a new level. For many English Catholics, a pilgrimage there was not, by then, an impossible feat: international tourism was developing, and Lourdes was accessible by trains and a boat ride across the channel. Thus, for example, three years before the consecration of the new church, on July 25, 1955, the bishop of Hexham and Newcastle, Joseph McCormack, sent a report to all priests in the diocese about the upcoming annual "Diocesan Pilgrimage to Our Lady's Shrine at Lourdes." Those traveling would go by a special train. He expected about 500 people, including twenty-one priests, sixty-three sick people, fifteen female and male nurses, and a doctor. He wanted the diocese's priests to share the information with their parishioners, so that "as many of our people as possible [will] be at the Railway Station as a sign and promise of their spiritual association with the pilgrimage, to give the pilgrimage a truly Catholic send-off . . . ."[61] A decade later, on July 30, 1965, *The Universe* published a charming photo of a large family with the caption: "They Saved for Two Years, Now They're Off: Family of 14 Set Off for Lourdes." For its readers, there was no need to explain the act. Moving a family of fourteen was a respectable feat, but the destination was a common one for those Catholics who were able to make the trip.[62]

Like all Catholics, the children of the parish were required to go to Mass every Sunday. There were five Masses, one after the other (one every hour, 7–11 a.m.). The advantages of attending one of the later Masses included a less stressful early Sunday rising, as well as a more elaborate and musical service. A disadvantage was that parishioners, including children, had to fast (no food or drink except water) for several hours before taking communion. Until 1957, the fasting had to begin at midnight. This is what the American author Mary Gordon, who was born two years before Sting and was also raised Catholic, said about her fear, as a child, of breaking the rule:

> One of the most important things to be drilled into our heads, and
> one of the greatest causes of anxiety, was the pre-Communion

61. HND, Ad Clerum Letters, February 1955–March 1966, MR8.

62. See http://links.stingandreligion.com/ld14. Among many popular works on Bernadette of Lourdes that were available to British Catholics at the time, one can note for example the small (and thus cheap and accessible) booklet by Martindale, *Bernadette of Lourdes*.

fast. In those pre-Vatican II days, one was required to fast from midnight of the night before taking the sacrament. I would, of course, be asleep for most of that time, but I had to be very careful, very very careful, vigilant to the point of death, not to pop something into my mouth on my way past the kitchen to the bathroom. I worried that even brushing my teeth might be a violation of the terms of the fast, but Sister Trinitas assured me it was not, when I raised my hand to ask the question. Did my classmates feel relief that I had voiced an anxiety they might have shared, or did they think I was a freak, ridiculous in my over-scrupulosity?[63]

Mary Gordon also mentions a saying the children had to repeat "like little soldiers": "Nothing must pass the lips after midnight." Then, in 1957, Pius XII shortened the required fasting to three hours. Thus, theoretically, for Gordon Sumner and his friends, who had their first communion in 1959, one could eat or drink early on Sunday and still take communion in the 11 a.m. Mass. Still, only very few were able to take communion during that late Mass. It should be remembered that, even in earlier Masses, many (at times, most) people did not take communion. As one of my interlocutors noted,

> For people of that generation, it was attending Mass, not receiving communion. It was attending Mass that mattered. The very word, "hearing" Mass. . . . If you want to remain a proper Catholic, you need to "hear Mass."[64]

At times the reality was more complex. Indeed, many who did not fast, or who did not make a confession, or who felt unworthy for many other reasons, did not proceed to receive the consecrated host. Sometimes, however, they found themselves in a precarious situation. Many children were not able to fast for many hours, and secretly (or not so secretly) broke the fast. Due, however, to family and social pressures, they still found themselves in church, and were expected, by those who did not know about their transgressive behavior, to take communion. Here they found themselves between a rock and a hard place. If they did not take communion, they would be revealing their misconduct. If they did take it, they would be committing a serious sin, and would suffer from remorse. It is likely that many chose the second option. As strong as faith is, fear of social pressure is generally stronger.[65] The result was children taking communion, and becoming, while

---

63. Gordon, "My First Communion," 335–36. See also Schultz, "Do This in Memory," 55.

64. L.I., interview by author, December 14, 2014, Durham, REC11:57.

65. See for example this idea in the Talmud, in *b. Ber.* 28b.

doing so, fearful of eternal damnation. The *Simple Prayer Book* that children generally used had this to say concerning Mass:

> To miss Mass on Sunday or on a Holyday of Obligation through your own fault, is a mortal or grievous sin. To come in late, willfully or through carelessness, when Mass has begun, is a sin. To miss Mass when you cannot help it, or when it would be very difficult for you to hear Mass, is not a sin. So, if you were to miss Mass because you were ill, or because you had to stay at home to mind a sick person or children, or because you were a long way from church, or if for some other reason you could not go, it would not be a sin. When you cannot go to Mass, say some prayers at home; but in no case may you join in the services of another religion.[66]

The children were normally expected to come to the 9 a.m. Mass on Sundays. According to some of my interlocutors, they generally did not sit with their parents in the pews, but rather in the front of the church, with their teachers: this was a part of the teachers' duties. According to others, they sat with their parents. Because the church was often very crowded, some people had to stand, and because there were several Masses each Sunday, the teachers could not for sure know if a child did not attend a Mass. Thus, if a teacher suspected that a student had not attended any Mass, that student would be questioned on Monday morning about the issue. This was often done by asking if the student knew the subject of the sermon and the reading from the Gospel. One older interlocutor remarked:

> A lot of older people always remember that on a Monday morning when they went to school, the teacher, not the priest, [made] trouble [for them] for not going to Mass. . . . That's terrible when you think about it because if you are a five or six years old you couldn't get up on a Sunday morning and go to church without your parents.[67]

Unlike the situation today in most places, the priest was standing on a high pulpit, so service was very much focused on listening to him.[68] Moreover, as some of my interlocutors insisted on reminding me, unlike today, when the entire service is performed in the vernacular, and in which

66. *A Simple Prayer Book (1965)*, 15. We will return to this booklet later. "Another religion" obviously mostly means non-Catholic Christians.

67. L.M.?., interview by author, June 27, 2014, Wallsend, REC18:11.

68. According to a reliable interlocutor on the matter, the Catholic use of high pulpits disappeared in much of Britain around 1968–69 (Z.E., interview by author, December 13, 2014, 2014, Wallsend, REC14:02).

the priest faces the congregation and delivers a sermon that is often not condemnatory,

> The priests were extremely distant. . . . [T]hey were of a very strong Irish background. . . . You were terrified of them . . . and on a Sunday, there would be the typical hellfire and brimstone sermon.[69] You had the Mass, where they mumble to the wall, then they came to the pulpit, will be telling off, and then went about to mumble at the wall again. . . . You were terrified, in case you missed Mass, or missed this. There was a lot of telling off. It was very authoritarian.[70]

Sting himself mentioned elsewhere, while thinking of a famous literary work by James Joyce they studied in class, this same style of preaching:

> Part of my education at school was to read *A Portrait of an Artist as a Young Man*, which is really about Catholic education in Ireland, and being brought up Catholic myself I related to a lot of the fire and brimstone. And the guilt.[71]

Sermons also included reading again, this time in English, the biblical texts that were read few minutes earlier in Latin. They were thus significantly longer and more predominant than what Catholics generally experience today. Hence, if a child could not report what was said in the sermon, there was a good chance that she or he had not been present.

Children raised in the Church of England had a slightly different experience. Often, when their parents went to the service (or even if they did not), the children had their "Sunday School." These "Sunday Schools" began in England in the late eighteenth century; their main purpose was to give poor children who worked during the week a basic education in reading, writing, and the Christian faith, while preventing them from participating in petty crimes on their only day of rest. Obviously, by the 1950s, long after elementary and then secondary education became free and compulsory in England, Sunday Schools had different goals. They served mostly as a site of religious education, and as a place to connect pupils to the religious community. The Vicar of St Luke's Anglican church, a neighbor of the Sumners, reminded the readers of *Wallsend News* of this in 1956:

---

69. On the reasons why priests were often indeed proud of not being intellectuals, see Wills, *Bare Ruined Choirs*, 24–25.

70. A.N.5., interview by author, December 15, 2014, Wallsend, REC10:54.

71. Sting, *All This Time*, CD-ROM, Part 9, "Library," 1:10, https://links.stingandreligion.com/cdr1.

> The Sunday School is not, as some people supposed it to be, a school of manners or deportment, still less reformatory. The Sunday School is the place where children learn what it is to be a member of the church—What it is to belong to the church.[72]

Despite the name, according to my Anglican informants, it was more a service adapted to children than a "school." It lasted about one hour. One of my Catholic interlocutors remembers hearing from her Anglican peers that they had a "Sunday School":

> Some of them they would tell me they go to Sunday School and, I mean, in my case, I did not want another school! To go to Sunday School on Sunday, and to go to church: oh!![73]

Because Catholic children almost universally attended Catholic schools and received their Catholic religious education during the week, they did not need such teachings on the weekend. Some of my Catholic interlocutors report that in reality they still spent much of Sunday in church, going to a service of "Benediction" in the afternoon. Some emphasized this as one of the only social activities possible. Shops were closed. Parents went to bed (to sleep, or to engage in other activities)[74] after Sunday lunch, and the children, in some families, had to be quiet. Playing outside was also not allowed, to prevent noise. Thus, there were only few attractive competitors to the service in church from the children's perspective. During this "Benedictions" service, in which a large consecrated host was presented in a monstrance and the participants were blessed, the children sang several hymns, among them the medieval *Tantum ergo Sacramentum,* which they sang to the tune of a famous melody by Joseph Haydn, the same tune that is used today for the *Deutschlandlied,* the German national anthem.[75]

Priests visited homes often. In a survey taken in a parish in Liverpool around the same time, 64 percent of those answering said that the main

72. "Sunday School."

73. L.I., interview by author, December 14, 2014, Durham, REC11:25.

74. On the desire (in more than one sense) of parents to have the children away from home on Sunday afternoon, see this in Purdue, *Newcastle: The Biography,* ch. 7: "Sunday Schools for younger children remained popular, though, popular gossip had it, more because it provided an opportunity for parents in crowded housing to have sex on Sunday afternoons, than because their offspring were experiencing religious education." See also in Common, *Kiddar's Luck:* "In working-class circles, Sunday afternoon is traditionally sacred to the worship of Venus and a nice lie-down."

75. S.E., interview by author, December 15, 2014, Newcastle upon Tyne, REC09:14. and B.G., interview by author, December 15, 2014, Wallsend, REC10:15. The *Tantum ergo Sacramentum* sung with this tune can be heard at http://links.stingandreligion.com/tant.

task of priests was to visit them in their homes, and 84 percent said that priests actually do that.[76] My interlocutors in Wallsend mentioned a saying that was common at the time: "A house-going priest makes a church-going people."[77] The belief, which might have been correct, that the visits would encourage people to come to church, was thus part of the incentive to do them. According to my interlocutors, the visiting clergy, who was most often an assistant priest, would generally, but not always, come in the afternoon.[78] Because many women stayed at home during the day, or because many men worked in shifts on the shipyards or in the collieries, there was usually someone at home at any point of the day. It should be remembered however that in Gordon's family the situation was slightly different. His father Ernest, except for a short period, did not work in the shipyard, but had a dairy store.

If possible, priests would call ahead to schedule their meeting. They would come for about fifteen to twenty minutes, and be served tea and cookies. Part of the visit consisted of a chat, while another part included verifying, using a black book they would have, the names and ages of the household members that were Catholic, as well as whether all were baptized, and if the children were going to Catholic schools. "A lot of the time," said one of my interlocutors, "it was information-gathering."[79] People who were considered more religious and more active in the parish were often visited more frequently, and by the senior priest. According to one interlocutor from such a family, the priest came to his grandmother's house every single Friday, where he would bless everybody, and then eat French fries.[80]

The visits were generally initiated using two sources of information: the priest's personal knowledge that a family at a particular address was Catholic, or a list of addresses held by the parish. When using a list, priests knew they were taking a risk, because the lists were not always updated. When people moved from place to place, they would rarely notify the local parish of their new address immediately. The priests often looked for other clues before knocking. The back of a statue of the Virgin Mary through the window, or a poster of the Sacred Heart of Jesus, was an assurance that this was a Catholic home. As one priest told me, it increased the likelihood

76. Ward, *Priests and People*, 114. Sting refers to this practice in one of his greatest hits, "All This Time" (2001).

77. A.N.6., interview by author, December 13, 2014, Wallsend, REC12:33. An online search of this expression shows it was already well-known in 1900.

78. It seems that many parishes had two or three assistant priests, each of whom spent about five to six years in one parish before moving to another one, often to be an assistant parish there as well.

79. A.N.7., interview by author, June 24, 2014, Wallsend, REC01:23.

80. I.N., interview by author, October 13, 2014, New York City, REC21:56.

that they would get a cup of tea and not a door slammed in their face.[81] If there was a specific reason for the visit, such as a discussion of an upcoming family event, it was more likely that the parish priest, and not an assistant, would make the visit. One interlocutor mentioned several other occasions in which a priest would make a visit: to bless a new home of a parishioner, to bless the room of a newborn, to bless the room of a child to be confirmed, and more.[82] Of course, priests also visited homes to perform the "Extreme Unction," the Catholic sacrament known today as the "Anointment of the Sick." Today people receive the sacrament even when they are not obviously going to die soon; this was not the case then. As one of those I interviewed said,

> My grandfather, he didn't receive the sacrament until a couple of days before he died. That was very much the approach. You sent for the priest if a person is going to die. . . . It was done at home. It would be done in privacy. It included a confession, so it was private.[83]

It should be noted that these practices were then already on their path toward extinction, even if, of course, this was not clear yet. A decade or two later, with the decline in the number of priests and the merging of parishes, the clergy no longer had the manpower to continue these home visits, and by the mid-1970s, when Gordon and his peers were already young adults, these visits practically disappeared. This marked the end of an extremely important tool for keeping the cohesiveness of the parishes, as well as the feeling of attachment to it for those who were unable, due to sickness, poverty, or age, to attend the church regularly.

The priests always wore a long black cassock and a white Roman collar in public, making their presence clearly visible when they approached a house. Even when the priests were allowed inside the home, their visits were not necessarily appreciated by the entire household. According to one interlocutor,

> If the priest was in the street, and they knew he was coming, the children would run out the back door as he came in the front door. . . . They were afraid of the priest because of his authority, for what he stood for, and what he was asking people to do.[84]

81. I.N., interview by author, October 13, 2014, New York City, REC21:57.

82. L.J., interview by author, June 23, 2014, Wallsend, REC15:32.

83. B.G., interview by author, December 16, 2014, Wallsend, REC20:20. See also the use of this motif in a song by Sting on pp. 77–78.

84. A.N.8., interview by author, June 24, 2014, Wallsend, REC01:23. See a very similar summary of the situation in a French village at the same time (based on a work

Not only the children were afraid of the priests. A female interlocutor who studied in a school for girls, but in another region, said,

> We were always taught by nuns. I cannot remember ever being taught by a man. . . . The nuns were usually as hard-lined [as the priests], but they were always terrified that the priests would come in and say something different. . . . They were terrified by the priests. . . . We did not have priests in the school as such but they would come in . . . for special occasion.

Her husband, a native of Wallsend, added his own perspective:

> I remember quite clearly that when a nun was in the presence of a priest, the priest was very much in charge. . . . He was the authority figure and the nun was a subservient to him. . . . The priest was very much put on a pedestal . . . .

While talking of nuns, he added, "Nuns were scary creatures really." The wife objected: "Some of them could be, yes. Some of them were lovely."[85]

Sadly, considering what we all know by now about cases of physical, verbal, and sexual abuses of minors by clergy and by male and female members of religious orders, it is highly unlikely that no children in the diocese of Hexham and Newcastle, which includes Wallsend's parishes, were abused during the time we explore. One of my interlocutors is aware of cases that were discovered, in which the priests involved were prosecuted (and at times jailed). In several of these cases, other priests, who were aware of these acts, did not report them. The cases that my interlocutor is aware of happened, however, after the period we are exploring in this study. And yet, as the same interlocutor said,

> There must be many cases of abuse which have not surfaced, and some people will have gone to their graves having not seen any justice or been unknown victims.

Thus, the lack of discussion here of the abuse of minors at the time by Catholic officials is not due to an assumption that it did not happen, but only because of a lack of information.[86] There were also cases of priests having relationships, which were considered inappropriate, with women; of course, such relationships, if they were between two consenting adults, are in an

---

by another scholar): "From an early age children learnt that priests were special: when a priest visited, adults behaved with respect and children were afraid. Priests were well aware of their authority . . ." (McLeod, *The Religious Crisis*, 46–47).

85. B.L.G., interview by author, December 13, 2014, Wallsend, REC13:20.

86. On this topic see also Scorer, *Betrayed*.

entirely different category: maybe problematic for the church, maybe at times morally questionable, but not criminal in a secular sense.

The Catholic high hierarchy had a negative opinion of other churches. Ecumenism, meaning, in this context, the desire and attempt to find ways to unite or at least bring closer together various Christian denominations, was not yet something the Catholic church was interested in. Some groups, like Jehovah's Witnesses, had an even harsher view of others, so Catholics were clearly not the most radical. On the other hand, there were other denominations who had a much more inclusive worldview. Catholics were somewhere in the middle.

Scholars often use the term "The Fortress Church" to describe the Catholic attitude of the time. I asked one of my Catholic interlocutors if he thought this was a good expression:

> Yes. In England, and Scotland, no doubt. For hundreds of years [the church] was persecuted. If the Catholic faith comes down through your family and you are all still taught about the persecution that your ancestors had received, . . . stories about being arrested, and fined, about [forced] to attend the Church of England, . . . you tend to look at your faith, . . . well, if they suffered all that, it's incumbent on me to carry it forward.[87]

This person of course refers to the laws that were enacted against Catholics following the break of the Church of England from Rome initiated by Henry VIII in the sixteenth century. In particular, the allusion is to the "Penal Laws" as they were practiced from the seventeenth to the nineteenth century. Catholic priests still faced high risks as before, but lay Catholics and other "non-conformists," other than in some notorious examples, did not have to sacrifice their very lives for their faith and practice. They suffered instead from various types of discrimination. To show conformity with the Church of England, one generally had to attend, in a more or less regular manner, services conducted according to the *Book of Common Prayer*, which defines how the reformed liturgy and rituals should take place. If one did not, one risked being classified as "non-conformist," "recusant," or "dissenter." Being in such a category meant ineligibility for many public offices, limits on studying and practicing certain professions, limits on assemblies, and more. It also meant having to pay various fines.

I asked some other interlocutors if they felt discrimination. Several said that they heard about the discrimination that affected their parents and grandparents in previous generations, and internalized some aspects of it, even if they did not have such experiences themselves. An interlocutor

---

87. S.E., interview by author, December 15, 2014, Newcastle upon Tyne, REC09:31.

quoted earlier, and who is slightly older than those of Gordon's generation, chose to answer about later periods in his life:

> Well, I felt . . . It's a bit like Northern Ireland. The minute when you have to write on forms what your school was, the minute you write your school, they know you are a Roman Catholic. It would be unusual if a state school were called "St Cuthbert's Grammar School." It wouldn't happen. So it means you identified yourself, and then anybody who feels that they hate Catholics, can now discriminate against you, and that used to happen at work, occasionally. . . . [Sometimes I would have preferred] I could have written another name [of a school] . . . .[88]

Interestingly, immediately after saying this, the same person began to accuse his own church, as if understanding parts of the objections others made to it:

> We always had the moral high ground. . . . We are raving we are the one true faith and the rest are all heretics. . . . I think that went on quite a bit. . . . I wouldn't say that Vatican II changed that attitude. I think we're still ranting that we are the one true faith . . . .[89]

I asked one of my Anglican interlocutors, who is from the same age group as Gordon and is also from Wallsend, if she was told that the Catholics were wrong. "No, no," she replied. "But the Catholics were told that you are wrong!" I insisted:

> Yes, I know. As Anglicans, we were never taught that any of the faiths was wrong. As Anglicans, we believe that there is only one God. We are all Christians of different denominations but we don't have different faiths. We were taught that the Church of England has exactly the same faith as the Roman Catholic faith. [The fact that] the services are very similar [was always emphasized].[90]

88. One article on English Anti-Catholicism notes that, "In a Gallup poll in 1957, 17 per cent of the sample professed to have a dislike for Roman Catholicism, about twice the proportion for all other denominations put together" (Wolffe, "Change and Continuity," 68).

89. S.E., interview by author, December 15, 2014, Newcastle upon Tyne, REC09:26, 31.

90. L.S., interview by author, June 25, 2014, Newcastle upon Tyne, REC04:06. It is of course impossible to know if this was indeed that person's attitude already in the 1950s, or if this is a later extrapolation.

One might wonder if the insistence of the Catholic hierarchy that Catholics not go to Church of England services was intensified because of the realization that people who do might ask themselves what, other than the issue of the pope, is the point of this painful dividing separation, when much else is so similar. It is important to remember that entering an Anglican church was considered a sin. In an extremely popular book of the time, we find a list entitled, "A short table of sins, to help the memory when we prepare for confession." In the very first category of sins, the penitent is asked: "[Have you] gone to places of worship belonging to other denominations?"[91] For lay Catholics, this situation was not simple. As one of my female interlocutors said,

> When we were young we weren't permitted to go into other churches. [When] someone was getting married there, we weren't allowed to go. . . . I suppose we were curious as children [and wanted to go].[92]

Interlocutors of both Catholic and Anglican backgrounds, however, insisted that children of different denominations were able to play together and to go to visit one another at their homes:

> You didn't even think about people's denomination. . . . If you talked about religion at all, [it was something like]: "Do you go to church? Oh yes, I go." But this was the end of it.

According to many of my informants, the separation happened at school and during church hours on Sunday, but generally not outside of these.[93] Perhaps because regular interaction was not prohibited (in this way, Catholics didn't exhibit what might be described as sectarian behavior), it was important for the clergy to remind their parishioners of the limits: "This was made very clear for us. You didn't go in a Church of England church. You should not go to a Church of England ceremony." "Could you play with the Anglican kids?" I asked.

> [You can] play with the kids; there were no problems with that. There were occasionally though battles behind the Ritz between the kids from the Western School and kids from St Columba's.[94]

Several mentioned that children from rivaling groups had particular insults for each other: Protestant children shouted "Catholic Cats" (or "Cathy

91. *Key of Heaven*, 215.

92. L.T., interview by author, June 24, 2014, Wallsend, REC01:25.

93. L.S., interview by author, June 25, 2014, Wallsend, REC04:21.

94. B.G., interview by author, December 13, 2014, Wallsend, REC12:50.

Cats," or "Cat-O-lics") towards the Catholic kids, and they responded with "Proddy Dogs."[95] Another female interlocutor discussed the relationship with non-Catholics:

> The priests wouldn't directly say negative things about them, but you were told that if you had a [non-Catholic] friend you shouldn't attend their wedding.[96]

She emphasized that this did not mean that having non-Catholic friends was frowned upon. Others from neighboring towns remember that most or all of their friends were Catholics. This was not necessarily because of some directive, but simply due to the fact that their friends were from school.[97] I asked another group if they were able to have non-Catholic friends: "Not really, not really, . . . I mean, if you're next door then yes. . . . We were fed stories [about] not mixing with Protestants." "Why?" I asked. "A fear it would lead to mixed marriages?"

> No, that wasn't really on the card at the time either *[group laughing]* . . . marrying a non-Catholic [was not expected anyway. Having non-Catholic friends] wouldn't be the norm, what people would want you to do . . . It's kind of you didn't need [non-Catholics kids] because you had plenty of Catholic friends. It wasn't that you didn't want them; you didn't need them.[98]

Of course, as mentioned earlier, no matter if it was expected or not, mixed marriages were in reality rather common. Another person from the community passionately talked about what seemed to be a painful childhood memory:

> All this reminds me, I very well remember, you don't follow the Salvation Army band. It was a music that attracted me, and the uniform. But because you are Catholic, you don't mix with these people.[99]

This interlocutor possibly referred to a major annual event, discussed every year in *Wallsend News*, which was mentioned many times in the interviews I

---

95. The association between cats and Catholics seems to be phonetic. "Proddy" was probably derived from "Protestant." See also Opie and Opie, *The Lore and Language*, 344. The book was initially published in 1959 and nicely reflects the period we are dealing with.

96. L.M.?, interview by author, June 27, 2014, Wallsend, REC18:27.

97. S.E., interview by author, December 15, 2014, Newcastle upon Tyne, REC09:23.

98. A.N.9., interview by author, June 27, 2014, Wallsend, REC17:29.

99. A.X.?, interview by author, December 13, 2014, Wallsend, REC12:51.

had: the Good Friday procession, arranged by the Methodists. Thousands of people participated in this procession, which had at its core large groups of marching Sunday School students. Such events were popular in many places. Local dignitaries led the Wallsend procession, which, with accompanying music, went through the area known as "The Green," and concluded in the local Richardson Dees Park. My Catholic informants said that they were always very intrigued by it, and wanted to join the fun, or at least watch it. They were not allowed to do so. Nevertheless, some did, half clandestinely.

Different people had different experiences regarding the question, possibly due mostly to the particular location of their homes and the neighbors they had. There were also cases in which children from different denominations met in an organized manner. This was particularly true at sports events, where teams from different schools or parishes competed with one another. Some sports clubs had religious/biblical/Christian names, such as the "Presbyterians," or the team from Gordon's parish, the "Corinthians."

Sports and playtime aside, the idea of celebrating religious rituals or prayers together with non-Catholics was still unacceptable to the Catholic hierarchy. Like many places worldwide, churches in Wallsend celebrated "The Week of Prayer for Christian Unity" annually, a tradition whose roots date back, in some places, to the late nineteenth century, and in others, to the early twentieth century. *Wallsend News* reported every year about the events. With some very rare exceptions, however, Catholics did not participate in them. They might have prayed for unity in the future, but they were forbidden from performing any act that could have shown an actual sense of unity with other Christians in the present.

Through the years this tradition of "The Week of Prayer for Christian Unity" went through several changes. Whereas in the early 1950s those praying together were mostly "Free Churches" with no participation from members of the Church of England, in later years Anglicans began to join the events. Catholics, however, continued to keep their distance, and probably very few thought this was going to change any time soon. This dynamic was so normal that in 1962, *Wallsend News* could write that "Tynemouth churches of all denominations will . . . hold joint intercessions this month," and that "delegates from all churches in the borough" would be present— even though Catholics were not part of it.[100] When ecumenism was discussed, Catholics were not even considered in the conversation.

Whereas Catholic leaders were not in favor of their people mixing and mingling with others, in some non-Catholic churches, a radically different attitude was held by the clergy. So for example, Rev. W. Rutherford Basham,

---

100. "Five services for unity of churches."

a minister in a local Methodist church, told his community that when they went on vacation, they should not only remember to read their Bible, but should also

> try worshipping with Christians of another sect. A Quaker
> meeting can be wondrously refreshing, a Roman Catholic ser-
> vice may teach you something of the majesty of God; and an
> Anglican service may be an uplifting experience if the prayers
> and lessons are well read. . . . If you are near London, you might
> even visit a Greek Orthodox church and learn how our Russian
> brothers and sisters worship. Such experiences save us from pa-
> rochialism in our outlook and remind us that Methodism is part
> of a greater whole.[101]

Catholics, and members of some other churches, might have been horrified to hear such an idea. For Catholics, it would take almost a decade for such a statement to become conceivable.

Another idea, that even now is still unacceptable in the eyes of the Vatican, although not so in the eyes of many Catholics, was manifested in Wallsend in 1956: female clergy. *Wallsend News* reported in November of 1956 that a woman, Miss Ella Gordon, was ordained and inducted as the new minister of a local community of the Presbyterian Church of England. The article says that "a new chapter in the history of the Presbyterian Church of England" was opened. Whether Rev. Gordon was indeed the first woman to serve in such a role I am not sure, but it is possible. Even if not, she was one of the first women to do so.[102] Words of welcome were pronounced during the ceremony by various local clergymen, as well as by the deputy mayor. Wallsend became thus a part of the history of the question of ordination of women, one of the most dividing issues for religious institutions worldwide through the late twentieth and early twenty-first centuries.

In March of 1958, when Gordon was six years old, the bishop of the diocese, James McCormack, died. Considering that McCormack was the local bishop for twenty-one years, it is likely that many of the teachers and the parents of the children did not have many memories of life under another bishop. This was thus a significant event. One can be sure it was discussed in school, and imagine the children were involved in some of the rituals related to his passing: perhaps a special Mass, perhaps a procession, perhaps

101. "Try churches."

102. See "Packed Church at Induction." In an article by Field-Bibb, "Women and Ministry," 162, a woman by the name of "A. I. Gordon" seems to be mentioned as the first woman to become a minister in 1956. It is unclear whether both articles refer to the same "Miss Gordon," who was ordained in Wallsend.

even something related to the funeral. Shortly before his death, a so-called "auxiliary bishop"—a title regularly given to someone who would replace the main, diocesan bishop after his retirement, resignation, or death—was appointed by Pope Pius XII, and ordained by the Archbishop of Liverpool, John Carmel Heenan (who would become the Archbishop of Westminster and leader of English Catholics six years later). The new bishop-to-be was James Cunningham from Manchester.[103] As a child, during the First World War, Cunningham spent some years in Ireland, a fact that possibly gave him a special understanding of Irish Catholicism.[104] In some places it was common for bishops to be appointed from either local clergy or from distant places; in the diocese of Hexham and Newcastle, however, all bishops since the diocese had been established in 1850 were local, including McCormack, who served in the diocese as a priest for decades before heading it. Thus, when the announcement came that a certain James Cunningham would be appointed auxiliary bishop, people thought that the man in question was James J. Cunningham, the vicar general of the diocese (the priest who was second-in-command after the bishop), and headmaster at the local St Cuthbert Grammar School (where Gordon would attend a few years later). They congratulated him, only to realize that the new auxiliary bishop was another James Cunningham. It seems that a local myth emerged, according to which the diocese of Westminster in London accidentally mixed the names, and mistakenly failed to appoint the local vicar general to the role of auxiliary bishop.

In the end, as planned, James Cunningham from Manchester became, on November 12, 1957, the auxiliary bishop, and eight months later, the bishop.[105] James J. Cunningham remained for several years in both his roles, as vicar general and headmaster. The pope, Pius XII, died a few months after James Cunningham's ordination, and the new bishop celebrated a solemn Pontifical Mass for the departed pope at the cathedral on October 17, 1958. The year 1958 was thus a year of two dramatic changes in leadership for the Catholics of the area: they had a new bishop, and a new pope.

The new pope was, it was later understood, a reformer. This was despite the fact that such a trait was probably not what those who elected him were looking for. After the long papacy of Pius XII, an effective and strong pope (who is today remembered often for his problematic actions, or mostly lack of action, during the Nazi period), the cardinals who were to elect his

103. An announcement of his appointment appeared in *The Tablet*, July 12, 1958, 18.

104. Some of the information here is taken from an obituary that was published in the *Northern Catholic Calendar* (1975), 155–57.

105. For a picture of Cunningham shortly after becoming the local bishop, see http://links.stingandreligion.com/cu01.

successor seem to have wanted someone who would serve a shorter period, and who would not rock the ecclesiastical boat too much. They elected Angelo Giuseppe Roncalli, an Italian like so many of his predecessors. For many years before his election, Roncalli had been a papal delegate in various countries, and then the bishop (or "patriarch") of Venice. He was seventy-seven years old; he chose for himself the papal name John XXIII.

Three months after his election, those cardinals who did not expect much from the new pope were in for a big surprise. John XXIII declared his intention to summon a council for the universal church, something that had not happened for nearly a century. Four days later, the decision was made public. In England, the Catholic journal *The Universe* announced it the next day in its main headline of January 30, 1959: "The First Ecumenical Council for 90 years is called. Unity: Pontiff Takes First Big step." It was clear that one of the main objectives of the council, which would begin its work only three years later, in 1962, would be to try to improve the relationship of the Catholic church with various Christian churches and denominations.

May and June were the typical time for the ceremony of first communion. (June 9 was an important day for another reason: it was the day of Columba, the patron saint of the parish.) It was during their time at the infants school, on May 9, 1959, that Gordon and his classmates had their first communion, preceded by a first confession two or three weeks earlier.[106] The children practiced beforehand how to behave during the ritual. Their teacher used a spoon to teach them how to open their mouths and receive the consecrated host on their tongue: at that time, laypeople were not allowed to touch the host with their hands.[107] Another Catholic, raised in England about a decade later, describes the instructions he received in this way:

> The round white wafer was God. . . . "You must not bite him," Sister Paul said. "You must not let him touch your teeth or the roof of your mouth. Let him rest on your tongue until you are ready to swallow him whole."[108]

This special care and attention are of course related to the famous Catholic dogma of "transubstantiation," according to which although the taste,

---

106. Archival material, 19. For a fascinating discussion of the past and present of this ritual in general, and in Britain in particular, see McGrail, *First Communion*.

107. A.N.10., interview by author, December 15, 2014, Wallsend, REC10:02.

108. Cornwell, *Seminary Boy*, 19. See also Mary Gordon (Gordon, "My First Communion," 340) describing her own first communion in 1956: "Or could I choke on the host, or my teeth could touch it—this, I knew was considered a sacrilege and in the very process of sanctification I could be involved in sin."

smell, appearance, and chemical composition of the bread and wine used in the Mass remain the same, during and following the recitation of the main prayers of the ritual by the celebrating minister, their essence is no longer that of bread and wine, but rather of the Body and Blood of Christ, who is, of course, the second person of the Divine Trinity.

The children could also review instructions about the ritual on their own. Many of them owned *A Simple Prayer Book*, in which they could find the following (italics in the original):

> In going to the altar-rails, and returning to your place, keep your *hands* joined, your *eyes* cast down, and your *thoughts* on Jesus Christ. At the altar-rails, take the communion plate and hold it under your chin. (Unless it is held by the server.) Hold your head straight up and motionless, keep your eyes closed, your mouth well open, and your tongue out, resting on your under-lip. Then, with great reverence, receive the Sacred Host, saying in your heart, with all the faith of St Thomas: "My Lord and my God." Your soul is God's temple. Jesus is now really present in it. Keep away all earthly thoughts and enjoy His presence.[109]

A few days before the first communion, on April 28, 1959, a representative of the diocese came to check the religious instruction in the school and the preparation of Gordon and his comrades for the ceremony. It should be noted that in Catholic elementary schools, the vast majority of the teachers were Catholic themselves, and generally the teacher in charge of the class, the so-called "Form Teacher," taught "Religious Instruction." These teach-ers were generally trained in Catholic Colleges of Education (or "Training Colleges"), and hence acquired the knowledge of how to run such classes. In Catholic secondary and grammar schools there was generally a much higher percentage of non-Catholic teachers, and the question of who was in charge of this aspect of student education was, at times, complicated. In the report, the inspector praised the school. Later, Bishop James Cunningham added his signature to the report:

> Every credit is due to the Head Teachers and the staff of this school for the piety, good behavior, eagerness and knowledge shown by the children. They answered questions from the Cat-echism very well, and showed, for their years, a good under-standing of the Doctrine. They recited their prayers slowly and with devotion. It is clear that candidates for first confession and first Holy Communion are being very well prepared.[110]

109. *A Simple Prayer Book* (1957), 58.

110. Archival material, 18. The report was also copied into the school's logbook on

In order to teach the "correct" faith, the Catholic church (and many other religious groups) uses both frontal teaching, generally for young children and
teenagers, as well as books that can guide the teachers, young people, and
other Catholic (or Catholic-to-be) adults about the faith. In many Christian denominations, including in Catholicism, these courses and books are
called "catechism," a word whose Greek origin means to teach orally. Several
official books of catechism, from different times and for different audiences,
were produced by the hierarchy, and countless have been produced by local
churches and individuals. During Gordon's childhood the most common
Catholic catechism in the United Kingdom for elementary schools was the
"Penny Catechism," called thus after its (initial) price. Its cover was red, and
thus it was also referred to as the "Red Catechism."[111] The children studied
the catechism every morning, following detailed instructions from the diocese that were adapted to each age group. One of my interlocutors described
these sessions thus:

> Every day, yes! . . . Starting the school day, you do your morning
> prayers, you do the catechism. That was first, before you done
> any of that. . . . It's called "Indoctrination." . . . It wasn't called
> [that by the teachers], but that what the whole thrust of it was.
> . . . Every morning, for about half an hour. . . . We all had the
> catechism, . . . it was a red one, . . . like Marx, you know, a red
> book. . . . That would be your homework. . . . Some did, some
> didn't care about it.[112]

Teachers often used supplementary sources in addition to the book of cat-
echism itself. *Catechism Stories*, a 1948 book by the Catholic Canon F. H.
Drinkwater, was one of the most popular books to accompany the teaching.
Thus, for example, when the children learned about the Trinity (paragraph
24: "Is there only one God?"; paragraph 25: "Are there three Persons in
God?") they might have heard this:

> Next morning, Easter Sunday, [St. Patrick] and his monks came
> to Tara in solemn procession singing the Litanies. There he en-
> countered and conquered the magic of the Druids,[113] and was
> given leave to speak of his God to the assembled rulers from all
> over Ireland. He plucked a shamrock from the ground and lifted

---

June 15, 1959. See Archival material, 122.

111. On the "Penny Catechism," see Marmion, "The Penny Catechism."

112. A.N.11., interview by author, June 24, 2014, Wallsend, REC01:31.

113. The Druids were apparently the clergy, the educated caste, in the Celtic culture
that was present in England and Ireland from around the fifth century BCE and that
slowly declined with the arrival of the Romans, and later, Christianity.

it up. "See this tiny plant—three leaves exactly equal—yet all one growth from one stem, The God I preach to you is likewise One and Three—Father, Son, and Holy Spirit, three Persons, one God."[114]

Patrick is, of course, the man who is traditionally considered to have brought Christianity to Ireland, the place from which the ancestors of many of the children came. This happened during the fifth century, while the Anglo-Saxons were settling in various parts of Britain, and when a young British man of about sixteen years old was captured by Irish pirates and taken as a slave to Ireland. The youth, later known as Patrick, was the son of a Christian deacon and the grandson of a Christian priest. After about six years in captivity, where, according to him, he became more attached to the faith that he had probably learned about at home, he managed to escape back to Britain. Following his return, he delved even more into the Christian message, received a classical Roman education, and was ordained a bishop; several years later, he decided to return to Ireland to spread the gospel.[115] Traditionally, the year this happened is said to be 432. His reputation as the one who brought Christianity to the Irish, whether historically correct or not, was solidified rather shortly after his death.

About a century after Patrick's mission we find in Ireland another crucial actor in the unfolding of Christianity in North East England: Columba, after which the parish we study was named. Born around 521 in Ireland, Columba was reportedly a learned man of impressive stature but not always good temper. Together with Patrick and Brigid (whose importance to our topic is less central), he is one of the three chief saints of Ireland. If his pastoral work in Ireland, and later among the "Picts," in what was to become Scotland, is of less significance for our discussion of North East England, he is still crucial for having founded a monastery around 563 on the island of Iona, which is today part of Scotland.[116] Together with other Irish monks, Columba created a thriving monastery there, whose learning and traditions

114. Quotes are from an American edition, but the text itself is identical to the original English edition. See Drinkwater, *Catechism Stories*, 27–28.

115. Thomas, *Christianity in Roman Britain*, 307–9.

116. The last centennial for this event was celebrated in 1963. In October 1962, *Wallsend News* reported: "A pilgrimage marking the 1,400 anniversary of the landing of St. Columba on the Island of Iona will take place next year on June 12, when both the Archbishop of Canterbury, Dr. Michael Ramsey, and the Primate of the Episcopal Church of Scotland will be present" (see "Plans for pilgrimage"). I am sure Catholics also celebrated the anniversary, but I do not know when and how. Clearly though, they did not join the other churches: such ecumenical acts would only be encouraged by the Catholic church about a year later, in 1964.

were spread by the monks it sent away. These monks had a dramatic impact on the region we are studying, and on the conversion of its Anglo-Saxon population during the sixth, seventh, and eighth centuries.

Hagiographic material tells us that St Columba's manner of living was very austere. We are told that, more than anything, he had always longed to die. Whether this is true or not we cannot say, but in 597, this supposed wish came true.

Back in the 1950s, when Gordon and his friends learned about the commandment, "Thou shalt not covet," they potentially heard a story about Columba, the patron saint of their own school:

> In his old age St. Columba one day saw an old woman gathering herbs for food, and she was so poor that she gathered even nettles. This filled him with self-reproach because he fed so much better than she. He went home to his monastery and gave orders that his dinner was to be nothing but wild herbs and nettles. One of the monks, however, put some butter into the saucepan where the nettles were boiling and the old saint was very displeased when he noticed it.[117]

Sting admitted that as a young boy he was very impressed with stories of saints such as these. At the same time, some confusion existed:

> You'd read the lives of the saints, St Columba, St Aidan, St Cuthbert, Roman saints like St Boniface, saints with strange names. . . . We were very proud of our [northern] saints. . . . [Still,] as young children we used to get Christopher Columbus and Saint Columba mixed up: Why did the saint go to America? [laughing].[118]

This attitude towards the saints is rather typical. As Andrew Greeley said,

> Saints are important to Catholics because their lives are stories of God's love . . . , of God's immediate care for humans, and of the response of some humans to that love. God hides in the lives and the images of the saints. . . . Saints are perhaps a bit mad. God sometimes seems to display bad taste in the choice of His special loves. But there is no accounting for tastes when it comes to love.[119]

---

117. Drinkwater, *Catechism Stories*, 252.

118. Sting, interview by author, July 23, 2017, Künzelsau, REC22:097, 003. For an account in which Gordon and his comrades apparently treated books about saints in a not-so-pious way, see Berryman, *Sting and I*, 109–13.

119. Greeley, *The Catholic Imagination*, 34.

Some of Sting's peers, both male and female, mentioned additional saints that were important to them as children: The northern Bede, whom we will mention soon, as well as Agnes, Charles Borromeo, Jude, Anthony, and Christopher.

The inspector's observations quoted above about the children's preparedness were possibly accurate. Gordon was, if we are to believe the memoir he wrote many decades later, actually very intrigued by the catechism:

> It was at St. Columba's [Primary School] that I began my lifelong fascination with religion and conversely my lifelong problem with it. All Catholic school children are taught the catechism, a little red book from which we are indoctrinated and expected to memorize verbatim, like proto-Maoists about to convert the world. *Who made you?* "God made me." *Why did God make you?* "To know him, love him, and serve him."[120]

All local Catholics with whom I spoke remember the catechism very well. This was especially true when several people met together:

> I still got mine! *[people laughing].* . . . Awful lot of people know it [by heart] absolutely all the way through. Yes. *[group agrees]* . . . We had to learn that. . . . We were inspected once a year, the priest came round and came in the classroom and said "You!" and asked you a question *[group laughs]* and you had to know it off by heart. [And if you didn't know it] it was not good, not good.[121]

Sting himself, when I asked him about a certain line in one of his songs, replied:

> "A sacrament is an outward sign of inward grace": This from the Catholic catechism, recited every morning before lessons. Indoctrinated and never forgotten.[122]

Gordon and his friends were very likely excited about their upcoming first communion, if not for its spiritual meaning, then at least for the nice new clothes and gifts they would get. Indeed, in a survey done among young Catholics a generation or two later, it was noted that one of the respondents

> remembers her first Communion but, like virtually all other interviewed, does not remember the sacrament but only the dressing up, the party and the gifts. The most important thing

---

120. Sting, *Broken Music*, 46.

121. A.N.12., interview by author, June 27, 2014, Wallsend, REC17:21.

122. Sting, email exchange with author, November 5, 2014.

> for her was its role as an initiation ritual: she would no longer
> be left alone when other family members went off to receive the
> sacraments; she would no longer "miss out"—it was all about
> being part of the gang.[123]

The special clothes, and for girls, white dresses, are something that my interlocutors also fondly remembered. The girls would wear the same dress again, and the boys their white shirts, on special processions in honor of Mary during the month of May. Some mentioned the other, darker side, of this custom: first communion was an expensive and economically challenging event for poor families.[124]

The children's certificates of baptism were checked, to make sure they are validly baptized. With regard to many of them, such as Gordon, this was a rather easy task: if they were baptized at St Columba's, the book recording all baptisms was available in the adjacent building. For many of the children, the upcoming ritual was likely to be their second memorable "rite of passage." Three years earlier they had their first day of school. Now, they were taking another step toward adulthood. After the first communion, they would be able to join their parents in partaking of the consecrated bread in the church. In a way, they would become "real" Catholics.[125]

Unfortunately for Gordon and his friends, the rules of the church said their communion should be preceded by a confession. Gordon and his seven-year-old peers needed to learn to identify the sins they should feel remorse for, so that they could regret them and later confess their own (real or imaginary) sins to a priest when they met him in a "confessional": a wooden furnishing that includes seats for a priest on one end and a confessant on the other, with the two separated by a thick mesh. The children were often encouraged to make a list of their sins and bring it with them. Some examples of what my interlocutors remember:

> Every two weeks . . . in the confession booth . . . with little list
> . . . with your own text. . . . "I was cheeky to my mom, called
> somebody some name I shouldn't use, I didn't say my prayers"
> . . . just childish things.

Generally, the priest instructed the children to say some prayers to complete the process after leaving the confessional:

123. Fulton, "Young Adult Catholics," 140.

124. See also Schultz, "Do This in Memory," 56.

125. Adequately, in former generations, and especially during the times priests were persecuted in England, saying that someone "learned trade" was a Catholic code to say he or she had made their first communion. See Smith, *Catholic Tyneside*, 68.

> It was always, always very [hard], . . . but then it felt great when
> you came out. . . . Just felt better . . . because it was over. . . . It was
> [hard simply because of] going into that dark box! . . . Saturday
> morning, 11 o'clock. They didn't put any lights on. Big queues
> of people. Adults and children. . . . It was a big thing, "confess
> your sins."[126]

Many speak about confession as a frightening event. An official brochure issued by the Catholic bishops of England and Wales in 1964 explained to the clergy how to celebrate the liturgy following the changes initiated by the Second Council of the Vatican (which was still underway then, but not yet even planned when Gordon was having his first communion). It says the following regarding confession:

> Confessors are reminded that the reference to excommunica-
> tion, suspension, and interdict may be omitted from the form of
> absolution where there is no serious likelihood of their having
> been incurred. This is important in the confession of children
> whose minds can only be confused by the mention of them.[127]

Using these terms of punishment had been a standard part of the ritual until that time. This text seems to suggest that they might not be beneficial, especially not in the confession of children. It is not hard to understand how the mere mention of these terms—each so closely associated to eternal damnation, for many—could have been terrifying.

All of that being said, it should be noted that some of those who grew up in this period do not harbor bad memories of confessions. One of them described the process in this way:

> Sometimes you had to struggle to invent sins to have something
> to say, tiny things. Examination of conscience . . . we did the list
> just before confession. It was a mental list, you would not write
> it.

One would kneel, and think about what sort of wrong things she or he had done since the last confession. Then, he or she would go to the priest. The same interlocutor continued describing the ritual:

> "Forgive me Father for I have sinned, it has been such and such
> a time since my last confession. Since my last confession I have
> . . ." and then talk about how you feel, how you could have been
> better. . . . The priest would then, in those days, give you some

---

126. R.C., Z.E., L.T., interview by author, June 24, 2014, Wallsend, REC01:35.

127. "The Sacred Liturgy."

encouragement about, well, just try the next time to be more
patient with your brother or whatever, and then give you a little
penance, say two *Hail Marys* or say *Our Father* or whatever, and
then you would make the act of contrition, . . . and then you
would be given absolution by the priest, and off you go. Usually,
because your penance was nominal, . . . say a couple of prayers,
you would just go to sit in the church and get that done and get
it out of the way, so off you went out of the church with a clean
soul and feeling fresh as a daisy. . . . There were some allegedly
fierce priests, but in conscience I couldn't say that I came across
that. So there were priests that would give you stiff penance, so
for example we always knew that if you went to Father D. . . . you
get a decade of the Rosary to pray, so you get ten *Hail Marys* to
do. You went to Father B., he might give you one *Hail Mary* to
say. So that was the only difference. I can't remember anybody
being shouted out or told off or that type of thing.[128]

It is hard to know how many Catholics of that generation (and later ones)
have negative memories about confession, but after speaking with many
people and much reading, I suspect many do. Sting seems to be among
them:

My biggest problem was confession. At the age of seven a child is
supposed to know good from evil, but most seven-year-olds, as
far as I know, don't commit evil acts. Yet the solemn sacrament
of confession requires that, kneeling in a closed cubicle and
facing a largely opaque scrim of canvas, you will confess your
sins to the shadowy form of a seated priest on the other side.
The form of the sacrament begins as follows: "Bless me, Father,
for I have sinned. My last confession was two weeks ago" (you
see, you're supposed to go once a fortnight), but I had difficulties with both of these statements. As far as I was concerned, I
hadn't committed any sins to speak of, but was too embarrassed
to tell the priest that I was sinless, so the first statement that I
had sinned was in itself a lie. I would then have to compound
the lie by making up a catalog of venial misdemeanors like, "I
have been disobedient" (I hadn't), or "I have told lies." Where
the only lies I had been involved in had been told at my last confession, within the sanctity of the sacrament, compounding the
lie with a sacrilege, which of course carried the penalty of eternal torment. This terrifying ontological conundrum and moral
paradox was frankly too much for my seven-year-old brain,
so I avoided confession like the plague, which of course made

128. B.G., interview by author, December 16, 2014, Wallsend, REC20:09.

matters even worse. One is supposed to receive the sacrament once a year at least, under pain of excommunication (another offense carrying a statutory minimum of eternal hellfire). So, simply to avoid embarrassment in the confessional, I had condemned myself to life outside of the communion of the church as well as everlasting torment in the Joycean version of hell that our Hibernian priests favored. Either I was a very stupid seven-year-old or I was overthinking things.[129]

Mary Gordon, in a piece about first communion, raises the same issue, and seems to have hard time forgiving this reality:

> The day arrived: 18 May[, 1956], the day of our First Confession, a day not of light but of darkness, the day of our reckoning, one of the *dies irae*, where we must acknowledge our sinfulness. . . . What were they thinking of? We were six, seven years old? How could we have sinned? . . . I felt bad. But I was not a bad child. I was a very good child. All of us were. We were six years old. How can we forgive them, why should we forgive them, for teaching us to say, when we had barely learned our ABCs, "Bless me Father, for I have sinned"?[130]

At the same time, Mary Gordon expresses an idea evoked by one of the previously quoted informants, who spoke of "feeling fresh as a daisy" following confession—namely, that after potentially harsh moments in the confessional, there was sometimes a great relief. According to her account, written half a century after the event, having confessed her "sin" to the priest in her first confession, this is what happened:

> If I was waiting for some words of enlightenment, none came. Only my penance: three *Hail Marys*. And the injunction to go in peace. And I did, and I was radiant, walking with my perfectly folded hands to the altar to say my penance. It was as if I had been dipped into a sea of sheerest silver, and walked out into the sunlight, my body brilliant as the sun.[131]

The very first question in a confession, in which the priest asks the penitent about when was her or his last confession, was the oil that kept the system rolling. The children were told they must confess twice a month, and they

---

129. Sting, *Broken Music*, 48–49.

130. Gordon, "My First Communion," 336–37. Bruce Springsteen, in his memoir of 2016, expresses very similar doubts about these practices, which he also had to go through as a child: "How much sinning could you actually have done at a second-grade level?" See Springsteen, *Born to Run*, 14.

131. Gordon, "My First Communion," 337.

believed that lying about it, in the confessional, would have particularly serious spiritual consequences. In order to protect themselves from reaching
such a situation, many of them went regularly to confession just so they
could say, every two weeks, that they confessed regularly. This also saved the
parishes' and schools' authorities from the need to follow up on confessions:
the fear of the children was possibly sufficient to ensure general obedience.

Priests and bishops knew obviously that many children, and perhaps
also adults, lied in the confessional. After all, other than the very few who
joined the Catholic church as adults, all these priests and bishops were also,
some decades earlier, frightened little boys doing the same. They tried their
best to discourage it. The future Cardinal Heenan said in a book for children:

> It is, of course, a fresh sin to tell a lie in confession, for the priest
> is in the place of God. When we tell a lie in confession, we are re-
> ally lying to God. But it is silly to tell a lie in confession because
> the priest is there only to help us.[132]

Whether the children were convinced is another matter.

Another custom that evoked strong memories among my interlocutors from Wallsend was the practice of "A penny for the black babies." The
Catholic church was heavily invested in missionary work in Africa, and the
children were asked regularly to bring a penny to school. Those pennies
were collected and marked on a special card, and when the card was completed, the children were congratulated for having amassed an amount that
would allow, they were told, to baptize another "black baby" to Catholicism
and give him or her a Christian name. Evidently, the feelings of my interlocutors today regarding this practice are complex.[133]

In addition to the catechism, and how to act during the sacraments
of confession and communion, the children learned to pray. Possibly the
most popular prayer book at the time was *A Simple Prayer Book,* which had
millions of copies in print, according to its publisher, the Catholic Truth
Society. The book had many editions. During their years in the elementary
school, many of my interlocutors probably had the 1957 edition.

Several prayers (discussed in more detail below) were included in that
edition (and at times, in later ones as well). Some of them would be seen by
many of today's Catholics as inappropriate in general, or inappropriate for
children in particular.

The *Memorare,* a prayer also known (erroneously) as "St Bernard's
Prayer," was placed in the book among the opening "Usual Prayers,"

132. Heenan, *Our Faith,* 140.

133. A.N.13., interview by author, June 24, 2014, Wallsend, REC01:49. On "Black/
Pagan Babies," see also Coffey, *Answers to Questions,* 5–6; Cascone, *Pagan Babies,* 52–57.

appearing on the second page (p. 4) of the small volume. It was apparently one of the most popular, memorized prayers of English Catholics: "It . . . seems to have been the devotional elasticity of the *Memorare* which led to its becoming, alone of modern prayers, nearly as familiar among English Catholics as the *Hail Mary* or *Our Father*."[134] The prayer begins with these words:

> Remember, O most loving Virgin Mary, that it is a thing unheard of, that anyone ever had recourse to thy protection, implored thy help, or sought thy intercession, and was left forsaken.

With all due respect to the Virgin and her believers, a less-than-pious reader cannot escape the feeling that countless reciters of this prayer, including many children, have had to reckon with the fact that, at times, they perhaps felt their prayers have gone unanswered, despite the unconditional promise given at its beginning. Obviously, the children were told their prayers are always answered, even if sometimes the outcome is not what they hoped for. How many were truly convinced it is impossible to know.

A bit later in the book, in the "Additional Prayers" section, an "Act of Resignation" is provided: "O Lord, my God, whatever manner of death is pleasing to Thee, with all its anguish, pains and sorrows, I now accept from Thy hand with a resigned and willing spirit." One can imagine the sort of terror that such a text could sow in a child's mind. Obviously, frightening stories and ideas are not something children are protected from (and according to many, should not be), but it seems Catholic children in England at the time had their particular share of terrifying ideas coming from their Catholic education in general, and prayer books in particular. Some of those that I interviewed mentioned this prayer in particular as one that brought about nightmares. This perhaps is in line with what an important observer and scholar of Catholicism, Henry Outram Evennett, wrote in 1944:

> The hierarchy of values taught by Catholicism is one which runs directly counter to much modern social and moral ideology. . . . Death and original sin are the constants in the light of which the Catholic church surveys humanity. Life is a preparatory stage and its values are secondary. . . . If education is what remains after we have forgotten all we learnt at school, the quintessential left by Catholic education is a lasting consciousness of the fact and meaning of death. . . . Death is seen as the focal point of life.[135]

---

134. Heimann, *Catholic Devotion*, 157 and 90–99.

135. Quoted from Hornsby-Smith, "The Catholic Church," 50.

A few other prayers that my interlocutors described as fundamental during their childhood included the "Come Holy Spirit Fill the Heart of Thy Faithful," the two penitential prayers, used in different contexts, "Confiteor" and "Act of Contrition," and the ancient "Glory Be," which appears, among other places, in various personal devotions, such as the Rosary discussed earlier.

Even if the young Gordon was unhappy with some of the elements in his Catholic education as he hints in various places, there were many people who had a more positive opinion of the issue. In fact, Catholic schools were often considered by parents to provide good education, and the church made great efforts to cater for Catholics wherever they were. Members of the Church of England were aware of it, and at times unhappy with the achievements of their own church in this field: "If the Church of England does not keep its day schools and provide others on the new housing estates, the Roman Catholic church will become the church of England within 100 years," warned Canon C. D. W. Davis, the Anglican rector of Wallsend and rural dean of Tynemouth, in June 1956. Noting that of 9,000 children in the borough, 2,000 go to Catholic schools, he added that,

> In the last 50 years the Church of England definitely failed [at building new schools]. . . . It does not realise that the day schools are a fundamental necessity to keep the masses of people and educate them within the fellowship of the church.[136]

The shared experience of the horrors, as well as the cooperative efforts of populations during World War II, which ended a decade earlier, broke some barriers between denominations.[137] Possibly due to post-war changes in sentiment, as well as the different wind blowing from the Vatican under John XXIII, relations between Catholics and Anglicans had begun also to warm up: in 1960, Archbishop Geoffrey Fisher of Canterbury made a visit to the Vatican without being invited, and was received by Pope John XXIII. This was the first time a pope and an archbishop of Canterbury had met since the Reformation. It is said that John XXIII asked the archbishop when the Anglicans would come back. Archbishop Fisher replied that it was not possible to go back; instead, both churches "must go forward together." The Vatican news channels did their best to downplay the importance of the visit, since it was impossible to conceal it altogether. In the Anglican world, however, the visit sparked a new hope for better relations. It was also reported in Catholic English media.

136. "Catholic Schools Are Commended."

137. See for example in Conway, *Catholic Politics*, 89.

In 1961, the Catholic church and Ireland celebrated 1,500 years of St Patrick's traditional date of death, March 17, 461. Gordon was nine years old, and it is likely that during that "Patrician Year," stories about Patrick and Catholic Ireland were particularly emphasized in the school and parish. In other years as well, a special Mass was celebrated on March 17, "St Patrick Day," in Wallsend churches as elsewhere. In some churches, including the neighboring Catholic parish St Aidan, those who attended the Mass were allowed to wear later, as a proof of their presence, buttonholes of Shamrock. At St Columba's though, the parish of Gordon's family, the practice was ended a few years earlier for practical reasons: "We found that the bad weather made shamrock difficult to obtain," said Father Timothy O'Brien of St Columba's in 1959, "and we discontinued the practice a few years ago."[138]

In the industrial towns of England, such as Newcastle and its neighbors, many Catholics had an Irish background. And yet, during the time of Gordon's childhood, the children of his age generally did not consider themselves "Irish," even if some of their ancestors came from Ireland. They saw themselves as English, partially because this is what the schools told them they were. They did not use Irish accents. For them, the only "Irish" around were the priests who came from Ireland. This was not seen as a badge of pride; rarely would someone self-identify as "Irish" gratuitously.[139] When I asked one of my interlocutors whether he considered himself to be Irish, he said

> No, no. We all considered we have Irish ancestors, and we all got Shamrock on St Patrick's day, but that was the end of it. . . .
> I think [the Irish background] was forgotten a long time ago.
> I mean people knew about it, but it wasn't a very significant fact.[140]

In my interviews, although most expressed somewhat similar ideas, a few felt they were raised with a stronger Irish identity. These were generally the children of actual Irish immigrants. One of them said, "We had a very, very Catholic Irish upbringing. Interesting, with no English saints, for example. We had no St Cuthbert for example, rather St Patrick."[141]

Cuthbert, mentioned by this interlocutor, was one of the most famous "Northern Saints" in England. We will meet his name often in a later chapter. His important legacy is not so much the result of his life story, but rather

138. "Wallsend Will Have," 14.

139. A.N.14., interview by author, December 15, 2014, Wallsend, REC10:68.

140. A.N.15., interview by author, December 13, 2014, Wallsend, REC12:67.

141. L.I., interview by author, December 14, 2014, Durham, REC11:02.

because of what was said to have happened, or more precisely, to not have happened, to his body after his death, and to the complicated story of its whereabouts.

We know much about Cuthbert thanks to Bede. Born around 672, Bede lived in a large monastery in Jarrow, four kilometers as the crow flies from the house in Wallsend where Gordon would spend his childhood almost 1,300 years later. Stones that were used to build his monastery were taken from the nearby Hadrian's Wall, built five centuries earlier. Bede had access to ancient texts, and also to oral traditions brought to his monastery by monks. Considering that the double monastery in Wearmouth-Jarrow was at times the home of hundreds of monks, many of which came from far away, he clearly had a treasure trove of information, and knew how to use it.

In addition to his monumental *Ecclesiastical History of the English People*, Bede is responsible for an extended revision of a previous anonymous work known as *The Life of St Cuthbert*. Bede did not meet Cuthbert, but he was able to speak with people who knew him, some of whom personally assisted Cuthbert or buried him.

Cuthbert was probably born in 634 not far from today's line separating England and Scotland. He most likely entered monastic life in his twenties, initially at the monasteries of Melrose and Ripon. Religious tensions were high in the region. Some Christians followed practices brought by the Italian missionary Paulinus a few decades earlier, reflecting the practices of Rome. Other Christians held dear the practices that were brought from the monastery on the island of Iona, which is today a part of Scotland, just a few years after Paulinus. Finally, in the so-called "Synod of Whitby" in 664, King Oswiu decided that the Roman practices are binding. A symbolic point in the history of Christianity in the North East took place, where subjecting to instructions from Rome became more important than guarding local customs.

Shortly after the dramatic decision at Whitby, Cuthbert (who seems not to have been involved in the synod) was transferred forty miles to the east, from the monastery in Melrose to the monastery of Lindisfarne, where he was appointed a prior, second to the abbot. That monastery was founded several decades earlier by another missionary from Iona, named Aidan. Due to the tide, the island of Lindisfarne (to be later known as "The Holy Island") on Northumbria's eastern coast, is cut off from the mainland twice a day, thus providing both a sense of "remoteness" for the monks living there (when the tide is high), as well as an opportunity to go and preach on the mainland (when the tide is low). Most of what we know about Cuthbert concerns his time there. According to the accounts we have, Cuthbert conducted an austere life as a monk, while providing physical healing and spiritual guidance to the many who came to meet him either on the island or during his many and long missionary travels. Cuthbert seems to have had the friendship and support of people of power, including royalty, abbots, and abbesses. In 676 he decided to lead the life of a hermit, first probably on an islet, and then on a bigger island southeast of Lindisfarne, where he worked the land, built a hermitage for himself, and a shelter for visitors.

In 684, while still on his island of Inner Farne and, we are told, against his wishes, Cuthbert was elected as the bishop of Hexham, about seventy miles to the south. Only after much persuasion did he agree to become a bishop, though not of Hexham, but of Lindisfarne. After his death in Inner Farne in 687, his body was taken back to be buried in Lindisfarne.

Bede and others tell us that eleven years after Cuthbert's death, his coffin was opened and it was discovered that his body remained intact—proof, of course, of his extreme sanctity. Countless miracles were reported to have happened to those seeking his help, and the wealth and fame of Lindisfarne only grew. The fact that Cuthbert began his career when the practices of so-called "Ionan Christianity" were common in the monasteries, and lived through and accepted the transition to Roman practices, possibly contributed to his great stature for later generations of hagiographers. Earlier figures, such as Columba and Aidan, were probably considered with some suspicion from Christian authors after the Romanization of the Northumbrian church.[142] With his glory growing, Cuthbert became the patron saint, and supposedly protector, of Northumbria. He was known to share his coffin with the skull of King Oswald, the brother of King Oswiu from the Synod of Whitby; this probably raised his status among royalty as well.

Vikings from Scandinavia began to arrive by the very end of the eighth century. Two of their first targets in the area were the Island of Lindisfarne, where Aidan and Cuthbert were buried, and the monasteries of Wearmouth-Jarrow, where Bede had lived merely sixty years earlier. The Vikings did not have theological problems with the monasteries and churches they sacked, nor particular interest in the bones these institutions kept: they wanted valuables, and these places were often rich and yet not well protected. After several decades of attacks, these northern invaders started to actually settle in the area.

Despite the great bloodshed, looting, and destruction that the community of Lindisfarne suffered during the Viking attack of 793, it managed to survive.[143] And yet, with the establishment of the Danes and the collapse of the Anglo-Saxon kingdoms around it, the monastery was abandoned about

---

142. See Nixon, *St Cuthbert of Durham*, 59.
143. See also Coupland, "The Vikings," 186–203.

eighty years later, in 875. The monks leaving it took Cuthbert's coffin and other relics and objects of value with them. After a complex journey lasting about eight years, the subject of countless legends of all kinds, they settled not far from Durham, about eighteen miles south of Wallsend. Slightly more than a century later, the coffin was moved to Durham itself.

Cuthbert came to represent Englishness. Patrick came to represented Irishness. In the family of an above-quoted interlocutor, the Irish saint Patrick was more central than the English saint Cuthbert. One can assume such families were the minority, since the big waves of Irish immigration to the area ended in the 1930s. Many in Gordon's generation were already the grandchildren, or great-grandchildren, of Irish immigrants. For them, the priests that often came from Ireland were Irish; they themselves were not. They were Catholic English children. Soon, some of them, Gordon included, would leave the school bearing the name of an Irish saint, Columba, and move to a school commemorating an English one, Cuthbert.

Chapter 3

CATHOLICISM IN STING'S WORK

I'm actually rather grateful for a Catholic upbringing. I think it's a great source
of symbolism and imagery, of guilt, blood, death, eternal damnation—
all of which are great for writing.[1]

WHICH ELEMENTS OR IMAGES from his early childhood and Catholic upbringing, explored in the previous chapter, remained with Gordon/Sting
during his career? Possibly the first obvious allusion to Christianity or Catholicism in his songs appears in the peculiarly named song "De Do Do Do,
De Da Da Da," included in The Police's third album, *Zenyatta Mondatta* of
1980:

> Poets, priests, and politicians,
>   have words to thank for their positions.
> Words that scream for your submission,
>   and no-one's jamming their transmission.
> And when their eloquence escapes you,
>   their logic ties you up and rapes you.

The choice of "poets, priest, and politicians" is interesting. On the one hand,
it is obvious the three groups were put together for alliteration, as the three
words begin with a "p." However, they are all also similar in that much of
their power derives from their use of words: they have "words to thank for
their positions." Priests (and poets, and politicians), says Sting, want to

---

1. Interview in *US Magazine*, April 1996. See http://links.stingandreligion.com/
us96.

control people, with eloquence or oratory. When they are successful, Sting compares their accomplishment to a very violent action: rape. Sting's interest in priests, and his, at times, criticism of them, first expressed here, would continue to appear throughout his work. We will meet priests again and again in later songs.

While during his time with The Police Sting did not use significant and obvious Catholic imagery in his lyrics (one should remember that the two other members of the band were not Catholics), he did so in his first solo album, *The Dream of the Blue Turtles* of 1985, in the song "Moon Over Bourbon Street." The song is a first-person account by a vampire who still has his previous human conscience. He is thus constantly doing things that he knows are wrong. In various places Sting has said that the song is based on the 1976 book *Interview with the Vampire* by Anne Rice (b. 1941).[2] Rice grew up in New Orleans, which is where Sting wrote this song recounting mysterious events that happened on the city's most famous street. Like Sting, Rice was also raised as Catholic. Her book is full of Catholic ideas and imagery: priests, rosaries, crosses, and confessions. In Sting's lyrics, the vampire uses prayer in order to be able to continue his acts: "I pray every day to be strong, for I know what I do must be wrong." Is he praying to God, or is this a secular use of the term? While the song does not seem to give a clear answer at first, it does so later when the vampire asks an existential theological question: how can a believer in God do so much evil? Or in the vampire's words, "How could I be this way when I pray to God above?" The vampire uses a biblical image, understood by Christians to refer to Jesus, to describe how he became what he is: "I was trapped in this life like an innocent lamb."[3]

The vampire employs what seems to be a Catholic image when he laments that his body physically expresses the dualism of his existence: "I've the face of a sinner, but the hands of a priest." When ordained, Catholic priests' hands are anointed with oil, a symbol of the special powers given to them. The priests' hands are supposed to be used to perform holy acts, the first among these is the consecration of bread and wine during Mass. This special devotion toward the priests' hands can be seen in some Catholic milieux, in which people gather after an ordination in order to kiss or at least touch the new priest's hands; in Orthodox Christianity, this devotion is found in many other contexts as well. About a decade before Sting wrote this song, in 1976, a song called "The Beautiful Hands of a Priest" was

2. Whether it was also influenced by "Thriller," released less than two years earlier by Michael Jackson, and dealing with vampires, zombies, and werewolves, I do not know.

3. See for example John 1:36 and 1 Peter 1:19.

released by a famous Irish traditional singer, Tom Lenihan (1905–90). It is not impossible Sting knew it, but even if not, the image of priests' hands has a strong place in Catholic visual culture, strong enough to explain its use in the song.

Another magnificent song, entirely Catholic in its origin and imagery, which Sting did not write the words for, but nevertheless chose to sing and record at the time, is "Gabriel's Message," a Basque song based on a medieval Latin carol. It appeared on a single with the song "Russians" in 1985, but was not included in the album that followed. Two years later, in 1987, Matt Mahurin (b. 1959) directed a stunning video for this song,[4] and the song appeared that same year on the collective album *A Very Special Christmas* produced to benefit the Special Olympics. The song finally appeared on one of Sting's own albums, *If on a Winter's Night . . .* of 2009.

In Sting's second solo album, . . . *Nothing Like the Sun*, there are some songs that use biblical references, and one, "The Secret Marriage," that mentions briefly a Christian/Catholic ritual, or, more precisely, the flouting of that ritual: "No earthly church has ever blessed our union . . . No Bible oath to swear." In some places, Sting was quoted saying that this song is a biographical one:

> [It] is my way of trying to justify or rationalize why I wasn't married to the woman I had lived with [Trudie Styler] for 10 years.[5]

Five years later, in 1992, Sting and Styler got married, and their union was actually blessed in a church, an Anglican one: St Andrew's church in Great Durnford, close to their estate in Wiltshire. "Our marriage is no longer a secret, it's official," Sting said about it in a recording released in 1995.[6]

While Sting's album of 1987, . . . *Nothing Like the Sun*, was marked by the sickness and then passing of his mother, *The Soul Cages* of 1991 was an obvious reaction to the death of his father. It is not surprising then that Catholicism, the religion of his father, was given a special, even if not always positive, place in the album. Sting was forty, and one might reasonably argue that this album represented a crucial moment in his dealing with the religion of his late father and of his childhood. The album's cover is a painting by the Scottish artist Steven Campbell of an object that might be interpreted as a boat under construction. In the background are four crosses on top of

4. See https://links.stingandreligion.com/gabr.

5. I was not able to locate a clear reference to this quote, even though it seems reliable.

6. Sting, *All This Time* CD-ROM ("Alchemical Laboratory").

what seem to be churches.[7] These crosses, over buildings and boats, appear again in illustrations, also by Campbell, inside the album's notes. In a video interview about the album, Sting said this:

> I was brought up a Catholic, so that's in the front line for me! . . . I was educated . . . with those sermons about hell and eternal torment, and torture, fire. It's pretty heavy stuff for a kid to accept. . . . We spent all of our days doing our work under this picture of a tortured man on a cross with blood pouring out of him. Pretty macabre! Again, I don't regret it, but I think you have to look at it objectively and say what is this . . . ?[8]

One of the most remarkable songs from the album, "All This Time," is a fast and upbeat song, a classic example of a technique Sting uses occasionally: cheerful-sounding musical accompaniment to a rather complex and dark narrative. "All This Time" includes a lengthy description of priests visiting the narrator's dying father:

> Two priests came round our house tonight,
>> one young, one old, to offer prayers for the dying, to serve the final rite.
> One to learn, one to teach, which way the cold wind blows,
>> fussing and flapping in priestly black like a murder of crows.

In the preceding song of the same album, "Island of Souls," a man is severely wounded in an "industrial accident," and has "maybe three weeks to live." His son, "Billy," clearly a reference to the young Gordon, imagines taking him on a boat to some remote place. In the song we analyze here, "All This Time," it seems the story continues, and the son reports he "saw two priests on the ferry." During Sting's childhood, priests were always dressed in black cassocks, resulting in the boy seeing them as "crows." And they definitely could have come on a ferry: until 1986, a ferry connected Hebburn, on the other side of the Tyne, and Wallsend. Apparently, these same two priests come to visit the dying man, and the son ponders again taking his father's body on a boat and burying him at sea.

Today, many Catholics who live in a church struggling with a severe shortage of priests, and in heavily industrialized societies in which death often occurs in an institution, never experience such visits to their homes. At best, a hospital chaplain might visit the sick and dying in the hospital or

---

7. See https://links.stingandreligion.com/scco.

8. The interview is available online, but no information about its exact date, location, or the name of the journalist, is provided. See http://links.stingandreligion.com/ncin. The quoted section begins on min. 10:43.

hospice. During Sting's childhood it was, on the other hand, rather common, as we saw earlier. Although complaints regarding the shortage of priests were frequent in Catholic newspapers already then,[9] their relative number was much higher than today, and a visit of a priest in a home was a rather frequent event. A study already mentioned above,[10] of a Catholic parish in Liverpool in 1957, when Gordon was six years old, showed that 64 percent of the interviewed said the most important duty of the priest was to visit parishioners in their homes (96 percent said the priest visited their house once every six weeks), and 42 percent said a priest's main role was to assist the sick and dying.[11] Assuming that the situation in Sting's hometown was not very different, a priest visiting a child's home was not a rare event.

The priests try to understand, and possibly to teach one another to discern, "which way the cold wind blows," meaning, I believe, how close is death. Because it is clearly approaching, they also perform the "final rite," also known during Gordon's childhood by its more formal name, "Extreme Unction" (today: "Anointing of the Sick").

Since the Middle Ages it is one of the seven Catholic sacraments, having at its core an anointing of an ailing person with previously consecrated oil. This sacrament rests upon various verses in the New Testament, including a text from James 5:14–15 (JB):

> If one of you is ill, he should send for the elders of the church, and they must anoint him with oil in the name of the Lord and pray over him. The prayer of faith will save the sick man and the Lord will raise him up again; and if he has committed any sins, he will be forgiven.

The Catholic belief in the existence of a world beyond this one and in the immortality of the soul is essential to understanding this sacrament. It is not a healing ritual, and there is no promise that it will contribute to the physical well-being of the sick person. Whatever the person's fate, Catholics believe that the sacrament will help him or her in the next stage of life, in body, spirit, or both, including by absolving his or her sins. At the time of Sting's childhood, prior to the reforms of the Second Vatican Council in the 1960s (which will be discussed in the following chapter), the anointing was accompanied by a Latin text, which was repeated while different organs of the dying (eyes, mouth, ears, legs, etc.) were anointed:

---

9. See below the mention of a letter from the local bishop when Gordon was eleven, on p. 106.

10. See pp. 45–46.

11. Ward, *Priests and People*, 47 and 57.

> Through this holy unction and His own most tender mercy may
> the Lord pardon thee whatever sins or faults thou hast commit-
> ted through [the relevant organ], Amen.[12]

The rite generally included a confession prior to the anointing, and a reception of "viaticum," a piece of consecrated bread. The priests who performed
the ritual in Sting's childhood parish recorded what they did in a special
book. Each log describes, other than the name, address, age, and complaint
of the ailing person, which one of the following five parts of the ritual were
performed: Pen(itence), Com(munion), Viat(icum), Ext(reme) Unc(tion),
and Ult(imate) Ben(ediction). In most cases, all these rituals were done,
but not always. Each log also includes a remark: whether the person died
shortly after (in that case, a "R.I.P." with the date), or if she or he recovered.[13]
The rite also incorporated (and still incorporates) various "prayers for the
dying." In the song, Sting has the priest utter these words:

> Blessed are the poor, for they shall inherit the earth.
> Better to be poor than be a fat man in the eye of a needle.

This is of course Sting's own version of Jesus's saying in the "Sermon on
the Mount,"[14] one of the texts actually recommended in the liturgical books
for this sacrament. Sting's version of the sermon is a play on texts found in
the New Testament. He took two parts of different verses—one speaking
about the poor (Matthew 5:3), another about the meek (Matthew 5:5)—and
merged them. He then added his own rephrasing of another proverb attributed to Jesus that is found elsewhere, that "it is easier for a camel to pass
through the eye of a needle than for a rich man to enter the kingdom of
heaven" (Matthew 19:24; Mark 10:24; Luke 18:24). Sting's rephrasing is an
ironic one: it is obvious that almost anything is better than being a "fat man
in the eye of a needle." One does not need Jesus to know that. Billy's father
hears the text quoted by the priests and remarks that indeed, the deal Jesus
offered to the poor—people like him—was not worthy. Inheriting the earth

---

12. Catholics of the late 1960s were told they had to modify many rituals they were
used to in order to be in tune with the time, and get rid of unnecessary elements. In this
ritual, the anointing of various organs of the dying was suppressed in 1974 and replaced
by only one anointing. This was exactly in line with the instructions in the *Book of
Common Prayer* of 1549, penned by the Catholics' biggest enemy, Thomas Cranmer
(1489–1556). In this case, like in countless others, English Catholics of the 1960s and
1970s were instructed to do what English Catholics of the sixteenth century tried to
fight. In the sixteenth century these instructions came from London and Canterbury.
In the twentieth century, they came from Rome and Westminster.

13. TWA, C.WA9/11 (Sick call book [Last Rites], 1961 to 1987).

14. On Sting's appreciation of this New Testament text, see above, pp. 6–7.

after others have already gotten their use of it does not sound to him like such an attractive reward:

> As these words were spoken, I swear I hear the old man laughing:
> "What good is a used up world, and how could it be worth having?"

Later in the song, the boy expresses his wish to bury his father at sea, an act not generally endorsed by the Catholic church for those dying on land. Clearly, neither the father nor the son are a model of piety. The boy, hearing and seeing the rite the priests perform, also asks a question. It is not clear if he is addressing one of the priests or his dying father when he says "Father, if Jesus exists, then how come he never lives here?"[15]

The song does not tell us if or how Billy's inquiry was answered. The question, which can be seen as rather irreverent, is in fact a serious Christological inquiry: if Jesus share(d) with humans their humanity, with all its difficulties, would it not be appropriate for him to also share the hard life of those living near the River Tyne, working—and dying—in the shipyards? Moreover, why, before his supposed resurrection, did he live in a remote place near the Mediterranean, and not in Wallsend, a place so much more important for the child?[16] Sting is not the first English poet to suggest that Jesus visited, or should have visited, the island. In fact, he might have been inspired by a poem by William Blake (1757–1827), which was made into a popular anthem, "Jerusalem," in 1916, by Hubert Parry. It begins with these words:

> And did those feet in ancient time, walk upon England's mountains green?
> And was the holy Lamb of God, on England's pleasant pastures seen![17]

Later in this same, intricate song, Sting refers to the ancient remains from the Roman period in his childhood region of Northumberland:

15. In some places, one can find "lived here" and not "lives here." In the official recording, Sting says "lives."

16. Bob Dylan had made a similar move in his song "Highway 61, Revisited" (1965), by placing the biblical story of Abraham's binding of Isaac in a place important to him, Highway 61 (officially called US Route 61), instead of on some distant Mediterranean mountain. See Yadin-Israel, *The Grace of God*, 27.

17. The Book of Mormon claims that after his resurrection Jesus visited America: such a narrative, written by a North American, might have quite similar psychological reasoning. See Book of Mormon, 3 Nephi 11.

[Our/The] teachers told us the Romans built this place.
They built a wall and a temple, [an/on the] edge of the empire
Garrison town.
They lived and they died, they prayed to their gods,
  but the stone gods did not make a sound,
and their empire crumbled 'til all that was left,
  were the stones the workmen found.

This stanza combines different sites and memories from Sting's youth. The stones that "the workmen found" are probably Roman vestiges, including parts of Hadrian's Wall, which were, in fact, discovered near the shipyard in Wallsend ("an edge of the empire Garrison town") some decades before, perhaps during Gordon's childhood. On the other hand, the workers did not find a temple in Wallsend (neither did anyone else for that matter), so it is likely that Sting is referring to something he saw elsewhere, such as the excavations of Housesteads, about thirty-five miles west of Wallsend. According to one of my interlocutors, it is possible that Sting is referring here to a field trip that he and his grammar school classmates went on at the age of fourteen.

The idea that the Romans had "stone gods" which "did not make a sound" is a common and old motif in Bible-related religions, meant to ridicule so-called "pagan" religions. Pope Gregory, who in 597 sent the man known later as Augustine of Canterbury to England, and who indeed brought Christianity to the Anglo-Saxons in the south, explicitly said the following about the locals: "The nation of the Angli, placed in a corner of the world, remained up to this time misbelieving in the worship of stocks and stones."[18] Similarly, in Jewish tradition, one finds a well-known ancient story in which Abraham ridicules the supposed "idols" of his pagan father Terah, by making his father admit that the idols can do nothing.[19] The same story was integrated into the Quran.[20] In the Bible itself, a verse from the Book of Psalms is often understood to be related to these types of discourse:

[Whereas] their idols, in silver and gold, products of human skill, have mouths, but never speak, eyes, but never see, ears, but never hear, noses, but never smell, hands, but never touch, feet, but never walk, and not a sound from their throats. Their

---

18. Gregory the Great, *Registrum Epistolarum*, Book VIII, Letter 30, Letter to Eulogius, bishop of Alexandria, translated by James Barmby. Quoted from Schaff and Wace, *Nicene and Post-Nicene*. See http://links.stingandreligion.com/greg.

19. Genesis Rabbah 38.

20. See Quran's *Surah Al-Anbiya* 21:51–71.

makers will end up like them, and so will anyone who relies on them.[21]

In fact, the word "prayed" in Sting's lyrics is more appropriate to religions such as Christianity, and less to Roman religions, where the central act of faith was worshipping the gods by performing acts that would please them (such as offering sacrifices). It should be noted that Sting does not say explicitly that the Romans prayed to these "stone gods." In fact, the words "They prayed to their gods, but the stone gods did not make a sound" can easily be understood to refer to two distinct things: the immaterial gods that they prayed to, on the one hand, and the visible representations of these gods in stone that played a part in their rituals. Moreover, the text represents what the teachers said to the children, not what Sting himself necessarily thinks. For the teacher who in reality, or only in Sting's imagination, uttered these words, all this was perhaps a kind of a local "sacred history." The stone gods of the Romans did not respond. They were false. Consequently—a child can definitely understand from such a description, if it was really said—their empire fell. Our Christian God is different. Our God is real. We will endure.

In another verse from this song, Sting says that "Men go crazy in congregations, they only get better one by one." It has been suggested already by others that Sting borrowed this idea from the nineteenth-century Scottish author Charles Mackay's statement: "Men, it has been well said, think in herds; it will be seen that they go mad in herds, while they only recover their senses slowly, and one by one."[22] That said, it is also possible that Sting was not aware of Mackay's text, but that he (and perhaps Mackay, as well) rephrased a common oral saying; Mackay himself says that what he is to affirm "has been well said." Sting rephrases the same idea so that it speaks unequivocally about religious groups, if the word "congregation" is given its common meaning. Such language probably does not qualify as being antireligious per se, although it likely reflects Sting's unease with some aspects of so-called "organized religion."

In other songs in the album, Catholic motifs appear momentarily. "Jeremiah Blues (Part 1)" speaks, among other issues, of a pope who "claimed that he'd been wrong in the past," and that "this was a big surprise." Sting had an audience with Pope John Paul II in 1989, two years before the release of this album, together with Chief Raoni from Brazil. Perhaps he is referring to something that was said at that time, perhaps to another papal statement. A few lines later, in four words that include two unexpected facts, we hear a rumor: that a "Cardinal's wife was jailed." Normally, a cardinal is

21. Psalm 115:4–8 (JB).

22. Mackay, *Memoirs of Extraordinary*, preface.

not supposed to have a wife, and even if a cardinal had one, we would not expect her to be a criminal. Misgivings about Catholic clergy has been, no doubt for many centuries, a major topic for gossip among Catholics and their neighbors.[23]

In an instrumental piece on the same album, "Saint Agnes & the Burning Train," Sting gives an "honorary sainthood" to his paternal grandmother Agnes, his only Catholic-raised grandparent, who happened to be once on a train when a fire broke out. With no relation to that event, she died seven years after the album came out, in 1998, at the age of ninety-five. For more than a decade, she was Sting's only surviving ancestor.

The title song, "The Soul Cages," includes nothing that is obviously Catholic, other than the topic of souls trapped and redeemed, to be discussed later.[24] Angels and fallen angels figure prominently in the album's final song, aptly titled "When the Angels Fall." The description of an act ("Take your father's cross gently from the wall; a shadow still remaining") might be on an actual deed that Sting did at one time: he mentions a similar object again in a song written more than two decades later ("Dead Man's Boots," 2013), when a rebelling son reminds his father that "all you've got left is that cross on the wall." Perhaps it is not a coincidence that "When the Angels Fall" also portrays a strong image of the destruction of Christian/Catholic monuments: "See the churches fall in mighty arcs of sound, and all that they're containing." Whether this was intentional or not is hard to say, but in practice, the album ends with powerful images that perhaps hint at a collapse of religiosity: a cross is removed, angels are falling, and churches, and their content, are in ruins. Sting was forty, having recently lost both his parents to cancer. The world became darker, and the religion he grew up in did not provide comfort anymore.

Two years later, Sting released a new album: *Ten Summoner's Tales* (1993). This title is an obvious wordplay on "The Summoner's Tale," one of the stories in the medieval English collection known as *The Canterbury Tales*, as well as a hint to his own last name, Sumner, which Sting says derives from "summoner," a person who summons others to court. Sting has said that he also chose the name because of the very irreverent nature of the medieval tale: "It's mainly about farting, I think. It's a very anti-religious tale. [The protagonist Thomas] has a running battle with a monk, who is also one of the pilgrims. It's about the corruption in the church basically, and farting. . . . It was a mild joke. People took it far more seriously."[25] Both Sting

23. See also Gable, *The Words and Music*, 59–60.

24. See pp. 160–61.

25. Sting, *All This Time* CD-ROM, Part 9 ("Library"), 12:51, https://links.stingandreligion.com/cdr3.

and others have described this album as an eclectic collection of relatively simple songs: a joyous work that counterbalances the dark, confessional album that preceded it. While this description may be, in part, appropriate, it is nonetheless a Sting album: some of the songs are deep explorations of love, relations, friendships, success, and existence. Catholic motifs occur in several of them.

The opening track, "If I Ever Lose My Faith in You," which became one of Sting's greatest hits, contains only one obvious line about Catholicism: "You could say I lost my belief in the holy church." Who the singer is referring to as "you," when he says, "If I ever lose my faith in you," is unclear. It seems to be a loved one, not a divine entity, although Sting himself said he intentionally left this vague:

> [The] "You" could be my producer, it could be faith in God. It could be a faith in myself or a faith in romantic love. It could be all of those things, but I don't define it.[26]

Two years later, Sting perhaps began to see his own song in a slightly different way:

> The song "If I Ever Lose My Faith in You" is a statement about, I suppose, my beliefs. And that I had lost a lot of faith in institutions. Institutions that were designed to sustain us, like government, church, television. And yet, I still maintain a faith in life itself, I still have a sense of hope and a sense of optimism, even though it's harder to define than things I have lost faith in. So I define very carefully the things I have lost faith in, and define quite vaguely what I keep faith in.[27]

Religious imagery, particularly Catholic imagery, figures prominently in the song's music video (directed by Howard Greenhalgh, b. 1963).[28] The video opens with Sting spinning crosses around himself, an image that reappears multiple times throughout. It also features monks, a church, possibly a group of pilgrims, and a monstrance. It was partially filmed in and around Glastonbury Tor, a peculiar site in South West England, which seems to have been viewed as sacred for thousands of years by various successive cultures. Famous myths and traditions claimed that King Arthur and his

---

26. Sting, *Ten Summoner's Tales Interview.*

27. Sting, *All This Time* CD-ROM, Part 1, "Gothic Cathedral," 9:55, https://links.stingandreligion.com/cdr4.

28. See https://links.stingandreligion.com/ife.

wife Guinevere were buried there, and that Jesus's Holy Grail was kept in the same place.[29]

Britain, unlike some other countries or nations, does not have a solid, ancient tradition about a founding figure of the earliest local Christian faith, such as an apostle or a missionary. This fact probably created space for the existence of many traditions on the issue. Various medieval legends, probably created in the twelfth century and later, claim that the first Christian to reach England was Joseph of Arimathea, who, according to various accounts in the New Testament, was a secret disciple of Jesus that obtained from Pilate the right to remove Jesus's body from the cross, and bury it in a burial cave he owned.[30] According to these medieval stories, Joseph later left Jerusalem and made it to England, to Glastonbury in the South. Joseph, so goes the story, brought with him the "Holy Grail." What the nature of this object was is not clear, but one common interpretation—adopted, for instance, by Monty Python and Indiana Jones—was that it was the cup used during Jesus and his disciples' "Last Supper," and/or in which Joseph collected the crucified master's blood.[31]

It is obvious that Sting was aware of all of this when he chose (or agreed) to film the video at Glastonbury Tor, and it seems likely that these sacred traditions were at least part of what attracted him and Greenhalgh to the site. And yet not everything in the video was his own idea, or should, according to him, be taken seriously:

> As I was doing that film . . . I was on this kind of wheel, and I was whirling around, there were kinds of crucifixes going around my head, and I was wondering "what the hell does this mean?" I have no idea. I think this was the director's idea. I am really not taking much responsibility for that. I think it was a cool visual image, but no, it doesn't have any particular meaning . . . . *[laughing]*.[32]

Sting appears in the video as a bishop with a staff at various points, and as himself using a carved bishop's seat. In one scene, he looks like the mythical King Arthur. He also stands in a pose that is reminiscent of the crucified Jesus, and then resembles Moses parting the sea. At another point, monks put a spell on him while he meditates (clearly hinting at his interest in and practice of Yoga, which began a few years earlier), turning him to a pig;

29. See Bowman, "Drawn to Glastonbury," 29–62.

30. See Matthew 27:57–60; Mark 15:42–46; Luke 23:50–53; John 19:38–40.

31. For other interpretations see Eco, *The Book of Legendary*, 248–78.

32. Sting, *All This Time* CD-ROM, Part 1, "Gothic Cathedral," 9:04, https://links. stingandreligion.com/cdr5.

later he is surrounded by fire that appears to symbolize hell. For a person with no knowledge of Catholicism and the Bible, the music video would be practically incomprehensible.

Another song from this album, "Saint Augustine in Hell," is one of Sting's most "Catholic" songs. Augustine of Hippo (354–430) is not someone a good Catholic would expect to find in hell, despite the fact that during his younger years, Augustine was not always a poster child for sanctity. For some reason, Sting places him in hell nevertheless. The song opens with a plea for redemption, and revelation, uttered by an agnostic who is unsure whether there really is somewhere "up there":

> If somebody up there likes me,
> somebody up there cares,
>> deliver me from evil,
>> save me from these wicked snares.
> Not into temptation,
> not to cliffs of fall,
>> on to revelation,
>> and lesson for us all.

The striving for a personal redemption here is clear, but a communal aspect exists as well; it contains a "lesson for us all." The agnostic is still of a Catholic type. To quote Michael Tylor Ross's words regarding another song by Sting, "Sting's sense of redemption does not fall into the trap of the personal salvation all too prevalent in many forms of Christianity. For Sting, we do not overcome our disorder by being saved alone . . . ."[33] Connections between this text and the famous Christian "Lord's Prayer" (a.k.a. the "Our Father"), in which saving from evil and temptation are also prominent, are rather obvious.[34] The song then merges a story of jealousy and possibly murder with a sharp criticism of various professions: judges, "failed saints," cardinals, archbishops, barristers, certified accountants, and music critics.[35] Intertwined in all of this is a phrase based on a famous statement of Augustine of Hippo's, who said that as a young man, he used to pray to God "Make me chaste, but not just yet."[36] Additionally, Sting says, "It's a promise or a lie, I'll repent before I die." Many early Christians, especially in the fourth century, had a similar attitude, and delayed their baptism (considered at that time,

---

33. Ross, "Sacred Love," 78.

34. See Matthew 6:9–13 and Luke 11:2–4.

35. The mention of "certified accountants" is a clear reference to an accountant who was in 1995 found guilty of stealing money from Sting. This part of the song is narrated by actor David Foxxe.

36. Augustine, *Confessions*, XIII, Chapter 7, 17.

before the sacrament of penitence was created, to be the only way to absolve sin) until they were on their deathbed. Sting then appeals to a handful of "saints"—including Theresa (which one, we shall see), his mother, Mary the mother of Jesus, and the so-called "whore of Babylon" from the New Testament—to explain the weakness of the flesh:

> Blessed St. Theresa, the whore of Babylon,
>   Madonna and my mother, all rolled into one.
> You've got to understand me, I'm not a piece of wood,
>   Francis of Assisi, could never be this good.

Mary the mother of Jesus (the "Madonna") had clearly, according to Catholic belief, issues with sexuality: she gave birth without having sex and remained a virgin thereafter, despite being married to Joseph. The "Whore of Babylon" is a mythical figure, or maybe a code-name for the Roman Empire, spoken about in the seventeenth chapter of the New Testament's Book of Revelation. She, or it, is the quintessential example of vice, including sexual vice. In England following the Reformation, the term was often used by Protestants to refer to Catholicism, the papacy, and Queen Mary Tudor. When calling upon Theresa, Sting is possibly referring to the Spanish Teresa of Ávila of the sixteenth century, who described some of her ecstatic spiritual encounters in almost orgasmic terms,[37] or perhaps to the French Thérèse de Lisieux, who already at the age of fifteen, and until her death nine years later, was enclosed in a cloister and detached from the surrounding world.[38] Finally, Sting's own mother Audrey was involved in an extra-marital affair, discovered by none other than the young Gordon.[39] To these four female figures, Sting added the male Italian Francis of Assisi of the twelfth and thirteenth centuries. Francis was known to fight temptations of the flesh by, for example, throwing himself into ice in the winter.[40] Even St Francis, Sting seems to say, would not be able to resist the temptations that the narrator (he himself?) faces in general, and perhaps in a particular case, when the previously mentioned four female figures are all rolled into one in the woman he encounters.

---

37. A famous example from her autobiography is to be found in Teresa, *The Life*, 275. In art, see for example the famous statue "Ecstasy of Saint Teresa" at https://links. stingandreligion.com/ecst. See also Winchester, "Sexualizing Saint Teresa."

38. English and Scottish Catholics were very instrumental both in the canonization of Thérèse de Lisieux as well as in spreading her cult. See more in Harris, "Thérèse de Lisieux," 262–78.

39. Sting, *Broken Music*, 66–67.

40. See for example in Thomas, *The First Life*, I.16.

A year later, in late 1994, Sting released a new album, *Fields of Gold*, celebrating ten years of his solo career. The album is mostly a compilation of some of his best-known hits up to then, with only two new songs: "When We Dance" (which was released as a single a few weeks earlier) and "This Cowboy Song" (which was distributed again in 1995 as a single). "When We Dance" mentions two topics common in Sting's work: souls (to be discussed in a later chapter) and angels. In one sentence of fourteen words, "The priest has said my soul's salvation is in the balance of the angels," Sting combines five images of great importance to Catholicism: a priest, the soul, salvation, judgment ("balance"), and angels.

Although the priest says that the angels will determine whether Sting will be saved, Sting disagrees. While speaking again of the issue of passion or temptation, which was hinted at in "Saint Augustine in Hell," he claims he is in charge of his own soul, and the ultimate judge of his own faith: "Underneath the wheels of passion, I keep the faith in my fashion." In fact, it seems that he wants to get rid of the entire idea of a heavenly judgment, and of those promoting it:

> If I could break down these walls
>   and shout my name at heaven's gate,
> I'd take these hands and I'd destroy
>   the dark machineries of fate.
> Cathedrals are broken, heaven's no longer above,
>   and hellfire's a promise away.

Sting's anger about the hellfire sermons he and his peers heard in childhood, which was mentioned above,[41] is obvious. Among other things, the "breaking" of cathedrals here seems to be a new take on ideas found in the previously analyzed "When the Angels Fall," where the listener was invited to "see the churches fall in mighty arcs of sound, and all that they're containing." Interestingly, the music video for "When We Dance" (also produced by Howard Greenhalgh) does not include Christian or religious imagery, despite the rather obvious religious motifs within the text.

The other new song from this same album, "This Cowboy Song," contains fascinating religious themes. The narrator is a cowboy, one of a group of riders who "lacked the consciences to pray." The night is frightening, and he is brooding over how and if he should pray. Wanting to avoid the "Devil to pay on judgement day," the cowboy asks, "Would Jesus strike me down if I should pray?" It seems he has two reasons to fear Jesus's wrath. On the one hand, he does not know actual prayers, and wonders if a song he knows can serve as a substitute:

41. See p. 44.

> This cowboy song is all I know,
>> to bring me back into your arms.
> Your distant sun, your shining light,
>> you'll be my Dog Star shining tonight.[42]

On the other hand, this cowboy recognizes his faults:

> I've been the lowest of the low on the planet,
>> I've been a sinner all my days.
> When I was living with my hand on the trigger,
>> I had no sense to change my ways.

What's more, he admits that he was previously offered another route by a preacher, which in Sting's Catholic world, is likely to mean a priest: "The preacher asked if I'd embrace the resurrection, to suck the poison from my life." He ignored the invitation to believe in a core element of the Christian faith, and seems to regret it now: "Just like an existential cowboy villain, his words were balanced on my knife." He now wants to try again: "This cowboy song is all I know, to bring me back into your arms."

The motif of a simple person wondering if he or she may pray to God using simple language is a common folkloristic theme in many religious stories around the world; the answer is often that such communication is not only possible, but also most desirable to the divinities. Sting probably knew this motif before using it in this song.

Howard Greenhalgh produced the music video for this song as well. He filmed it as a traditional Western (shot I believe at Sting's residence in the South of England), hinting at the religious motifs in a simple but obvious way: in two of the primary settings where Sting sings (in a prison and in a bed with several women) a large and very visible cross is hung on the wall. The redemption of the cross is offered to this sinner wherever he is.

The song "Valparaiso," from Sting's later album, *Mercury Falling* of 1996, includes another cross. The song describes the navigation of a ship around the southern tip of South America.[43] While navigating, the sailor is aided by a "Cross in the sky," and the "Star of the sea." The first reference may refer to the "Southern Cross," a famous bright star that is a part of the "Crux Constellation," visible indeed in the Southern Hemisphere, and crucial for navigation. It may also refer to the Christian faith in general, or to the cross

---

42. "Dog Star" is a common name for Sirius, the brightest star visible on Earth at night. The name comes from its being the most obvious part of the "Greater Dog" (*Canis Major*) constellation. Sting mentions the "Dog Star" again in the same album, in the song "Valparaiso."

43. On Sting's fascination, since childhood, with South America, see Sting, *Lyrics*, 210.

that, according to legend, appeared in the sky (or in a vision, or in a dream) to Emperor Constantine in the fourth century CE, and influenced his later conversion to Christianity. The second reference, to the "Star of the sea" (*Stella Maris*), seems to be more specific, hinting at the Virgin Mary. Since his childhood, Sting found this image to be powerful:

> Mary the Star of the Sea became my icon as a child, floating above the ocean in her blue veil, her head ringed by stars and tilted gently to one side, her eyes modestly downcast as if in thought. Her smile was delicate, Venusian, and held the promise of infinite patience and compassion. She was a being who could intercede for me in the court of heaven. My favorite childhood hymn had ended "Virgin, most pure star of the sea, pray for the wonderer, pray for me."[44]

Sting's quote is from the hymn "Hail Queen of Heaven" (*Salve Regina*), hymn 101 in the *Westminster Hymnal*, which was widely used by English Catholics during his childhood, and which will be discussed later.[45] The topic of burial at sea, mentioned already in "All This Time" of 1991, appears again in this song. It suggests that without a proper Christian burial, the fate of the dead is hard to determine: "If I should die, and water's my grave, she'll never know if I'm damned or I'm saved."

Just before the new millennium began, Sting released another album: *Brand New Day* (1999). He intended to show optimism for the future:

> At the time that we were working on this album, there was a lot of premillennial hokum about the "end being nigh," doomsday, and Y2K. I wanted to go against all that and sing something optimistic.[46]

One song on the album stands apart to one looking for explicit Christian references: "Fill Her Up." In this song, the man to whom the narrator is speaking is asked to "fill her up," with "her" referring (at the song's beginning) to a car in need of gas. Later, however, the "her" seems to refer to a

---

44. Sting, *Broken Music*, 330. It is possible that the image Sting remembers is more or less similar to this one: https://links.stingandreligion.com/stma, perhaps blended in his memory with a mosaic of Mary on the wall of his childhood church, here: https://links.stingandreligion.com/mos1. On that mosaic, see also pp. 104–5.

45. See below, pp. 111–12. In 1953, when Sting/Gordon was two years old, Pope Pius XII published an encyclical on the medieval theologian Bernard of Clairvaux, which he concluded with a praise of Bernard's sermon about Mary's title "Star of the Sea." It is not impossible that this created a surge in the appreciation of this title among the clergy and then laity. See Pius XII, *Doctor Mellifluus*, May 1953.

46. Sting, *Lyrics*, 228.

woman that needs to be filled with very different things. The future wife of
the protagonist of the song needs to be, if we use a term that is not found
in the text itself, converted, before he can spend the rest of his life with her.
Instead of stealing a box with cash as he had considered doing, filling his girl
with shame, he should do something else:

> You gotta fill her up with Jesus,
>   you gotta fill her up with light;
> You gotta fill her up with spirit,
>   you gotta fill her up with grace;
> You gotta fill her up with heaven,
>   you got the rest of life to face.

A song that was released three years later, "Dead Man's Rope," in the album
Sacred Love of 2003, includes again explicit references to none other than
the Son of God himself:

> With Hell below me,
>   and Heaven in the sky above,
> I've been walking,
>   I've been walking away from Jesus' love.

It is a remarkable text, one that seems to be a psychological biography. According to Sting, he wrote the song while working on his memoir, an act that
naturally made him think of his past. Whether the song's narrator is Sting's
own self-reflection, or whether he has created an imaginary persona, I cannot say with certainty, even though there is no obvious reason why it cannot
be autobiographic. The song starts with a dark description of the person's
past, and slowly but surely moves to a brighter, more positive, optimistic,
and literally faithful, present. The line that seems to separate the two sections refers to a "sweet rain of forgiveness." Other than Jesus, hell, heaven,
and forgiveness, the song also discusses the creation of the world, "the hand
of an angel," and grace. All the Catholic keywords that we have already seen
in other songs appear again here. It is a song that could fit perfectly within a
religious ceremony, similarly perhaps (according to various reports) to the
way that some of U2's songs are used.[47] Does this song describe a "return"
to—or at least a consideration of—the traditional Christian belief in Jesus
and his promise of forgiveness? Is this "rain of forgiveness" an allusion to
Christian baptism? Sting does not tell us, but if he wrote it about himself, it
is hard to avoid such an interpretation, particularly when this song is a part

---

47. See for example Rothman, "The Church of U2." On some interesting differences
between Sting and U2 with regard to religion see Ross, "Sacred Love," 87–88. See also
Calhoun, *U2*.

of an album packed with religious and spiritual themes. Twelve years had passed, and Sting's distance from Christianity that was evident in his album of 1991 had perhaps been reduced by the time of the release of this album in 2003.

Three other songs in the album include Christian concepts. "This War," a powerful anti-war song, is about the invasion of Iraq by a force composed mostly of American and British troops in March of 2003, a few months before the release of the album. It is hard to avoid the impression that Tony Blair—the British Prime Minister at that time who cooperated with the American President George W. Bush, despite very strong opposition in his own country—is one of those harshly criticized in the song. Whether Sting speaks to Blair, or to Bush—both leaders having robust Christian beliefs— or to someone else, the words are strong, and incomprehensible without some knowledge of Christian traditions. The very first sentence of the song, "You've got the mouth of a she wolf, inside the mask of an innocent lamb," clearly refers to Matthew 7:15, concerning false prophets being like wolves dressed as sheep.

Shortly after, more religious associations appear: "In the temple that was Mammon's, you were ordained the parish priest," Sting says. Mammon, one should remember, is a word coming from Aramaic, a language close to Hebrew, which entered many other languages through its mention in the New Testament.[48] Originally meaning simply money and wealth, it gained a pejorative sense in Christianity. In the Middle Ages, the belief that Mammon is the name of the demon of greed was developed. Sting clearly uses the term in this way: Mammon has a temple, and the person he speaks to is serving him. One can hardly avoid the thought this is related to charges that the war was, among other things, fueled by the urge to control Kuwait's and Iraq's oil fields. Those Sting admonish are in a way guilty of idolatry: they serve the demon-god of money. Sting continues the attack, aiming explicitly at a British person who stands "on the white Cliffs of Dover":

> You may ask, what does it profit a man
> to gain the whole world and suffer the loss of his soul?

Again, this line comes from a Christian context: it is a quote from the New Testament Gospel of Mark 8:36, using either the Darby or the Douay-Rheims translations, both of which are translations made by English Christians, and versions Sting might have known in his childhood. Towards the end of the song, Sting highlights the fact that there are indeed many parallel wars at present. One of them, he says, is among religious people in general, and

48. See Matthew 6:24; Luke 16:9, 11, 13.

Christians in particular: "There's a war inside religion, and what Jesus might have meant."

"Sacred Love," the album's title song, has religious motifs in almost every line. After a text that includes many biblical motifs, Sting describes a prayer. If in many common Christian images, all bow to Christ, here, they all bow to Love:

> So I got down on my knees and I prayed to the skies,
> when I looked up could I trust my eyes?
> All the saints and angels and the stars up above,
> they all bowed down to the flower of creation.
> Every man, every woman,
> every race, every nation,
> it all comes down to this
> sacred love.

Although Sting occasionally sings songs written by others, such performances are rarely part of his major albums. Two successive albums he released soon after (2006 and 2009) were an exception to this rule. The first did not include any songs written by himself, and the second includes only three or four with original lyrics (depending on how they are evaluated). Most of the authors of the lyrics in both of these albums lived in the rather distant past. *Songs from the Labyrinth* (2006) is based entirely on music composed by John Dowland (1563–1626), with the exception of one tune ("Have You Seen the Bright Lily Grow"), composed by his contemporary, Robert Johnson (c. 1583–1633). Most of the lyrics are by Dowland as well. A few are by his contemporaries: the aforementioned Robert Johnson, and Edward Dyer (1543–1607). Some are of unknown origin.

Dowland was born five years after Queen Elizabeth ascended to the throne: the first four decades of his life were during the long reign of this Protestant monarch. Elizabeth was, of course, the daughter of Henry VIII, who began the official process of Reformation in England, which ultimately brought about the existence of a "Church of England" not subordinated to the popes in Rome. An exceptionally accomplished lute player, Dowland hoped to become a lutenist at Elizabeth's court, but the position was given to someone else. Highly disappointed, he accepted a lucrative position in the court of the King of Denmark. When he returned to England, King James VI and I had assumed the throne, and a few years later Dowland was appointed as one of his lutenists. Dowland spent his final year under yet another monarch, King Charles I.

The songs performed by Sting in this album are remarkably free from any religious notions, perhaps with the exception of the first track, an instrumental piece, entitled "Walsingham." Walsingham Priory, in Norfolk, has been a major site of Christian pilgrimage for centuries. Like countless other ecclesiastical sites, it was destroyed in 1538, during the reign of Henry VIII. About half a century later, during Dowland's lifetime, an anonymous and popular ballad, lamenting this destruction, appeared.

It is not that Dowland did not write lyrics with religious content, or that he did not compose music to existing texts with religious content. He did both. Sting, however, intentionally or not, only selected pieces that were secular in nature. Judging by its content, the album is of little importance to our study. And yet, Sting's very interest in Dowland might be related, in part, to the fact that Dowland was a convert to Catholicism—one who believed he was not awarded the position he hoped for in Elizabeth's court because of his religion. Dowland had to navigate his Catholic identity while surrounded by many members of the Church of England. He had to keep his distance from Catholic monarchs, and even the pope himself, out of reasonable fear it would mark him as a traitor, a title that could have led him to the gallows. It is reasonable to imagine that Sting felt a certain affinity for this English Catholic of many generations earlier. Unlike the unlucky Dowland, Sting received in 2003 an award of recognition, "For services to the Music Industry," from Queen Elizabeth.[49] Obviously, this was from Elizabeth II, not from the Elizabeth of Dowland's time.

In 2009, Sting released another album based almost exclusively on lyrics and tunes composed by others: *If on a Winter's Night . . .* is a collection of songs composed mostly by other authors and musicians (some of whom are unknown) from the sixteenth to the twenty-first centuries. Out of the eighteen/nineteen songs that appear in various editions of this album, only a few do not seem to have any religious references.[50] Some of those that do are of entirely religious nature. The songs that were not written by Sting are obviously not relevant to this study, even though their very selection by him (from, it seems, many options suggested by the musical director Robert Sadin) can definitely be seen as another form of religious and Catholic expression in his biography. A good example is "Christmas at Sea," a poem written by the nineteenth-century poet Robert Louis Stevenson, an author much

49. See https://links.stingandreligion.com/scbe.

50. Songs with religious references of some kind include: "Gabriel's Message," "Soul Cake" (and the musical riff of "God Rest Ye Merry Gentlemen"), "There Is No Rose of Such Virtue," "Christmas at Sea," "Lo How a Rose E'er Blooming," "The Burning Babe" (a sixteenth-century poem that Sting speaks about in a documentary on this album), "Balulalow," "Cherry Tree Carol," "You Only Cross My Mind in Winter," "A Cradle Song," "Bethlehem Down," and "The Coventry Carol." In some cases, the religious references are relatively minor; in others, they are quite significant. We will refer to some of these songs later.

appreciated by the young Gordon. Sting, together with the Scottish musician Mary Macmaster, put the poem to music and included it in the album. In the song, a sailor realizes to his shame that he is working on Christmas day. What could be a better example of the type of remorse felt by many of those who leave the religion of their youth—or who, at least, do not practice it as carefully as they were taught to?

Among the album's songs that Sting actually wrote, religion appears only once: in "You Only Cross My Mind in Winter" Sting recalls engaging in a debate on faith with the person the song addresses.

A video recording of a live performance of these songs at Durham Cathedral accompanied the release of the album. In addition to the performance itself, this documentary includes a long interview with Sting. Even though one might expect religious and Catholic themes to come up in the interview—on account of the themes of many of the songs as well as the location of the concert—there are only a few. Sting emphasizes that he sees in the album a mixture of themes, connecting the idea of the resurrection of Christ with "the resurrection of the seasons through the winter." Both, he says, "[are] very related to me. I wanted to join the sacred and the secular thing together . . . to show that they are the same thing."[51] He reveals that he was asked to do a Christmas album, but refused; he wanted instead to do a winter album, as winter is a spiritual time for him. In the interview, he says he had not been in Durham Cathedral "for almost forty years." Since he graduated from St Cuthbert's Grammar School (about which we will speak in the next chapter), exactly forty years earlier (1969), and because we know he visited the cathedral during those school years, it is possible that this was in fact his first visit to the cathedral as an adult. He notes that, "I feel very at home here," but does not explain where the idea to perform in Durham Cathedral came from. When I asked him about his choice to perform in that cathedral, he referred in his answer to incidents as far back as the conquest of 1066, when the Normans, coming from the continent, defeated the Anglo-Saxon kingdoms. When he spoke about controlling one's own activities, he probably referred to the bells of these churches, which indeed marked small and big moments of life:

> When I go to Durham cathedral, as much as I love it, it is a demonstration of power, the architecture. Saying "We're controlling you in this life, and we're controlling you in the next life." It was really a demonstration of Norman power over the Saxons. The Saxon churches were much smaller. The cathedrals were a piece

---

51. For another example of Sting's use of the motif of the resurrection, see our discussion of *The Last Ship*, pp. 13–17.

of architectural theatre designed to control you. They controlled time, they controlled when you woke up, when you went to sleep, went to work. It's all about control. . . . Despite all that, there is something inside these cathedrals that still works for me. I think you could still be spiritual in those places. You can still find solace.[52]

He said similar things about a much smaller church, St Andrew's church in Great Durnford (which happens to be Anglican also), close to his home in Wiltshire:

> I like this church. I would visit [it] when it was empty and I'd find a great solace there. I like the architecture, I like the quiet, I like the slightly cold atmosphere, I can sit and meditate. I like stain-glass windows. For me it's . . . about a spiritual connection to God.[53]

Like Sting himself, Durham Cathedral is a place where Catholicism and Anglicanism merge. Gordon Sumner, the Catholic boy who once went with his class, as we will learn soon,[54] to this magnificent Anglican cathedral to see the graves of those they considered to be Catholic saints, took control of the place (a place that some Catholics feel was stolen from them by the heretic Anglicans), and found solace in it.

As mentioned earlier, in 2013 Sting released an album entitled *The Last Ship*, which was the basis for a musical of the same name. The biblical references in this album were discussed in a previous chapter. It is time now to look at the Catholic references. Many of them are found in the musical itself in its original American version. Sadly, that version is unlikely to be staged anymore, having been replaced by the much more secularized, and commercially more successful it seems, British version.

In some of the songs printed in the liner notes for the studio version of *The Last Ship*, it is noted which figure in the musical should sing them. Therefore, we can know, even without the book for the musical (which was not written by Sting), Sting's early intentions for the songs. No information of this kind is given for the title song, "The Last Ship," analyzed at length earlier. In the musical itself, in its American version, the first person to sing part of the song is the local priest, Father O'Brien,[55] who wears full liturgical garb in which the dominant color is green, associated with those parts of the

52. Sting, interview by author, July 23, 2017, Künzelsau, REC22:098.

53. Sting, interview by author, July 23, 2017, Künzelsau, REC22:007.

54. See below, pp. 116–18.

55. In the studio album's liner notes he is spelled, constantly, O'Brian.

year known as "Ordinary Time."[56] "I loved that priest [from *The Last Ship*]," Sting told me about a year and a half after the end of the musical's run in New York. "He was a perfect priest for me. He was a combination of a few people I knew."[57] One can assume that among these were some of the more left-leaning, socially aware priests that Sting knew in St Cuthbert's grammar school in Newcastle, mentioned in the following chapter. By having the priest tell the story, the text is no longer just a modern reworking of a biblical story; it becomes a homily. It is not clear if this idea was Sting's, or if it came from the musical's book's authors (American version), John Logan and Brian Yorkey.[58]

Another song, "Shipyard," is central to the studio album, and even more so to the musical. Several of the protagonists of the story speak about their life in the shipyard.[59] "Jackie White," the foreman of the yard, introduces himself, and then says to the workers:

> Now ye could die and hope for Heaven, but ye'd need to work your shift; And I'd expect ye's all to back us to the hilt. And if St. Peter at his gate were to ask ye why yr late, why you'd tell him that ye had to get a ship built.

Jackie's words are a mixture of pious Catholic imagery—St Peter waiting at the gate of heaven—and irreverent irony: Peter or not, ships have to be built, and on time. It is unclear whether Jackie knew that the idea that Peter acts as gatekeeper to heaven was possibly introduced into Christian lore by someone from his own region: The Northumbrian king Oswiu more than 1,300 years earlier in the "Synod of Whitby" of 664, mentioned above.[60] Following Jackie White's intervention, the priest, Father O'Brien, joins and speaks both about his own life and the lives of those he serves:

56. This happens in Act 1, Scene 7. Father O'Brien was played on Broadway by Fred Applegate. See https://links.stingandreligion.com/frap. For most of my analysis of the American version of the musical I use my own recollections from the productions that I have seen in New York on October 13, 2014, when it was still in previews, and again on January 10, 2015, as well as a copy of the musical's book, dated August 26, 2013. This scene appears on page 27.

57. Sting, interview by author, July 23, 2017, Künzelsau, REC22:083.

58. John Logan also has strong attachments to shipbuilding: his father worked in a shipyard in Belfast. See Logan interviewed by Hedy Weiss for the *Chicago Sun-Times* (June 2014) at https://links.stingandreligion.com/loga. My attempts to contact Yorkey and Logan to ask them about this and other issues have failed.

59. Sting wrote this song (or its tune) with others: Rob Mathes, Kathryn Tickell, Peter Tickell, Julian Sutton, and Jo Lawry. Several paragraphs that are included in the liner notes do not appear in the song itself.

60. The idea is based on a particular interpretation of Matthew 16:19. About this synod see above, p. 70.

Well, me name is James O'Brien, it's from Ireland I was sent, to be the pastor of this flock, and your spiritual guide.[61] I might suggest to all of you heathens what you might give up for Lent, but[62] ye won't give up your dignity, ye can't give up your pride. And ye can't give up your history, ye can't give up the ghost. For on the last day of judgment, a heavenly host will descend on this community to separate the just from the damned and the wicked and the ones ye couldn't trust. And there are times when the good Lord might ask for sacrifice, but it's the devil that be tempting ye, even if he's paid you twice. For their souls cannot be purchased as they haven't got a price, and they won't give up.

This text is filled with Catholic imagery we have already encountered in Sting's work, among them the day of judgment, angels ("heavenly host"), damnation, the devil, and souls. Father O'Brien refers to the locals as "heathens" in what seems to be an ironic tone. In this, he revisits the idea that the English are pagans who need to be Christianized by the Irish. At some historical periods this was indeed, more or less, the case (from a Christian perspective). Aidan, and to a lesser degree Columba, are examples of this type of movement of missionaries. In other cases, Christian missionary activity worked in the opposite direction. Patrick is a good example for such a direction.[63] In recent decades, many Catholic priests in North East England and in many other parts of the country have come from Ireland. Father O'Brien says he may be able to suggest "what you might give up for Lent," a period of mourning in the Catholic calendar, but it sounds like he does not see this as his central role. He also speaks of the "Day of Judgement," a time when God, and God's "heavenly host, will descend on this community to separate the just from the damned and the wicked and the ones ye couldn't trust." He of course refers to an ancient belief, found already in the Hebrew Bible (Old Testament) and the Christian Bible (New Testament), that at the end of times, God will judge humanity in a mighty cosmic event.[64]

61. In one of the performances I watched, it is possible, but not certain, that the words "spiritual guide" were replaced by the word "healer."

62. The words "to all of you heathens, what you might give up for Lent, but," were not sung during the performance I attended in January 2015. The same was the case for the ensuing phrase "on the last day of judgment."

63. On Aidan, see above, p. 70. On Patrick and Columba, see above, pp. 58–60.

64. See for example Micah 4:1–5; Isaiah 2:1–4; Zechariah 8–9; Matthew 7:13–25; 25; Luke 13:22–28; Revelation 20.

Sting kindly provided me with some verses that he wrote for "my unruly priest" (as he called him) that were not included in the album or musical.[65] He prefaced them with this:

> My paternal grandfather [and grandmother] were penniless and ended up living in a Catholic Convent in Newcastle . . . looking after the resident priest, whose name was Father Jim. Father Jim was the name I gave to the heterodox priest in *The Last Ship*, while the real Father Jim was more conventional in his outlook.

These verses are presented here. For the sake of analysis and the formatting used elsewhere in this book, they are arranged in paragraphs, intercut with my own comments:

> I'm Father O'Brien from the county of Clare,
>   but how long I've been here? Well I wouldn't swear.
> Perhaps thirty-five years if I'm not mistaken,
>   to look after this parish of blessed St Aidan.
> But I'm not what you'd call a good Vatican man,
>   I don't always see eye to eye with that plan.
> I follow the liturgy but not to a fault,
>   I prefer the old dogma with a wee pinch of salt.

County Clare in Ireland is heavily Catholic, but Father O'Brien seems to have been in Wallsend for several decades already. It is not clear why Sting chose to make him the priest of the parish of St Aidan, also in Wallsend, and not of his parish of origin, Our Lady and St Columba. Perhaps he wanted to reduce similarities in the story to his own biography. In the musical though, Father O'Brien serves Sting's true childhood parish.[66] Father O'Brien makes it clear he is not a "good Vatican man." During Sting's childhood, there were three popes: Pius XII, John XXIII, and Paul VI. During the 1980s and 1990s, the years when the story seems to be set, the pope was John Paul II. Three of these four popes, during at least a part of their papacy, and with some simplification, tended to be on the conservative side, requiring strict obedience, and a certain return to old decorum. Father O'Brien seems not to like it:

> Religion's the cause of so many troubles,
>   and not worth a candle when it boils and it bubbles.
> A soup of conjecture and exegesis,
>   like they've somehow tapped into the mind of Jesus.
> Where the man himself was a man of the people,

---

65. Sting sent me this text on November 4, 2014, and reconfirmed I could use it on July 23, 2017.

66. Logan, *The Last Ship*, 13.

> he'd no need of a church with a great towering steeple,
> or a throne in a palace with a big white hat,
>> you'd never see me wearing something like that!

O'Brien's statement on religion—that in some cases, it is worthless ("not worth a candle")—is obviously rather strong, especially when it comes from a clergyman. Those who know Catholicism will agree though that hearing such statements from priests is not extremely rare, even if it can be shocking for some members as well as outsiders. Father O'Brien opposes complex interpretations ("conjecture and exegesis") of Jesus's words, seeing Jesus as a simple "man of the people." Although he serves in a church that indeed has a "towering steeple" (though not a huge one),[67] he affirms he does not believe it is needed. He also criticizes bishops, and specifically the behavior of popes, who have "a throne in a palace with a big white hat."

The remaining stanzas of this never-used text likewise show Sting's desire to depict Father O'Brien as a progressive priest. O'Brien strongly believes in the importance of being "where the flock is," or as the current bishop of Rome, Pope Francis (whom Sting has said he admires), says, "shepherds living with the smell of the sheep":

> My ministry's here with the men from the dock.
>> I've abandoned the pulpit to tend to my flock.
> To comfort the dying and heard from their lips,
>> that God is amongst us, the builders of ships.

> Where Jesus sought comfort among rough men like these,
>> the likes of poor fishermen, beggars, and thieves.
> This is my ministry, this is my calling.
>> Do you hear that sound? Is it angels falling?

> I've christened most of ye's here, and one day I'll be hearing your last confession.
>> But I've a sneakin' suspicion we'll need more than one session.
> For the list of y'r sins, still you'll carry no guilt.
>> For you've earned absolution in the ships that you built.

> There's a sacrament here in the bending of steel.
>> In the welding of plates, fashioned into keel.
> An outward sign for the work of the soul,
>> an ark of the covenant the ship in the hole.

---

67. See http://links.stingandreligion.com/olc5.

Even though these lines are not included in the final lyrics, Father O'Brien expresses a similar theological idea in another scene of the American version of the musical, in a narrative section, not a song:

> A man's work is a sacrament—an outward sign of inward grace. . . . And to build ships well enough that other men will sail in them—to make other men safe—well if that's not God's work I don't know what is.[68]

This idea is close to the hearts and the theology of the working priests, the *Prêtres ouvriers*, a movement Sting was exposed to while in grammar school in the 1960s.[69] In one of the songs of the album/musical, "Show Some Respect," the idea that work itself is a means for salvation is expressed forcefully:

> Each of us well appointed,
>   we've all but been anointed,
> such was our occupation,
>   this means of our salvation.

For Father O'Brien, "good deeds" (in this case, a life devoted to hard work, providing for family and community) can bring salvation. Pious rituals, on the other hand, might not. When in the musical, a major character, Gideon (standing for Sting himself) asks Father O'Brien if, after saying "Twenty *Our Fathers* and ten *Hail Marys*," he will be absolved of his sins, O'Brien answers "God, no, are ye fucking daft? Ye've got work to do, son."[70] Such statements by an actual clergyman would have shocked some Protestants (for whom faith is what counts), and some Catholics (for whom rituals are of great importance), but they are not unheard of in Catholic circles. The fictional priest that Sting created is perhaps not the ideal in the eyes of conservative bishops or some lay people, but he is not unrealistic. Priests like this have probably always existed in the Catholic church.

Father O'Brien admits, following his speech, his great fondness for drinking. I suspect it was not Sting who decided to make him an alcoholic. At least initially, in the studio version of the album, the person who sings about his alcoholism is a certain "Davy Harrison."[71] Yet, there is indeed an

---

68. Logan, *The Last Ship*, 27. See also the comment Sting wrote to me regarding this line on p. 61.

69. See below, pp. 132–33.

70. Logan, *The Last Ship*. 14.

71. According to Sting, many, if not all, of the names used in the play are those of people he knew. Among them, he mentioned Davy Harrison and Jackie White. See the video interview he gave to the *New York Times* on October 20, 2014, https://links. stingandreligion.com/ny14, 7:49.

old cliché about priests being drunkards.[72] Considering that the priest in the musical is Irish, another group often portrayed as fond of alcohol, the use of these stereotypes is not surprising.

A few other songs from the album/musical have Christian/Catholic themes. "Dead Man's Boots," for example, mentions a cross on the wall of Gideon's father's room, very possibly related to an actual cross referred to in Sting's song "When the Angels Fall" (1991).

Father O'Brien, who is dying of cancer, says "this ship is ready to sail," referring to his dying body. In 1963, Pope John XXIII was dying, and it was reported that shortly before his death he confided to his doctor, "My bags are packed and I am ready, very ready, to go."[73] It is not impossible that the young Sumner heard this quote; he was twelve at the time, a student in a Catholic school. Appropriately, while the pope who had been previously a diplomat for decades had described himself as someone with packed bags, Sting made the priest of Wallsend speak of himself as a boat.

A song mentioned above, "Show Some Respect," employs a term used by Sting in many songs, and which we will analyze extensively later: the soul.[74] The builders of the (last) ship plan to bury Father O'Brien, who died shortly before the launch of the boat, at sea, fulfilling his request. In this, they follow the motif of burial at sea in Sting's "All This Time" of 1991. It is possible to understand the "net of souls" that the builders say they will "cast upon the sea" as a reference to the priest: it might be a hidden allusion to Matthew 4:19, where Jesus says that he will make his disciples "fishers of men." After serving the community for many years, the good priest is a "net of souls" himself.

During the festive, Irish-style wake, following Father O'Brien's death, the group sings a song simply entitled "Hymn" in the musical's book and program:

> And as ye sleep, the angels round thee,
>   have brought ye safely home, across the oceans;
> Rest ye well, all those who toil upon the sea,
>   trust in this, within the darkest night;
> Thy dreams will find safe passage
>   to the morning.[75]

72. Like many clichés, it is far from accurate, but is still based on a certain sad reality. See for example Lucie-Smith, "Why Are so Many."

73. This sentence is often quoted in Catholic sources about John XXIII. See for example in https://links.stingandreligion.com/john. It should be noted that an identical phrase appears in John Denver's song "Leaving on a Jet Plane" of 1966.

74. See pp. 158–61.

75. Logan, *The Last Ship*, 54.

This text sounds very much like an actual hymn originating in a maritime community, where sailors "toil upon the sea," go "across the oceans," and need a "safe passage." It is, though, according to Sting, an original piece he wrote, not based on already existing material.

It is likely that, in a community like the one Gordon grew up in, the comparison between the Christian community (or church, or the individual's soul) and a ship was not unheard of. It is an old metaphor, accompanying Christianity since its very first centuries. It appears in the writings of Tertullian and Clement of Alexandria, two authors of the second and early third centuries CE. Some think that the idea is already in the background of New Testament texts such as 1 Peter 3:20–21 and Mark 4:35–41. Ships are also seen by many as upside-down churches (or as Sting said in one recording, "maybe a church is an upside-down ship").[76] One can imagine that in a place where boats were so visible, priests would make the comparison. If this was the case, it might explain why the priest sees the building of a (last) ship as an appropriate answer to the needs of his community. This seems to have been the case with the story from Poland that inspired Sting to write the musical. There, as in the musical, the priest suggested the project and helped fund it.[77]

In person, Sting said to me regarding the imagined fate of the last ship, "Where they're going? They're going to death. The ship is about death." In his introduction to the liner notes of the studio album, Sting offers a different explanation:

> In all honesty, it is only a ship of dreams, an allegory for what might have been, an allegory about the importance of work, the importance of community as well as the underlying themes of fatherhood, exile, alienation, religion, redemption, mortality, passion, humour and the courage that sometimes emerges from desperation.[78]

As in the story the play is based on, and as mentioned above, Father O'Brien dies from cancer at what seems to be a rather young age. Sting's adoption of this motif might very well be a tribute to his own father, as well as to his mother, who shared the same fate. The fact that Sting depicts the priest as a very likable person demonstrates that although he no longer considers himself a Catholic or a member of any organized religion, he is not anticlerics. This attitude toward the clergy is not hard to find in his memoir,

76. *All This Time* CD-ROM, Part 13, "Seaside," 9:12, https://links.stingandreligion.com/cdr6.

77. Kulish, "Homeless in Poland, Preparing an Odyssey at Sea."

78. Introduction to the liner notes of *The Last Ship* (Studio Version, 2013).

Broken Music, published in 2003. There were priests he abhorred; there were priests he admired. Much of the musical in its American version evinces a positive opinion on priests, or at least on some of them. It is the priest who initiates the idea to build a "last ship"; it is the priest who finds the money for it; it is the priest who is said to be most understanding of Meg, the young and unwed pregnant protagonist in the musical; it is the priest who helps people through confession; it is the priest who assures people that if they do good deeds—whether working in the shipyard, or taking care of their family—their sins will be absolved; and it is the priest who welcomes the lost "prodigal son" Gideon to the community. Finally, the "Last Ship" itself is named after him: "S.S. James Francis O'Brien."[79] *The Last Ship* is about boats, and love, and sickness, and a crumbling economy. But it also about sin and redemption, saints, priests, sacraments, and the Bible. In this, it describes well the reality and mentality of the community Sting grew up in the 1950s, where Catholicism was a central component of the group's identity, and Catholic clergy had an important social role. In a way, it is a summary of much that was seen in this chapter: Catholic images and their power on the imagination of an artist who grew up in a strong Catholic milieu.

---

79. "S.S" as a prefix for a ship historically meant "Steam Ship" or "Single-Screw Steamship." In recent decades, it often seems to mean "Sailing Ship."

Chapter 4

RELIGION SURROUNDING GORDON SUMNER: PART II

Men go crazy in congregations
They only get better one by one.[1]

WHAT TYPE OF RELIGIOUS world surrounded Gordon after he graduated, with his friends, from the local parochial elementary school, and until he became known to the world as Sting?

By 1961, the new Church of Our Lady and St Columba's in his parish of Wallsend had been open, blessed, and had been in use for four years, even though something was still missing: a formal and complex ritual of consecration that only a bishop can perform. This had not taken place right away on account of the custom to consecrate a church only after it was free of debt and its future is assured. This happened in 1961, when two beautiful mosaics were added to the interior of both sides of the church—one of Mary the mother of Jesus ("Our Lady") and one of Columba. "I remember looking at that mosaic a lot," Sting recalls.[2] The two mosaic pieces were done by a well-known and respected company in Manchester, which was founded in 1865 by Ludwig Oppenheimer, a German Jew who converted to Christianity. It was a family-based company that used the talents of many of its own

1. "All This Time" (1991).

2. Sting, interview by author, July 23, 2017, Künzelsau, REC22:003. See an image of the mosaic of Mary and an image of an early planned version of it here: https://links.stingandreligion.com/mos2. Same regarding the mosaic of Columba: https://links.stingandreligion.com/mos4.

members as well as artists from other places, including many Italians. Its works adorn many churches in England, but also in Ireland, France, and elsewhere. It was closed in 1965: the mosaics in Wallsend represent some of the company's work during its last years of existence.[3]

Completed and free of debt, with a universal saint, Mary, on one of its walls, and a local one, Columba, on the wall facing it, it was consecrated on June 13, 1961. The local secular newspaper *Wallsend News* described it with obvious fascination for the peculiar, rare, and complex ritual:

> The £70,000 Roman Catholic church of St. Columba in Carville Road, Wallsend, was consecrated by the Bishop of Hexham and Newcastle, the Right Rev. J. Cunningham. . . . A crowd of about 50 people gathered at the church gates to watch the beginning of the four-hour ceremony as the Bishop said prayers at the main entrance and sprinkled the main door with Holy Water. About 20 priests attended the ceremony. After the Bishop circled the outside of the building to sprinkle the walls the procession moved into the church where the Bishop blessed and anointed the five crosses on the altar and the 12 crosses on the wall. The relics of the Roman martyrs to be sealed in the altar were carried in procession round the outside of the church and then placed in their sepulchre on the altar stone.[4]

An almost identical article appeared a few days earlier, on the day the consecration ceremony took place, in the *Evening Chronicle*, which had the advantage over *Wallsend News* of being published daily. One interesting and amusing difference is that in the *Chronicle* it is said that most of the fifty people gathered were women. It should be noted that such a small crowd of laypeople is rather surprising. One could have suspected that perhaps the ceremony was not highly publicized, or that because it was, according to another source, early on a Tuesday morning, many people who worked outside of the home during the day could not attend. The articles seem to hint that the church itself was not open to laypeople, something not unusual in a pre-Vatican II mentality. In the thinking of many members of the clergy at that time, in a holy and ritualized ceremony of consecrating

3. To see many other magnificent examples of mosaics produced by the company, and more information about its history, see a paper given by Field, "L. Oppenheimer." The church is a very impressive one, and was justly a finalist in a national competition, "Best Modern Places of Worship," managed by the National Churches Trust in 2013.

4. *Wallsend News*, June 16, 1961. I have not found a picture from the consecration, but the same ritual, done by the same people three years earlier for the sister parish of St Bernadette, was immortalized by *Wallsend News*, and was probably almost identical in nature. See http://links.stingandreligion.com/cobe.

a building, the potential presence of not-so-holy laymen, and worse still, laywomen, might have been considered inappropriate. And yet, an article about the consecration of another new Catholic church in Wallsend, St Bernadette, which took place in July 1958, describes a rather different level of attendance: Five hundred people were present at the ceremony, and all were allowed in the church, according to a that other article.[5] If both numbers are reliable, the poor attendance at the consecration of St Columba can perhaps be explained by the fact that it was no longer a new church, but rather one that had already functioned for several years. Still, one can imagine that this low attendance was disappointing for the clergy.

Five days after the consecration of his church, on June 18, 1961, having witnessed the fulfillment of a mission that he had started many years earlier, Father Timothy O'Brien retired due to failing eyesight. Father O'Brien's tenure as a priest at Wallsend had lasted exactly twenty years, including a period of war. A good Irish after all, he moved to Dublin.[6] During his two decades of service in Wallsend, O'Brien was personally responsible for overseeing the construction of two new Catholic churches (St Columba and St Bernadette), as well as the development of the parish school. He also actively promoted the creation and development of certain pious associations in the parish. Gordon was almost ten years old when O'Brien, who had married his parents, retired. An era has ended.

A new era, that of the Second Council of the Vatican and its aftermath, was about to begin. Even before the council was opened, things were changing. For example, *The Universe* reported in April 1962 that a priest, Father Leslie McCallum, had "made history" by speaking in an Anglican church. McCallum made sure, however, not to participate in any service, and devoted his talk to "explaining the four distinguishing marks by which Our Lord made it possible for all to identify His Church": The Catholic one, obviously.[7]

On October 12, 1962, *Wallsend News* reported on a letter sent from Bishop Cunningham to the diocese's Catholics about the lack of new priests. The Second Council of the Vatican had begun the day before, but there is no mention of it anywhere in the article. In fact, in all of the issues of *Wallsend News* that I reviewed, I did not find a single mention of that major event for Catholics. One might have noticed that changes were happening within local Catholic parishes starting around 1963, but based on the *Wallsend News* alone, one would not know why. In Sting's memoir of 2003, and in

5. See "Consecration Ceremony Watched," 12.

6. "Catholic Priest to Retire."

7. "Priest Speaks," 1 and 20.

the memoir by his childhood friend James Berryman,[8] the council is also never mentioned, even though both speak extensively about their Catholic environment. All of this seems rather strange, though a poll from 1978 revealed that 46 percent of English Catholics had never heard of the council that ended thirteen years earlier.[9] There is no question that the Catholic church in England went through major changes following the council, but it is possible that many people did not associate the changes, some of which were gradual, with the council.

Bishop Cunningham was probably in Rome at the time the article was published in *Wallsend News*.[10] Surely, like all bishops, he did not know he was going to be a part of an ecclesiastical earthquake. After three years of preparation, in a festive ceremony in the Basilica of Saint Peter in the Vatican, the council opened. Known as "The Second Vatican Council" or simply "Vatican II," it would become the most significant event in the history of the Catholic church in the modern era.

The council convened for four sessions, each lasting for a period of two months during the autumns of 1962, 1963, 1964, and 1965. Pope John XXIII died shortly after the first session, but his successor, Paul VI (formerly Cardinal Giovanni Battista Montini of Milan), immediately made the decision to continue the council. Paul VI effectively steered the direction of the council in its last three sessions, during which its decisions were formulated and promulgated. The council's decisions were, to a great extent, the prelude to many more changes that were to take place in the Catholic church over the next decades. Without delving into the contents of the sixteen documents promulgated by the council, it is probably fair to characterize them as displaying relative openness, optimism, flexibility, and permissibility of various types of changes in the life of the church.

The application of some of these decisions took time. But much of this was still in the future. The year was 1962. The council, the outcome of which Bishop Cunningham certainly could not imagine, had just begun. He was more concerned about urgent problems in his own diocese.

The lack of new priests that Cunningham lamented became a common and growing Catholic concern beginning in the middle of the twentieth

---

8. Berryman, *Sting and I*.

9. See Norman, *Roman Catholicism*, 108.

10. Although I cannot with certainty vouch for his presence in the opening days, it is likely that he was there. He was definitely present at some, if not all, of the council's four sessions, as one can see in the documents he wrote during the council, kept in the diocese's archive. For a picture of him in Rome during the council, see http://links.stingandreligion.com/cu02. It is possible that the person that is shaking the hand of Pope Paul VI in picture http://links.stingandreligion.com/cu03 is also Cunningham.

century. Gordon probably heard about this problem. Many thought, per-haps with good reason, that the best way to get new priests was to encourage (or compel) boys towards such a vocation. Many of those who later became priests were encouraged toward that path in their early teens. They were sent to study in "Minor Seminaries," a type of institution that is rather rare today in many parts of the world, but was still popular and respected in England during Gordon's childhood. The Catholic *Code of Canon Law* of 1917 ex-plained how to identify such boys, and what is the role of these seminaries:

> Priests and bishops, especially pastors are to work so that boys who give signs of an ecclesiastical vocation are kept with special care from the contagion of the world, to form piety, and from their first studies of letters are imbued with divine things that will encourage the seed of vocation in them.[11]

The British historian John Cornwell was born about a decade before Gor-don, in 1940, and was sent to such a seminary:

> When Father Cooney put my name forward to the bishop as a candidate for the priesthood I was approaching my thirteenth birthday. I was already a Johnny-come-lately: many boys of my generation had begun their priestly formation at the age of eleven.[12]

Two of Gordon's father's younger brothers, Paul and Anthony Sumner, studied at such a seminary, Ushaw College, about twenty miles south of Wallsend. This institution was created in the early nineteenth century after a college that had been founded in Douai, France, to train English priests, when training priests had become illegal in England following the Reforma-tion, was forced to close in 1795, due to the French Revolution. Neither Paul nor Anthony attained the priesthood. Both joined the armed forces instead.[13] Going to seminary did not mean an assured future as clergy.

Gordon was eleven when Cunningham's letter about the lack of priests was published. He was at the perfect age to answer the call. Earlier, he did something that served as a way for priests to verify whether certain boys were good candidates for minor seminaries: he became an altar boy.[14] In the interview I had with him, he said "I became an altar boy when the new church was built."[15] The new church was opened in 1957, when he was six

11. Peters, *The 1917*, Canon 1353.

12. Cornwell, *Seminary Boy*, 7.

13. Sting, email exchange with author, May 16, 2017.

14. Sting, *Broken Music*, 47.

15. Sting, interview by author, July 23, 2017, Künzelsau, REC22:002

years old. I do not know if he meant that he literally became an altar boy immediately then, or later, but still in the new church.

From some of my interlocutors I learned that in order to assume this role, one had to go through several training sessions, and that not all those who began the training were invited to continue. Needless to say, there were no "altar girls" at the time: women were not even allowed to approach the altar, other than during their own marriage ceremony, as one of my female interlocutors bitterly noted. The invitation for boys to serve in that role was at times related to whether one had a brother who was doing it, or to other special connections and traits. Gordon possibly had the honor because of his good looks and voice. Serving as an altar boy not only offered social benefits, but financial ones as well: at funerals and weddings the altar boys received tips.[16] It should be remembered that altar boys played a rather significant public role during the liturgy. Prior to the council there was almost no interaction between the priest and the congregation (some would say, the "audience," to highlight this fact) during the service, other than in the so-called "Dialog Mass," which was done in some places starting in the 1950s. The priest would recite his part (in Latin), and the altar boy would reply (in Latin). The people merely watched, or recited other prayers such as the Rosary or prayers from books such as *The Garden of the Soul*.

And yet, as both his testimony and testimonies of others reflect, Gordon's short career as an altar boy was not the beginning of a beautiful route towards priesthood:

> Paradoxically, [serving as an altar boy] relieved some of the boredom of the liturgy. I could parrot the Latin Mass with the best of them, although my understanding of the text was negligible. I'm sure I was far from alone in this, but I think I must have enjoyed the dressing up, a full-length black robe under a white surplice on a weekday and red on a Sunday—it was basically a dress—and the theatricality and the solemn pomp of the ritual must have appealed to the performer in me.[17]

Clearly, Gordon was not made of the kind of "priestly" material that the bishop had hoped for when looking for future clergy. Crucially perhaps, he did not have what was often essential to push a young boy towards the career of a priest: a very pious Catholic family, where parents (or at least one of them) actively hope that one or more of their sons will become priest(s), and one or more of their daughters will become nun(s). John Cornwell,

16. A.N.16., interview by author, December 15, 2014, Wallsend, REC10:12.

17. Sting, *Broken Music*, 47. Bruce Springsteen was also an "altar boy" as a child. He apparently failed miserably: see Springsteen, *Born to Run*, 16.

mentioned earlier, says that his father was not practicing at all: "never went to church, even at Christmas." On the other hand, when the young Cornwell was offered the possibility to attend a seminary, his mother told him, "I should be so proud! And as your saintly grandmother used to say: Gain a priest—never lose a son."[18]

During Gordon's childhood, only one or two children from the parish attended the seminary at Ushaw College. Not all saw such moves with admiration: it was sometimes said by cynical parishioners that going to a seminary was a good way to get a grammar school education for those who failed the entrance exams to regular grammar schools.

Cornwell and Sumner did not become priests, but many English boys of that generation who were sent to minor seminaries did. One of my interlocutors, a priest, who grew up in another part of Britain, had such a trajectory:

> I went to seminary at age eleven. . . . We had a grammar school education, with Latin and Greek and French and the sciences . . . in the seminary. . . . A very small minority [of the boys went to seminaries]. . . . We were fifty in my year, from the seven northern dioceses, and out of those fifty, I think eight of us got ordained [to priesthood]. There was a huge drop-out. It is a vocation, not everybody is called. . . . Some people ran away as well. . . . They couldn't stand it![19]

Another interlocutor, a classmate of Gordon in grammar school, became a priest without going to a minor seminary. He recalls that he had considered priesthood from the age of eight, and admits that his own family was "a very Catholic family, pillars of the parish."[20] Although children can obviously choose routes that are absolutely not in line with their parents' worldview or wishes, it is reasonable to assume that a very religious family can be instrumental in the decision of a child to pursue a religious vocation, or in pushing such a child towards such a direction.

Most of my conversants say that they were not actively encouraged to consider a vocation in orders or priesthood. Many, however, remember going to a "Religious Vocations Exhibition," in which various Catholic organizations and orders presented themselves to the curious public. So many of them mentioned these exhibitions that it is clear that they made an impression on them. I was able to find information on one such exhibition in their area in the relevant years: between the 12th and the 19th of May 1963,

18. Cornwell, *Seminary Boy*, 9.

19. Z.E., interview by author, June 24, 2014, Wallsend, REC01:29.

20. I.N., interview by author, October 13, 2014, New York City, REC21:08.

such an event took place on the Town Moor in Newcastle. The organizers expected 100,000 people to visit it.[21]

Regardless of their interest in religious life, all Catholic children and adults, and even more so, those who played an active part in the services—such as altar boys, members of choirs, or other assistants to the priest and members of some parish associations—were exposed continuously to the hymns sung in liturgy, whether during Mass, or services such as Benedictions and Processions. Children also practiced them at school, often on Friday mornings. There were several books of hymns for the Catholics of England, but there was one that claimed superior authority, and which included the musical notation for each hymn. This was *The Westminster Hymnal*, which declared on its cover page that it was "The only collection authorized by the hierarchy of England and Wales." Asserting that the hymnal came from Westminster not only indicated that, as the introduction says, "The tunes have been in part selected and in part composed by Mr. E. E. Terry, Mus.D., Organist and Choirmaster of Westminster Cathedral," nor that it had been "issued with the sanction of the Archbishops and Bishops of the Provinces of Westminster, Birmingham and Liverpool," but also gave this collection the allure of supreme authority. The self-esteem of the editors was high, and the aims of the hymnal were ambitious:

> The Hymns [included] are what we have been accustomed to, but the musical setting is, on the whole, far more scientific and satisfying than anything that has hitherto appeared. There can be no doubt that it will conduce very much to the devotion and decorum of extra-liturgical worship and popular services to have one common manual of Hymns, which at once offers a suitable variety and prevents the undesirable introduction of amateur efforts and unedifying novelties. . . . Some of [the tunes used in England and included in the hymnal] are good, some are indifferent, and some bad. But it has been felt that since those of the last-named class have been—for one genera-tion at least—bound up with the pious associations of so many holy lives, this is hardly the occasion for their suppression. They have therefore been retained, although this retention cannot be justified on musical or other artistic grounds. Alternative tunes have been provided to most of them, so that they need not be used by those to whom they are distasteful. . . . It is too much to expect that adult members of congregations accustomed to

21. See a letter of Bishop James Cunningham on the matter, sent to the diocese's priests, on April 4, 1963 (HND, Ad Clerum Letters, February 1955–March 1966, MR8). For a review of an earlier exhibition of this kind from another area of England, see "The Vocations Exhibition," 44.

mutilated or transformed melodies, will at once assimilate the correct form of them. But if one standard version is carefully and consistently taught in the schools, the next generation will see English Catholics in all parts of the country singing, at any rate, the same form of the same tune to any given hymn.[22]

One may doubt this lofty goal was ever achieved, but the children knew many, if not all, of the book's 263 hymns, many of which came with various texts and tunes. My interlocutors insisted that it is hard to give a list of the "best of," or a list of most frequently used hymns at the time, but they still mentioned several in particular, including: "Faith of Our Fathers" (No. 138) with its combative words and glorification of the suffering and martyrdom of earlier generations; "Full in the Panting Heart of Rome" (No. 139) with its words of admiration for the Vatican and the pope; "Come Holy Ghost" (No. 47), particularly used in Pentecost; "Hail Queen of Heaven" (No. 101) about Mary and including the expression "Star of the Sea," which very likely resonated well with these children living close to the sea ("I love that hymn," said Sting);[23] and "Soul of My Saviour" (No. 74) about Christ. Some of the popular hymns that they mentioned came from other sources: "Immaculate Mary" (also known as "The Lourdes Hymn"), and the lengthy "For All the Saints," which was composed by an Anglican bishop, but contains nothing problematic from a Catholic perspective.

According to one of my interlocutors, Gordon was strongly impressed and influenced by the *Westminster Hymnal*. Sting confirmed it himself. What impact all these hymns had on others is hard to say. Some of my interlocutors stressed the fact that many of the hymns and prayers were not really understood by the children. They memorized them, but the texts were never explained. Thus, while these interlocutors believe that the prayers and hymns contributed to a certain habit of Catholic practice among the children, as well as to their knowledge of musical and textual formulas, it is hard to know how the hymns actually contributed to the children's faith, despite the familiar Catholic Latin expression *Lex orandi, lex credendi*, which suggests faith is shaped by liturgy. To my question of whether the Catholic liturgy had an impact on him, conscious or unconscious, as a composer and songwriter in later years, Sting replied strongly:

22. All quotes are from the opening parts of the hymnal, i–xii.

23. Sting, interview by author, July 23, 2017, Künzelsau, REC22:049. See also above, in the discussion of his song "Valparaiso" (1999), pp. 88–89. Similar expressions about Mary (for example, "Hail, thou Star of ocean!") appear also in "The Blessed Virgin / Ave Maris Stella" (No. 109/110).

> Absolutely! I was an altar boy and I learned the Mass in Latin, and I would sing Gregorian chant, the Kyrie, the Credo. I can sing it now. So that affected my musical sensibility greatly. I love hymns. It is part of my culture. Every day I would hear and take part in religious music. It is inherent in my musical sensibilities. The cadences I'm fond of are very church-like in many ways. But that should not surprise you. There are cadences in my music which are clearly from this connection, this familiarly with church music, and a love for it. A real love for it. We had a very good organist in St Columba's, and a good choir. I loved those hymns. We'd sang [hymns] every morning at school. And I can still sing the Latin Mass, if I am forced to! *[laughing]*.[24]

Other elements that probably shaped the children's religious views were books and movies. Regarding books, several of my interlocutors surprisingly agreed that they cannot recall many that were particularly popular among Catholic children or that were formative to their Catholic worldview. Several movies, however, were mentioned as widely popular among Catholic children. One should remember that during that time, movies were extremely well attended, and it was common for many to go to the cinema once a week (often, on Saturday morning, it seems), and sometimes as an official classroom activity.[25] My interlocutors mentioned the following films: *The Song of Bernadette* (1943) on a famous supposed apparition of Mary in the French town of Lourdes; *The Robe* (1953), which tells the story of a fictional Roman military officer who executes Jesus and later, regretting it, becomes Christian; *The Ten Commandments* (1956); *The Inn of the Sixth Happiness* (1958) about a Christian (almost certainly not a Catholic) English missionary woman in China, who, in a classic colonial worldview, saves Chinese children and adults both spiritually and physically; *Ben Hur* (1959); *The Nun's Story* (1959); and *The Greatest Story Ever Told* (1965). *The Sound of Music* (1965) was mentioned as the only movie that nuns were allowed to see, a rather interesting permission considering the movie's content.

The BBC was also important in framing a religious mindset. Sir William Haley, a former General Director, referred to Britons as "citizens of a Christian country," and affirmed that "the BBC . . . bases its policy upon a

---

24. Sting, interview by author, July 23, 2017, Künzelsau, REC22:050. See also Sting, *Broken Music*, 84, and Pentin, "Sting."

25. On the views on cinema among German Catholics leaders of the time see Ruff, *The Wayward Flock*, 71–75. According to Ruff (p. 226, n. 83), in England, the average number of times people went to movies at the time was twenty per year. He does not give his sources for this information or indicate to which age groups it refers.

positive attitude towards Christian values." In a book on the era, one learns that

> [The BBC was broadcasting] a daily radio service and a short re-
> ligious talk (*Lift up Your Hearts*) on weekdays. . . . [It] provided
> an extensive menu of religious programmes on radio and televi-
> sion on Sundays, and in the case of television the period from
> 6 to 7.30 on a Sunday evening was preserved as a "God slot."[26]

The early 1960s were a period of great anxiety in Wallsend, since the local shipyard, Swan Hunter, which employed thousands of people from Wallsend and the surrounding area, was having difficulty securing new orders. Some years earlier, in 1956, *Wallsend News* still reported,

> Never before have the possibilities at shipbuilding been so good
> and the trade can look forward to full employment for several
> years to come.[27]

By 1962, the local situation and mood had changed. Occasionally there was good news, such as when the *Wallsend News* announced that the town got a "Christmas Gift" in November 1962. Its main headline reported what people clearly knew by then: "Big Tanker Order News Welcomed by All: Whole Town Delighted at Work Ahead." Building two new super tankers would provide, it was said, full employment at the yard for about two years, just when the previous big project was ending.[28] This was crucial for the community; around that time, a sociological study tells us, about 20 per-cent of Wallsend's employed men worked in shipbuilding and in ship repair. About a further 9 percent worked in the closely related marine engineering industry.[29]

Gordon surely heard the news about the new projects in the shipyard, but was too young to even consider going to work there. Earlier that same year, in 1962, when he was almost eleven, he took the notorious "11-plus" examination that decided (and in some places, still decides) the academic fate of British students. Gordon passed it successfully and had thus the right to be admitted to the highest-level category of schools, a "Grammar School."[30] According to one interview with Sting, his father still wanted him

26. McLeod, *The Religious Crisis*, 40.

27. "Possibilities in Shipbuilding."

28. *Wallsend News*, November 30, 1962, 1.

29. See Brown and Brannen, "Social Relations," part one, 72. The numbers provided are for the year 1966, when Gordon was fifteen years old.

30. In Sting's musical *The Last Ship*, in its British version (2018), Gideon, who is, at least partially, made in the image of Sting, does not pass the exam. The girl he loves,

to go a Technical School to learn a trade. There was a family fight, and then, when his father went off to the pub,

> my mother said, "Come here, we'll fix the form." So we fixed the form. We put a piece of white paper where he'd put the technical school and we put grammar.[31]

One should remember that only a minority of the children passed this exam and pursued such a trajectory. This low rate was due mostly to the fact that there were simply not enough places available in the local grammar schools so, according to my interlocutors, passing meant being in the top 20 percent.[32] Most of those who did not get into them went to a Technical School (where the expected destinations of the students were the crafts and more cerebral trades in manufacturing and commerce) or to a Secondary Modern School (where the students were expected to work at low-level factory jobs), schools in which the education was considered to be of lower quality. Due to this, going to a Grammar School often meant, on the one hand, great academic possibilities, but on the other, partial or complete ostracization by those who were not given that option and felt, justly, left behind.[33]

The school Gordon went to in the fall of 1962 was also Catholic: St Cuthbert's Grammar School, which was a train and a bus ride of about an hour from Wallsend into the west end of Newcastle. It was one of the two Catholic Grammar Schools in the area, the other being "Sacred Heart," for girls. Gordon would spend the following seven years in this boys-only school until graduating in the summer of 1970. It should be noted that there were Catholic schools in the area that were mixed (boys/girls), such as St Joseph's in Hebburn. Thus, a separated education was not the only conceivable way to have a Catholic school. If until then Gordon had been exposed mainly to the style of Catholicism of his own parish, he was now exposed to a slightly broader Catholic world.

St Cuthbert's Grammar School was founded in 1881.[34] It was a "Direct Grant Grammar School," which meant that it received money directly from the government, and not, like many schools, from local authorities. Among other things, such an arrangement gave a school more liberty. The choice of

---

Meg, does. Gideon watches her going to school every morning. By doing this, Sting, or those working with him, portrayed him as one of those who failed in the exam and were jealous of those who passed. See Campbell, *The Last Ship*, 71.

31. Whetstone, "Sting Talks."

32. See also Conway, "An Investigation," 59.

33. See Brown and Brannen, "Social Relations," part one, 72.

34. See Hart, *The Early Story*. This "founding" was actually the reestablishment of a defunct school that had originally opened in 1870.

its name was related to local pride. The island of Lindisfarne, also known as "Holy Island," located sixty miles to the north of Newcastle, was one of the places from which Christianity came to the English Isles, particularly to the northeastern kingdom of Northumbria. One of the famous monks based on the island was the seventh-century's Cuthbert, whose story we discussed earlier.[35] Not surprisingly, the school that bore Cuthbert's name was founded in order to educate the most academically talented Catholic boys of the area. Until now Gordon had studied in a school bearing the name of an Irish saint, Columba; now he was attending a school named after an English saint, Cuthbert. A coincidence, but maybe one with some symbolism: the Irish identity of his childhood, even if already very limited, was taken over by an English one.

Local Catholics had a painful problem related to Cuthbert: his remains were close by, but were not under Catholic control. As noted, Cuthbert's remains are supposedly in Durham Cathedral, to the south of Newcastle.[36] Catholics lost, in a sense, the physical Cuthbert, when worship in the cathedral, as in countless others, came to be performed by those later referred to as "Anglicans," loyal to the monarch and not to the pope. Catholics did not, however, lose their veneration of Cuthbert: the school, as well as countless other Catholic (and some Anglican) institutions in the area, still commemorated the local hero. In fact, a tradition that Cuthbert's remains are not even in his grave, and that their secret location is known only to a few Catholic monks, has helped Catholics to feel Cuthbert is still, even physically, in their hands. Here is how a book from 1980, written from a perspective that is clearly nourished both by scholarship and Catholic tradition, tells this story:

> At the destruction of the shrines in around 1537 [following the orders of Henry VIII, as part of his reformation efforts], commissioners were embarrassed to find Cuthbert "lying whole, uncorrupt." The incorrupt body was left in the sacristy until 1541 when instruction came for it to be buried underneath where the shrine had been. The official position is that the body buried under the blueish slab carrying the word "Cuthbertus" is that of the Saint. The tomb was opened in 1827 and again in 1899. Remains were found as were the relics now on display at Durham. But there are insistent Catholic traditions that these human remains are not those of the Saint. As early as the 1620s references are found to a supposed removal of the body and to its being hidden elsewhere in the cathedral. Three members of

35. See pp. 69–72.

36. See http://links.stingandreligion.com/du01 and http://links.stingandreligion.com/du02.

the English Benedictine Congregation were custodians of the
secret of the resting place, and as one died the secret was passed
on to another. The secret is still extant and is held by the Abbot
President and by certain other members of the English Benedictine Congregation. But perhaps the time is ripe for the tradition
to be tested by excavation.[37]

Several of my informants mentioned this tradition. One of them told me,
while we visited the cathedral together, that he had heard the tradition
whispered by a teacher and that the teacher had pointed to the "correct"
place of burial in another location inside the cathedral. Thus, the children
themselves felt that they possessed a secret tradition that the ignorant Anglicans around them did not. Another interlocutor remembers that during
a school trip to Durham's Cathedral (something that was emotionally and
religiously complicated for both children and teachers since it meant entering an Anglican church), they saw the graves of Bede and Cuthbert and
it was said that the saints were "held hostage by foreign religion." During
one of these visits, the teacher/priest showed the students the list of priors
and deans of the cathedral on display in one corner. Pointing to the first
Protestant among them, that teacher said, "Look boys, look where the line
of priors ends? The reverend so and so? He is as much a priest as Charlie
Chaplin!"[38] The teacher was referring to the comedic persona of Charlie
Chaplin (1889–1977), but he almost surely knew that Chaplin, still alive
then, was born in England, and was baptized in the Church of England:
in other words, even Chaplin the man was very far from being a Catholic
priest. Any inferiority that these Catholic children may have felt when they
entered a majestic Anglican church—in order to see the resting place of a
hero they considered to have been Catholic—was turned upside down by
the assertion that they, after all, held religious superiority. The fact that Pope
Leo XIII had declared that all Anglican ordinations were "absolutely null
and utterly void" in his 1866 bull *Apostolicae curae*, a declaration that was
never retracted,[39] gave the teacher, and the children, a solid basis for their
mockery of the list.

37. Power, "St. Cuthbert," 67.

38. I.N., interview by author, October 13, 2014, New York City, REC21:32.

39. In recent years, one can find various opinions about this statement. On one
hand, it has been reaffirmed several times by the Vatican hierarchy. On another, various acts and gestures show that the declaration by Leo XIII is not something that all
celebrate: for instance, when Pope Paul VI met Michael Ramsey, the archbishop of
Canterbury, in 1966, he presented him with the gift of chalice, an object that a non-
ordained person should not have. One could likewise cite various statements by different Catholic theologians and organizations regarding the declaration. For a major

Another female interlocutor, who became a scholar in the field of religious studies, also remembers visiting the cathedral:

> Catholics, a lot of them, didn't think that St Cuthbert was buried there anyway. I was taken to the cathedral when I was about nine I think, by my great aunt, who was Anglican, [she was] my father's relative, and I can remember, standing and thinking, "Gosh, what a huge building," but I knew St Cuthbert was not buried there. The story was that the body has been spirited away at the time when the shrine was despoiled, and buried somewhere which was known only to two Benedictine monks. . . . That is the story which was firmly believed by quite a lot of people, particularly in the nineteenth century.[40]

St Cuthbert's Grammar School was run by priests. According to one of my conversants, this was rather unusual.[41] During Gordon's time there, Father Martin Cassidy (from Wallsend) was the headmaster, and Father Michael Walsh, in charge of discipline, was his deputy. They were assisted by four other priests. Cassidy was a "canon," a priest attached to the cathedral and the bishop (the "cathedral chapter").[42] These priests saw themselves as a certain clerical elite, and due to their academic degrees and close relations with the bishop (whose residence was a few minutes' walk away), they were considered as such by many others. Some of the priests only taught religion. A few also taught the sciences. All of the other members of the faculty were laymen: there were no female teachers.[43]

The school's boundaries (its "catchment area") were very large, as it was the only Catholic grammar school for boys in the North East. Some students had to travel sixty miles daily to reach this dorm-less school; they came from places as far as the Scottish border to the north, or Carlisle in the west. In Gordon's time, there were about 1,200 students at St Cuthbert's.

---

document on the question, issued by the United States Conference of Catholic Bishops in 1990, see http://links.stingandreligion.com/anor.

40. L.I., interview by author, December 14, 2014, Durham, REC11:34. A search in the archives of the British Catholic newspaper *The Tablet* shows indeed that there was a great interest in the topic in the decades around the turn of the twentieth century, and then again in the late 1950s.

41. I.N., interview by author, October 13, 2014, New York City, REC21:01.

42. Normally, "cathedral canons" share common life similar to members of orders. In nineteenth-century England, this was not the case. I do not know whether this had changed by the middle of the twentieth century. See Norman, *The English Catholic*, 108.

43. A female interlocutor from Wallsend said that in the girls' grammar school, the ratio of nuns to laywomen was "around fifty-fifty." (L.T., interview by author, December 13, 2014, Wallsend, REC14:06). Another interlocutor, about a decade older, said that most teachers were laywomen. Still, there were no male teachers according to both.

Not all of them actually passed with success the "11-plus" examination. On the one hand, the bishop and the school authorities were aware of the fact that some intellectually gifted students failed the examination for various reasons. They were also aware that, in many cases, students who were not accepted would end up in non-Catholic schools. Pressure from parents, especially if they had good relations with their local priests, helped some students to be accepted regardless of their performance on the examination.[44] Aware of this situation, the school had its own internal divisions into classes of various levels. It had some extremely successful students who were encouraged to finish school in six years instead of seven, yet it also had students who were constantly struggling to pass exams and who left without graduating or graduating at the age of fifteen or sixteen.

St Cuthbert was a school with strict discipline. Some of the priests wore black Roman cassocks, with thirty-three red buttons, and birettas. Some of the lay teachers wore academic gowns, and students, like in any self-respecting British school, wore uniforms and ties. Extreme formality was the rule, and cane strokes were used to punish deviations of all kinds. Canon Cassidy and his deputy, Father Walsh (who later replaced Cassidy), were those in charge of the cane. It should be noted that this was not unique at the time. Boys, but generally not girls, were subject to corporal punishment in schools in England and Wales until 1987.[45] The testimonies of several of my interlocutors about how and why they were beaten by teachers were gut-wrenching. Reacting to my bewilderment, they said that the children did not tell their parents about such acts because they were afraid, probably justly, that admitting they had problems at school would only result in them being punished again at home. There was, as one said, "definitely a fear of adults in general," so children simply had no one they could complain to about such acts other than their peers.[46] Several said that the humiliation was stronger than the actual pain. If we are to believe Sting's own recollection, he was beaten often:

44. I.N., interview by author, October 13, 2014, New York City, REC21:04.

45. This was true if the school was at least partially funded by public money. Private schools were allowed to continue this practice as late as 1999. See http://links.stingandreligion.com/cpuk. When I asked a female interlocutor if there was corporal punishment in Sacred Heart, the girls' grammar school, she said, "No, never. It wouldn't be lady-like at all. No, never." (L.T., interview by author, December 13, 2014, Wallsend, REC14:06). Another source, speaking of another Catholic school, in another part of England, and about three decades earlier, describes a priest hitting a schoolgirl, the mother of the author. See Cornwell, *Seminary Boy*, 14.

46. For example in A.N.17., interview by author, December 15, 2014, Wallsend, REC10:61.

[I had to] bend over in front of Jesus on the cross, to be whipped. . . . And that's all that particular priest did in the school.[47] That was his sole function. I have seen the same in a Buddhist monastery in Tibet. A discipline master with a whip. Controlling the young monks. Did such discipline harm me? I don't know. I wouldn't have my own children suffer that way. After three or four strokes of the cane, you're feeling murderous, after six forget about it! It's like being cut with a knife, in the same place. And "six of the best" they called it. In one year I suffered forty-two strokes, and I honestly wasn't a bad child. I wasn't delinquent. Just in the wrong place at the wrong time, and the wrong attitude. That's how they kept discipline, with violence, or the threat of violence. A lot of the priests were terrifying. And in the junior school we were hit with the belt [making the sound of such a hit on the table]. It was humiliating.[48]

According to both him and his peers, Gordon was in fact a good student. One thing that possibly got him in trouble was not being shy of standing on his own, including criticizing aspects of the school system, and not caring enough about some rules that the school had. One of his classmates said that Gordon was punished almost more than anybody else, for offenses such as being late, wearing the wrong color sweater, having long hair, etc.[49] Another added this on the matter:

One of my big regrets is that I wasn't more challenging to authority. Gordon was. He was much more a challenge to authority than I was, because he had the, I think, something, the right to challenge was given to some and not to others, within our grammar school. [Maybe because] he was great in football. Great athlete. Very clever boy. He made great challenge to authority.[50]

The school presented high academic standards for those capable. Many of the teachers were alumni of prestigious British universities such as Cambridge and Oxford, and their implicit or explicit intention was to educate the barbarian northern boys so that they would take the same route.[51] Some of these teachers are indeed remembered by alumni as beacons of academic excellence and instillers of knowledge and critical thinking in their students. Sting has also acknowledged this. After speaking about the violence used as

47. I believe he referred to Father Walsh. See also Sting, *Broken Music*, 91–92.
48. Sting, interview by author, July 23, 2017, Künzelsau, REC22:095.
49. See Berryman, *Sting and I*, 72–76. See also Sting, *Broken Music*, 91–95.
50. B.G., interview by author, December 13, 2014, Wallsend, REC13:27.
51. I.N., interview by author, October 13, 2014, New York City, REC21:01.

a disciplinary tool, and about a teacher who expressed anti-Semitic ideas, a story that will be mentioned later, he added,

> I am giving you an extreme example that I have never forgotten, but on the other side there were also kindly priests, and dedicated teachers, who were genuinely good people and the faith was something that supported them in that, so that we were exposed to a range of religious and irreligious ideas.[52]

The school day was opened with a prayer as part of the "Assembly" of the entire student body. The priests celebrated Mass every morning: separately, as was the custom before the Second Council of the Vatican, and possibly together, in a "con-celebration," at a later period. This was for the priests themselves, as students were generally not expected to be present. Lunch marked the end of the morning session, and it was preceded by a grace before the meal recited by a priest:

> At school, there would be rigorously grace before meals and grace after meals. . . . One of the priests would bang on the table, everybody would stand up, whether they started the meal or not, and [the priest] said a grace before meal: "Bless us, O Lord, and these Thy gifts which we are going to receive, through Thy bounty through Christ our Lord. Amen."[53]

During lunchtime, there was a Mass that students could attend. They were also able to take communion, though as noted already, taking communion at that time was not as common as it is today, and attending a Mass without taking communion was rather normal. Students were encouraged to go to this service, but did not have to. Generally, only a few dozen students were apparently present. Some of them were regulars, while others had decided, for whatever reason, to attend on specific days or seasons:

> Perhaps if you started Lent,[54] you said "Oh I am going to communion [at school] every day," and then by the end of the second week you were "Perhaps not. I go for a game of football." . . . But then the problem was . . . you felt a failure.[55]

---

52. Sting, interview by author, July 23, 2017, Künzelsau, REC22:013. See also Sting, *Broken Music*, 95.

53. B.G., interview by author, December 16, 2014, Wallsend, REC20:25.

54. Lent is a period of preparation for Easter, when Catholics have the practice of giving up some food, or committing to other acts that are intended as signs of piety and repentance.

55. B.G., interview by author, December 16, 2014, Wallsend, REC20:05.

When Gordon began his studies at St Cuthbert's, the Mass was celebrated in Latin, with the priest's face to the altar, and his back to those
attending. The students answered in Latin in various places in the Mass,
and my interlocutors were easily able to repeat these answers from memory.
During and more so after the council, major changes took place in the liturgy. Well before Gordon left the school, the Mass was celebrated in English, with the priest possibly facing the students. Possibly, but not surely:
On June 30, 1965, Cardinal Lercaro, an important figure in charge of the
liturgical changes, sent a letter to all the national hierarchies, with regard
to the changes in the liturgy. On September 10, 1965, Bishop Cunningham
sent his clergy a summary of this letter.[56] Several parts of it were reported in
the Catholic media. Thus, for example, one could find the following:

> Cardinal Lercaro, Archbishop of Bologna, head of the commis-
> sion for the implementation of the Constitution on the Liturgy,
> in a message to bishops throughout the world states that Mass
> facing the people is the most helpful manner of celebration from
> the pastoral point of view.[57]

In reality, I do not know if this was done at Gordon's school. The fact that
Lercaro found it important to write this to bishops (and through them, to
priests) worldwide suggests this practice was still not a given. Celebration
of the so-called "Liturgy of the Word" (the first part of the Mass, centered
around readings from the Bible) while facing the congregation was already
the norm, and did not require any physical adaptation of the church. But full
celebration of the Mass, including the "Liturgy of the Eucharist," facing the
congregation, often demanded massive and costly changes in the physical
organization of the church and the place and shape of its altar. In Gordon's
home parish, St Columba, permanent changes of this kind happened only
in the mid 1970s.[58] I do not know if the Eucharist was celebrated at St Columba's, prior to that, facing the congregation, or not. In a letter to his clergy,
written on January 4, 1965, therefore six months before Lercaro's statement
appeared, Bishop Cunningham wrote the following:

> In accordance with the recommendation [in a Vatican docu-
> ment] . . . new high altars should be constructed in such a way
> that they can be used for Mass facing the people. With regard to
> existing altars, structural changes may not, of course, be made

56. HND, Ad Clerum Letters, February 1955–March 1966, MR8.

57. "Mass Facing People Best," 4.

58. *Our Lady and Saint Columba Centenary, 1885–1985*, 27. This happened in 1970
itself according to the website of the parish.

without permission. In many existing churches the high altar is so far away from the congregation that there is little point in remodeling the altar in its present position. In such cases, it would be better to use an altar placed nearer to the Congregation. If you intend to ask for permission to say Mass facing the people, please let me know what you have in mind before making any arrangement.[59]

It seems that, in general, institutions that were under the direct control of bishops, such as seminaries and schools, reacted to the changes of the council more quickly than those that were one step further from the bishop: in parishes, the changes sometimes were slower. Some think this was due to the time needed for clergy and parishioners to get used to the new rules. Others suggest that this was mostly due to the priests' reservations, not the parishioners:

> Yes, yes, [it was slow]. It went on, seemed like years to me. . . . It was a lot of "pre," you know. To get us used to the idea of English. Yeah, English! What do we need to be told about English? I think the clergy were [more afraid than] the laity about the changes [from Latin to English]. I think they still had that *inner sanctum*, I think quite many [priests] still think like that, that they are delivering something to you that is outside. When the Latin was no longer the language, they were afraid of losing something, some great honors. . . . They were in fact right, it turned out to be that way. It was a Pandora box. . . . I suppose that this is in a typical English manner. We never get rid of anything. We introduce something new, say like the metric system, but we don't get rid of feet and yards. And we introduce the vernacular, but we don't get rid of the Latin. . . . In my recollection, Latin Masses and English Masses ran in parallel for quite some time. . . . Older priests just couldn't give it up.[60] . . . My recollection is that the Latin Mass went on [for a long time], and the priest stood with his back to you anyway [even] in English. . . . I think the younger people were quite thrilled with English, while older people were against it, for whatever reason, even though I suspect they did not understand a word of what they said [in Latin].[61]

59. HND, Ad Clerum Letters, February 1955–March 1966, MR8.

60. In the instructions composed on March 1965 by the bishops of England and Wales for the second stage of the reform of the Eucharist, it is acknowledged that some priests might decide to continue in Latin, due, for example, to "small texts and failing sight." This is not forbidden, but such priests need to get a permission to do so from their bishop.

61. S.E., interview by author, December 15, 2014, Newcastle upon Tyne, REC09:18.

Another interlocutor mentioned a joke people would tell in order to dismiss
the pre-council position that Latin was vital: "If the Church really valued
Latin, it would preach for money in Latin!"[62] Yet another confirmed that the
laity was generally thrilled with the change to English. She also remembers
that the process was gradual and careful, even though the transformation
in her parish was completed in only a few weeks: "Our parish priest introduced it very carefully over several weeks. He took us through it, and
he explained it." But this was not the case throughout England. That same
woman remembers visiting a parish in the West of England at around the
same time, in which, by sheer luck, she witnessed the change effected immediately; the priest simply said that from now on, they would do the Mass
in English, and that "we will probably all hate it." In her opinion, as a scholar
of liturgical issues,

> It would depend very much more on the parish priest [than on
> the bishop], because the bishop would send these orders out,
> "It's going to happen," but the parish priest had to put it across
> to the people.[63]

Similar issues were noted by scholars regarding the American Catholic
church. Mark Massa, a priest, historian, and theologian, said this about the
question:

> I think priests were very ill prepared to explain to their con-
> gregations what was going on. Some of the bishops, even those
> most in favor of the reforms, . . . feared that there would be a
> rebellion in the pews. The surprising thing is that most people
> liked the new Mass. There were a few strong rejections, but the
> expected explosion never materialized. Sociologist Father An-
> drew Greeley said that within two years around 73 percent of
> American Catholics said they liked the changes in the liturgy,
> which was astonishing. Nobody expected that.[64]

In fact, at times bishops had to stop parishes and priests from using the
vernacular too early. Thus, Bishop Cunningham instructed his priests, on
February 14, 1964, that,

> No vernacular may be introduced until the translation has been
> approved by the Holy See. Therefore, in England and Wales, no
> vernacular in the Mass may be permitted for the time being.[65]

62. A.N.18., interview by author, December 13, 2014, Wallsend, REC12:48.

63. L.I., interview by author, December 14, 2014, Durham, REC11:27.

64. Massa, "The Times."

65. HND, Ad Clerum Letters, February 1955–March 1966, MR8.

The bishops of England and Wales released several documents with instructions concerning the changes to the liturgy. The first official document seems to have been a pamphlet entitled "The Sacred Liturgy," issued on October 20, 1964, shortly after a related document directed to the universal church, "*Instructio ad Exsecutionem Constitutionis de Sacra Liturgia Recte Ordinandam*" was made public. In their document, the English hierarchy explained many of the changes, and the schedule of putting them into practice:

> Although the *Instructio* does not take full effect until the First Sunday of Lent 1965 [March 7, 1965], [some] changes . . . will take effect from the First Sunday of Advent this year [November 29, 1964].

Bishops, however, were temporarily allowed some local diversity:

> In view of different circumstances in various parts of the country, each Ordinary [=bishop] will inform his clergy of the days and conditions when the various changes in the Liturgy are to be regarded as obligatory and when they are merely permissive.[66]

Bishop Cunningham, during his stay in Rome for the third session of the council, sent a letter back to his diocese on November 2, 1964, four weeks before the English liturgy would become the norm. In it, he set up the local rules:

> Because the next twelve months or so will be in some ways experimental, the bishops [of England and Wales] decided not to impose uniformity on the whole country. Each diocese will make its own regulations until Advent 1965 [November 1965]. The following are the rules for this diocese . . . 1. The use of English is not allowed if there is no congregation. Thus, e.g., Mass at which only the altar server assists must be in Latin. 2. The use of English is obligatory at all Low Masses—at the which there is a congregation—on the following occasions: a. On Sundays and Holy Days of Obligation.; b. On weekday evenings.; c. Funeral and Nuptial Masses.; d. Masses for school children. ; e. The Community Mass in Convents and other institutions except on one weekday each week.[67]

Bishop Cunningham clearly understood the importance of instructing the priests about the changes. Under his direction, the diocese published a series

---

66. A copy of this brochure exists at HND, Vatican II Papers, MR49.
67. HND, Ad Clerum Letters, February 1955–March 1966, MR8.

of brochures to explain the council to the local clergy. In the introduction of one of them, Bishop Cunningham said

> The Council has given us a programme for the renewal of Catholic life. The impact it will have will depend largely on the priest becoming thoroughly familiar with the decrees, explaining them to his people, and guiding them in applying the teaching of the Council to their daily life.[68]

Having seen these and other documents, and having spoken to many people, I believe the pivotal day was the same one for many Catholics worldwide: November 29, 1964, the First Sunday of the Advent season. From that day on, Catholics had a different liturgy, whether they liked it (and most of them probably did) or not.[69] It seems clear that (recollections of some of my interlocutors aside) from that day on, all Masses in the diocese, both in parishes and at schools, were conducted in English, other than in rare exceptions. This does not mean Latin was no longer used in them. In fact, some parts of the service continued in Latin. Six months later, on April 11, 1965 (Palm Sunday), the second stage of "The Reform of the Sacred Liturgy" occurred, and, among other things, the use of the vernacular was extended further. Other than during some of its core parts and in sections spoken silently by the priest, the most common type of Mass, a low Mass with a congregation, was celebrated almost entirely in English.[70] By the end of 1967, priests were allowed to use English for almost all of the sections that were still recited in Latin.

Before that, and later, priests were flooded with letters from the bishop regarding minor and major changes to the liturgy and sacraments in general. One can only imagine the frustration that many felt from the endless stream of amendments that they were supposed to follow and put in practice. At times though, they got instructions many of them were probably

---

68. Diocese of Hexham and Newcastle, *Instructions on the Decrees of the Second Vatican Council, De Ecclesia, Chapters I-II-III*, p. 2 (HND, Vatican II Papers, MR49). The brochure does not have a date, but I believe it was released in 1964.

69. The "Pastoral Letter" by Bishop Cunningham that was to be read in all parishes that day can be seen at http://links.stingandreligion.com/cu04. The original is available at HND, B04, Bishop's Pastoral Letters, MR112.

70. It seems that Bishop Cunningham actually had some reservations about what was done, soon after the English Masses began. In a letter to his priests on January 20, 1965, he seems to ask sincerely for their advice: "The Constitution on the Liturgy insists that "steps must be taken to ensure that the faithful are able to say or to sing together also in Latin, those parts of the Ordinary of the Mass which are rightfully theirs." (No. 54). Would it therefore be a good idea to have one Low Mass on Sundays entirely in Latin?" (HND, Ad Clerum Letters, February 1955–March 1966, MR8).

happy to comply with. Thus, in late 1964, Pope Paul VI reduced the fast required before Mass to one hour only, a time that is rather negligible for most people, considering that about half of it can occur from the start of the service until communion. Then, in a letter one can be sure many of the priests were delighted to find in their mailbox, Bishop Cunningham informed the entire clergy of his diocese that,

> It was stated [in a previous letter] that the fast from solid food had been reduced to one hour before the time of receiving Holy Communion, but that the fast from alcoholic refreshment remained at three hours before Holy Communion. A statement from the Holy See makes it clear that the fast from alcoholic refreshment has also been reduced to one hour . . . with moderation.[71]

During the final stages of the transformation of Mass to English, Bishop Cunningham asked his diocese's priests whether the very core of Mass, the "Canon," should be recited in English. At the time, most parts of the Mass were already said in English, but it was not yet permitted to recite the "Canon" in the vernacular. Cunningham wanted to hear the opinions of those in his diocese because the Catholic bishops of England and Wales were about to discuss the issue. In a letter on July 11, 1967, he summarizes the results he received to his inquiry:

> Translation of the Canon of the Mass into English: 191 replies were received. 110 replies were generally in favour, 30 contained results of parish voting, 27 recorded divided opinions and 24 were generally against the translation of the Canons into English. 177 priests would favour the use of an English translation, whilst 55 would not. The parish voting results generally varied between 60 and 70 percent in favour of translation. The total of known voting figures showed 60 percent for English, 30 percent for Latin, and 10 percent uncertain.[72]

It seems fair to deduce from the numbers he provides that a significant majority of parishioners in the diocese—and interestingly, an even larger majority of priests—supported the Anglicization process of the Mass and wanted it to include practically the entire ritual.

It is likely that shortly after Gordon's thirteenth birthday, most of the Masses he attended were almost entirely in English. One should remember,

---

71. Letter of December 8, 1964. HND, Ad Clerum Letters, February 1955–March 1966, MR8.

72. Letter of July 11, 1967, HND, Ad Clerum Letters, March 1966–December 1972, MR8.

however, that the language change was just one aspect of the transformation of this central Catholic ritual. Many changes to texts, acts of the priest, and acts of the congregation, made the ceremony very different than the way it had been celebrated for many decades, if not centuries. Gordon, his friends, and their extended families had to adjust to a different ritual than the one they had known until then.

One thing, however, seems to have gone unchanged for some time: the exclusion of women from leading roles during the liturgy. Thus, in November 1967, when Mass was already almost entirely in English and ecumenism became a given, Bishop Cunningham still gave these instructions, reaffirming the inferiority of laywomen when compared to laymen, and insisting they should not be allowed near the altar, most probably due to the long tradition, even if generally implicit and not spoken about, that menstruation makes women impure, and thus not compatible with the sacred:

> In the case of communities of Sister(s) or girls' schools where a competent male reader for the Epistle at Mass is not available, a woman or girl may read the Epistle. She must be outside the communion rail.[73]

The "Assembly"[74] at St Cuthbert's Grammar School included several prayers (such as the "Angelus"), and on specific days of the week it included additional parts. The afternoon session started with grace after the meal. The day ended with a prayer as well—a *Hail Mary*, an *Our Father*, or another blessing—and a time for reflection. Some students participated in other religious devotional practices. Thus, for example, members of the Catholic association "The Legion of Mary" would meet in the school's chapel or in a classroom to recite the Rosary, an act cherished by many of the school's priests. Others never added of their own will religious components to their life at school except those that were obligatory and monitored.

The slogan "A family that prays together stays together," mentioned earlier,[75] was a well-known one during Sting's childhood. When I asked him about it, and if his family was a praying one, he laughed and said, "My family didn't stay together so obviously we didn't pray together."[76] Personal prayer however is, or was, not unknown to him. I do not have proof that Gordon ever participated in non-obligatory events such as those that took place at

73. Letter of November 23, 1967, HND, Ad Clerum Letters, March 1966–December 1972, MR8.

74. "Assemblies" were and are also conducted in state schools: the law (Education Act 1944) requires that the morning begins with a "collective act of worship."

75. See above, p. 32.

76. Sting, interview by author, July 23, 2017, Künzelsau, REC22:049.

school, but he admits liking, very much in fact, the Rosary, as a youngster. This is what he told me in 2017 when I asked about a statement he made in his memoir:

> [I had a special relation to Mary]. I would say the Rosary more than anything else. It became my sort of mantra. I suppose I had Obsessive-Compulsive Disorder. So I would just say the Rosary constantly, when I was walking to school or I was troubled I would say the Rosary. It would comfort me. It seemed that my devotion was towards a female deity more than the male. There was a kindness there, there was gentleness. Which is one of the good things about the Catholic church. It has this female [figure].[77]

Students were able to confess at St Cuthbert's a few times a week during lunch time: "Confessions were held in the school chapel every lunchtime, with some 1,200 boys, potential penitents, all reeling off the same sins," according to one of Gordon's classmates, James Berryman.[78] From other alumni I learned that this possibility to confess in school during lunchtime was used by some and not by others. In reality, there was never a situation in which the entire student population was waiting to confess. A testimony of another friend of Gordon, who was in the same class, shows, not surprisingly, that during their teenage years issues of sexuality were present, explicitly or not, in the pupils' minds while confessing:

> You were at a confession, and you said "Oh my father, I had impure thoughts," and the priest would say behind the curtain, "Did you entertain these thoughts?" "No, the thoughts entertained me!"[79]

James Berryman recounted several experiences with regard to confession in which he and Gordon were involved.[80] Obviously, these recollections were written decades after the events, so we cannot vouch for their exactitude. Still, they seem to reflect a certain atmosphere that is attested in many descriptions of Catholic life at the time. In one case that he recounts, the twelve-year-old Berryman answered in the positive to a priest asking him during confession if he had transgressed "The Seventh Commandment." He

---

77. Sting, interview by author, July 23, 2017, Künzelsau, REC22:040.

78. Berryman, *Sting and I*, 32. In Sting's memoir, he says that at the time there were more than 2,000 boys in the school. See Sting, *Broken Music*, 90. Berryman's number is, as far as I was able to verify, more accurate.

79. B.G., interview by author, December 13, 2014, Wallsend, REC13:11.

80. Berryman, *Sting and I*, 29–36.

did it without knowing that that commandment is about adultery, something he had very little understanding of or experience with.[81] Humor aside, the story does reflect a common issue attested in countless sources of many periods: the sacrament of penitence was not designed for children. Berryman describes well the rather absurd situation in which good behaving boys (and girls) in their pre-puberty years were supposed to regularly confess sins, although in their mind they had not committed any. Just like Sting's testimony quoted in an earlier chapter, and that of several of my interlocutors, Berryman reports that inventing sins, without even understanding what they meant, was often the only approach the children were able to think of.

This unease with the ritual was perhaps one of the reasons why many chose to confess elsewhere, not in school: in their parish, in another parish, or in St Mary's Cathedral in the heart of Newcastle. Attending confession was kept to each student's conscience and was not registered in any way at school. Berryman himself says he never thought about confession at school before Gordon suggested it to him. It was supposed to help him protect his anonymity from the priest while doing it, something he never succeeded in doing at his home parish.

Many of the priests teaching at St Cuthbert's adopted the type of piety that was the hallmark of the previous pope, Pope Pius XII, who died in 1958. Some of them had affinities to the French priest and preacher Louis-Marie Grignion de Montfort (canonized by Pius XII in 1947), who called for a rather extreme adoration of the Virgin Mary.[82] They quoted his words that "God wishes that His Holy Mother should now be more known, more loved, more honored, than ever she has been" and tried their best, with unknown success, to instill this attitude in the heart of their disciples. Ideas such as "you should love Mary more than your own mother" were also a part of it. Having as a model Pope Pius XII, they were supporters of a strong papacy, or in Catholic parlance, "ultramontanism." These "Marian" priests celebrated many rituals (or in that time's parlance, "devotions" and "benedictions"),[83] which often included veneration of the Eucharist in

81. For an analysis of this genre of stories told by Catholics, see Krasniewicz, "Growing Up Catholic," 51–67.

82. I.N., interview by author, October 13, 2014, New York City, REC21:10.

83. The rituals that today are officially called "sacramentals" (meaning, everything other than the seven Catholic "sacraments") were referred to by all my interlocutors as "devotions" and "services." See also Heimann, "Devotional Stereotypes," 21. On Benediction Service in general and in English-speaking lands in particular, see http://links.stingandreligion.com/bene. Although it was very popular for a century or more, it was first officially recognized by Rome in 1958, something that probably made it even more esteemed in the eyes of Rome-leaning English priests.

glorious monstrances on a high altar, and images of Mary surrounded with flowers. Hymns to Mary or to the consecrated bread (for example, the medieval "O Salutaris Hostia") were central in these celebrations. It should be remembered that English Catholics were surrounded by many Anglicans of the Anglo-Catholic tradition, for whom devotions to Mary and to the Eucharist were also important.[84] As such, these rituals did not set English Catholics apart from many of their non-Catholic neighbors.

The priests encouraged belief in the power of devotional scapulars, square pieces of cloth with holy images, some of which, if worn at the time of death, were considered to save one from the torments of hell. They preached about the efficacy of devotions such as the "Novena," according to which, in exchange for one saying a certain prayer nine times, one's time in purgatory (or one's relatives' time) would be shortened. Not all students appreciated it. One of my interlocutors, who also studied at St Cuthbert's, and considers himself to this day a good Catholic, did not mince words:

> We used to have things called indulgences, where if you said a prayer nine times, you got hundred days off in purgatory, that kind of rubbish. Which is now, generally accepted as rubbish. But to do the nine prayers you had to do it nine times in and out, so you said your prayer, went out of the church, got back again, said another prayer, in and out nine times. Hundred days off [from purgatory], and off to the cinemas. The logic of that completely failed me! I thought, "what an absolute rubbish!" It does not make sense.... I did not do that, cause I did not believe it! It wasn't an item of faith. I thought it is ridiculous. If there is a God, and there is a God, I was saying, if he is looking down at these lunatics! He is saying something else: not that I give you 100 days off, but I give you another 100 days for that stupidity!

When I asked him if he was happy when these things were abolished after the council he said,

> Oh, yes, . . . but the trouble is that they never actually said that what we used to tell you in the past is rubbish, they just sort of quietly let it slip away down the drains so that nobody does it now and it is not taught, . . . so they keep themselves morally correct and don't admit the stupidities of the past.[85]

---

84. By then, acts of devotion to Mary already seemed natural to Anglo-Catholics, since the process of integrating her in some parts of the Church of England had begun more than a century earlier with the "Oxford Movement" and other thinkers. See Engelhardt Herringer, "The Virgin Mary," 46.

85. S.E., interview by author, December 15, 2014, Newcastle upon Tyne, REC09:15.

Two of the priests at school, one of whom was Father Craven, were, according to some, more liberal than the others. Other students remember Father Craven as a very authoritarian and unforgiving teacher, noting, however, that something he did years later may have signaled another aspect of his personality: he left the priesthood to get married. Encouraged by the winds that came from the council starting in 1962, some priests brought new ideas to the school. The same can be said about some of the lay teachers, who presented the students with a progressive, middle-class, highly educated, lay Catholicism. They exposed some students to the thought of the famous John Henry Newman, who converted from Anglicanism to Catholicism in 1845 and was part of the influential "Oxford Movement" that propelled the attitude known in the Anglican world as "Anglo-Catholicism." Among other things, Newman's ideas about the need for so-called "development of doctrine" caused him to be considered by many progressive, learned Catholics, as a "prophet for the council." Those from the conservative sides appreciated his ideas less. Not surprisingly, then, Newman was mentioned by lay teachers at St Cuthbert but not by the more conservative priests. The same fate befell another Anglican who converted to Catholicism but in more recent times: Ronald Knox, who became a Catholic priest in 1918. His most famous work, *The Belief of Catholics*, published in 1927, presented an intellectual type of Catholicism far from the pious Irish model that was preferred by the conservative priests. According to one of my interlocutors, during and after the council there was a growing split between the more liberal and the more conservative teaching priests.[86] Sting also recalls such a dynamic:

> In the sixties when I was in grammar school there was a left-wing church and there was a right-wing church, and I could see that the priests within school were in two camps. You could sense it.[87]

Some of the more progressive priests and teachers referred to an idea popular then, summarized as "See, Judge, Act": a method for social intervention which prided itself on taking notice of reality. Its author was the Belgian priest (and later Cardinal) Joseph Leo Cardijn (1882–1967), who convinced Pope John XXIII to speak about it and endorse it in *Mater et Magistra*, an encyclical on Christianity and social progress John XXIII released in 1961:

> There are three stages which should normally be followed in the reduction of social principles into practice. First, one reviews the concrete situation; secondly, one forms a judgment on it in

86. I.N., interview by author, October 13, 2014, New York City, REC21:20.

87. Sting, interview by author, July 23, 2017, Künzelsau, REC22:013.

the light of these same principles; thirdly, one decides what in the circumstances can and should be done to implement these principles. These are the three stages that are usually expressed in the three terms: see, judge, act.

These priests also supported the Catholic Worker movement, which was founded in 1933 in the United States by Peter Maurin and Dorothy Day, and then spread to some other parts of the world, in particular to English-speaking countries. It was a left-leaning movement with great emphasis on social justice.[88] Those progressive teachers also exposed some of the students to the French movement *prêtres ouvriers*, the "worker priests," who believed priests should integrate into the working class by working in factories, ports, shipyards, mines, or agriculture. It is there, among the people, that they can share the gospel, on the one hand, and understand their flock on the other. The movement, which began a few decades earlier, was condemned by Pope Pius XII in 1954 but then re-established by Pope Paul VI in 1965, when Gordon and his friends were at St Cuthbert's. Much later in life, in his album and musical *The Last Ship*, Sting would place the kind and compassionate character of a priest among the shipyard workers, and have him express ideas typical of that clerical movement.[89]

It is possible that concelebrated Masses, in which several priests celebrated the Eucharist together, began to take place at the school at some point during those years. Until the council, these were reserved for very specific cases, such as priestly ordination; the council, however, changed the rules, overcoming vehement opposition to it by, most prominently, Cardinal Francis Spellman of New York. Basing his position, it seems, on the words of a theologian he had heard previously, Spellman was apparently of the opinion that the grace produced by the celebration of Masses depends on their numbers: when several priests concelebrate one Mass, less grace is produced than when they celebrate Masses separately.[90] Clearly, a certain "divine arithmetic" was popular in some corners of the church, as was also evident above in the testimony regarding Novenas. In the end, Spellman and those who held similar opinions lost, and concelebrations became a relatively common procedure. Still, at the time, it was a new and exciting event. The secular *Wallsend News* itself reported in 1968 that in a certain local parish, the first ever concelebrated Mass took place.[91] To the list of significant dates, especially for carnivores, one should also include the last

88. On the movement and some of its founders see Coy (ed.), *A Revolution*.

89. See above, pp. 95–101.

90. See Rynne, *Vatican Council II*, 66–67.

91. "Teams to meet at Mass," 13.

day of 1967, when another centuries-old rule was changed: the obligation to abstain from meat every Friday was dropped.

Another novelty, holding services together with non-Catholics, was also beginning to become common. In 1964, when Gordon was thirteen years old, with the promulgation of the *Decree on Ecumenism* by the council, the door for such events was opened:

> In certain special circumstances, such as the prescribed prayers "for unity," and during ecumenical gatherings, it is allowable, indeed desirable that Catholics should join in prayer with their separated brethren. Such prayers in common are certainly an effective means of obtaining the grace of unity, and they are a true expression of the ties which still bind Catholics to their separated brethren.[92]

Ten days after the release of this text, back in Newcastle, Bishop Cunningham sent a letter to his diocese's priests. The letter ordered them to read a "Statement about Ecumenism" produced by the bishops of England and Wales "at every Mass in every church and chapel of the diocese" on the upcoming Sunday, December 6, 1964. Two days after the letter was written, the statement was also sent to the press, ensuring that non-Catholics learned about these new Catholic rules on the same day that Catholics did. In very blunt and clear terms, the statement allowed acts that only recently had been considered absolutely unacceptable:

> In certain circumstances . . . joint prayer [of Catholics and non-Catholic Christians] is to be commended as a most valuable way of promoting unity. . . . [Catholic] elected representatives and public officials may in future attend services in non-Catholic churches in the course of their civic duties. . . . It is permissible for Catholics, for reasons of friendship or courtesy, to attend religious ceremonies in non-Catholic churches on social occasions such as weddings or funerals. . . . A Catholic may be bridesmaid or best man at a wedding between non-Catholics. . . . As friendship between Christians grows, invitations are increasingly extended to certain Catholics to attend non-Catholic churches on special occasions such as the induction of a new Vicar or Minister. These invitations may now be accepted. . . . On Remembrance Day Catholics are sometimes asked to attend services at the local War Memorial. This invitation they may now accept . . . .[93]

92. *Unitatis Redintegratio* (November 21, 1964), II:8.

93. HND, Ad Clerum Letters, February 1955–March 1966, MR8. See http://links.

It is fascinating to envision the faces of those Catholics that sat in their pews on that Sunday morning as they heard this striking text being read aloud. How many of them had, on the one hand, deeply internalized the prohibitions that were valid until that moment, and on the other hand, thought of all the pain and discomfort these rules had caused them? How many weddings and funerals of friends and family had they missed? How many events had they wanted to attend, such as memorial ceremonies for fallen soldiers, but could not? A week ago, to the day, they began praying in English, something that English Catholics resisted for centuries. Now, they were being told that they are encouraged to do what was strictly forbidden until recent months. One can only imagine the shock and silence when this text was read, and the lively discussions about it on the streets and in Catholic homes following the service. It is obvious that some were happy and felt relief. It is certain that others felt betrayed by their church, and may have wondered if it had not become a heretical one.

Regardless of the possible reactions of some in the pews, the changes were put in practice very quickly. Less than two months after the publication of the council's document, *Wallsend News* reported about this new reality:

> Although the Week of Prayer [for Unity] will follow the same pattern in the borough as in past years, a notable and important exception is that, for the first time, Catholics will be participating. . . . During the week, the Rev. Derek Simpson, of St. John's [Anglican] Church, Wallsend, together with a small group of his church people, will be attending an evening Mass at one of the Catholic churches in the borough as a gesture towards unity.[94]

I suspect that it took some time before Catholics dared to go a service in a non-Catholic church. A year later, when Bishop Cunningham returned to the diocese from the fourth and last session of the council in late 1965, a celebratory reception was organized. Apparently, at his request, and for the first time, representatives of other Christian denominations and of the local Jewish community were invited as well.[95] Some months later, in April 1966, the *Newcastle Journal* reported on yet another move by Wallsend's Catholics towards other Christians:

> St Columba's Catholic Women's League has invited 50 women from each of the Anglican churches of St Luke's and St John to join them at a social evening and supper in their church hall.

stingandreligion.com/ecu1.

94. "Churches Unite," 8.

95. *Northern Catholic Calendar* (1975), 155–57.

Clergy of both denominations will be there. Mrs Mary G Willson of Station Road, chairman of the St Columba's Guild,[96] said last night: "We are all very pleased our invitation was so readily accepted. . . . I think it is best that this should be done by the people themselves rather than those at the top. We all believe in God and the sooner we get together the better." Mrs Mary Richardson, of St Aidan's Road, enrolling member of [the Anglican] St Luke's Mothers Union, said: "They have extended the hand of friendship and we are going to grasp it. I hope it is just the start of continued meetings." . . . Father J. Kelly, St Columba's parish priest, said: "We have a great regard for our non-Catholic brethren and are very pleased."[97]

Things had clearly changed since the days, only a few years earlier, when almost any type of cooperation with non-Catholics, unless done to promote clear Catholic interests, would have been viewed negatively by the hierarchy.

From some oral accounts, it seems that not all non-Catholics were treated equally: Anglo-Anglicans were a relatively easy group to relate to. On the other hand, Methodists, for example, were still kept at a distance.[98] And yet changes were taking place. Three years later, by 1968, *Wallsend News* was reporting on joint services and meetings during the Week for Christian Unity, with Catholic participation, as almost a matter of fact.[99] Slowly, cooperation in events outside of that week was also starting to take place. This happened, for example, at the annual service on the ruins of the ancient medieval church of Holy Cross in Wallsend, generally celebrated only by members of the Church of England.[100] This time, Canon Michael O'Leary, from the Wallsend's parish of St Aidan's, represented the Catholic bishop:

96. Should have been "Catholic Women's League."

97. "Step towards Unity."

98. I.N., interview by author, October 13, 2014, New York City, REC21:31.

99. "Hundreds Take Part," 6.

100. The Church of the Holy Cross was built around 1150, about a century after the Norman conquest of England. For the next four centuries, until the Reformation, Wallsend was part of the parish of Jarrow (where Bede, whom we mentioned above, was previously composing his works). Priests from the area served this chapel, which was probably used for private prayer, baptisms, marriages, and funerals, with only the occasional Mass being said. The chapel was a necessary one, as there were no others around for miles. It is likely that some of the stones used to build this chapel were taken, just like in Bede's monastery, from Roman remains. Around the end of the eighteenth century, this church, by then in Anglican hands, became unusable after six centuries of serving the community. Due to its small size and its location on a hill far from the center of modern Wallsend, repairing it for use was no longer justifiable. See Knowles, *The Church*, 8.

Although annual services at Holy Cross have taken place during recent years, the event on Sunday was the first occasion when church people of beliefs other than Anglicans have been invited to participate and Roman Catholics as well as Non Conformists were present.[101]

In Grammar School, another catechism, no longer the red "Penny Catechism" mentioned earlier, was used. The children referred to it as the "blue catechism" (officially the "Catechism of Christian Doctrine . . . with Explanation") due to the color of its cover. It was more advanced than the "Red Catechism" in the sense that the answers to the questions were longer and more detailed. Many said that they rarely reached its end due to its length. Several of my informants described this part of schooling as extremely rigid, and as something in which questions were not allowed. Called at the time "Religious Instruction" (RI), and not yet "Religious Education" (RE), some students had their own way to show their dislike of it, especially those who were old enough to study physics. In the British Isles, the so-called "two-fingered salute," in which a V sign is done with the fingers while the palm is facing the person giving the sign, has long been considered an insulting gesture. Older students learned in physics class Ohm's law in electricity that "$V=RI$," and considered this formula to perfectly describe their feelings about the Religious Instruction they were subjected to:

> We hated [Religious Instructions]. We hated the priests that taught that. . . . Because it was so narrow-minded. Because it was so didactic. . . . They taught us "You SHOULD go to confession every week, you MUST do this, you MUST do that. . . . We would be tested on this. The priest [in secondary school] would come and test you on this. We were told what we had to think. What we were given was absolute certainty. This is what you [believe]. This is what you do.[102]

Sting seems to agree, and also recalls explicit problematic teachings:

> [I had] a teacher who in hindsight was genuinely anti-Semitic. That teacher would say, "Who started the war?" [We answered:] "The Germans." [The teacher then replied] "No, it was the Jews!" And we did not know who Jews were, we didn't know any Jews. "So who are the Jews?" [we asked]. [The teacher answered:] "Well, who do you pay the money to, when you pay for your [leased] furniture every week? Mr. Hardy? He's a Jew!" It was

101. "Service," 13.

102. B.G., interview by author, December 13, 2014, Wallsend, REC13:09.

indoctrination and hideous antisemitism, that I instinctively
knew was bad.[103]

In 1965, during the last stage of the council, a new and revised edition of
the *Catechism* was published. From my inquiries among my interlocutors,
it seems that the children began to use it in school rather quickly. It had
some changes in details and in style, but these changes were still rather minor. Gordon's generation would already be out of school when entirely new
books of the catechism would appear.

During the same year, on February 21, 1965, Gordon received the
sacrament of confirmation in a ceremony celebrated by Bishop James Cunningham in his home parish of St Columba's, together with another 134
boys and 130 girls.

The person to be confirmed, the "confirmand," chooses a "sponsor," an
adult Catholic in good standing, that will accompany her or him. In many
places, including in Britain, the confirmand also chooses a "confirmation
name": a name of a saint she or he identifies with. During the ritual, the
sponsor comes with the confirmand to the bishop, and the bishop performs
the ritual. Today the bishop gives, in many places, a "sign of peace" (such
as a handshake) to the confirmed person. During Gordon's childhood, he
would have given the children a pat on the cheek upon completion of the
ritual.

The large number of children at Gordon's confirmation was due to the
fact that children from various parishes were confirmed together in what
seems to be a rotation system between the parishes. This was necessary because of the large number of parishes and children, and the fact that only
one person in the entire diocese, the bishop, would normally perform it. For
this reason, this sacrament was often performed only once every few years
in Wallsend. Thus, children of various cohorts received it together when the
occasion came. With possible exceptions, the children from St Columba's
who were confirmed on that day seem to have been born between March
1948 and September 1954. In other words, the youngest was ten years old,
while the oldest was sixteen years old. My interlocutors told me that the
ceremony was not much of a big deal at the time. Unlike today, it included
only minimal preparation, and was not awaited for by the children with
great anticipation. Thus, a delay of some years in celebrating it was not a
major issue. Most children went through it, although a minority chose not

103. Sting, interview by author, July 23, 2017, Künzelsau, REC22:010. The idea that
"the Jews" are responsible for World War II was promoted by Hitler himself, in a speech
he gave in the Reichstag on January 30, 1939. An English translation of this speech,
together with selections from many other speeches given by Hitler, were published in
book issued by Oxford University Press already in 1942.

to: these were generally those who had already decided that Catholicism was not "their thing."

Each of the participants had to choose a "confirmation name." Gordon, who was thirteen, chose the name "Thomas."[104] He was the only one to choose this name. There were a few other children that chose a name that no one else did (for example "Frederick," "George," and "Gerard," among the boys, and "Anastasia," "Bridget," and "Monica," among the girls), but they were the exception. Most children chose names that were selected by others as well: among the boys, there were seventeen John's, twenty-five Paul's, eleven Peter's, six Christopher's, six Anthony's, six Patrick's, nine Michael's, and eight Joseph's. Among the girls, there were nineteen Teresa's (and twelve Theresa's), eighteen Mary/Maria/Marie's, fifteen Bernadette's, ten Catherine's (and two Katherine's), nine Anne's (and three Ann's), nine Margaret's, eight Veronica's, and five Elizabeth's.

The choice of "Thomas" is peculiar. The first famous Christian Thomas, "Thomas the Apostle," appears for the first time just after the story of the resurrection of Lazarus in John 11. There, and in some other places, he is not particularly skeptical. Later though, in John 20, he doubts the claim of the other disciples, that the person they reported seeing was the resurrected Jesus. Only after he sees Jesus, and is invited by him to touch his wounds, he begins to believe that Jesus has indeed returned. He gets mildly rebuked for this by Jesus: "You believe because you can see me. Happy are those who have not seen and yet believe."[105] He is thus popularly known as "Doubting Thomas." Did Gordon want to hint that he was a skeptic? Or at least, a "sophisticated" believer? Or maybe he chose the name after another Thomas? The answer might be a mix of all. This is how Sting currently explains his choice:

> I chose Thomas as my confirmation name after my paternal grandfather, but yes, I always thought the disciple's initial scepticism was reasonable in the circumstances.[106]

An important book appeared around the same time, in 1966: An English version of the French *Jerusalem Bible*. Being, I believe, the first Catholic English translation of the Bible done scientifically in the twentieth century, it represented something new and exciting. Very quickly, British Catholics acquired copies for themselves. One of Gordon's classmates from Wallsend

---

104. Archival material, 116.

105. John 20:29 (JB).

106. Sting, email exchange with author, July 8, 2017.

describes the experience of not having a Bible and then buying one. His experience is possibly reflective of a common reality in Catholic families:

> We did not have a Bible in the house. We only bought a Bible when the new *Jerusalem Bible* was published. I remember being in my teens when that was first published. [Before that] we had the missal from church and that had the readings that you use on Sundays and the daily lessons which are daily readings, but it didn't have the whole Bible or the whole New Testament. [The result is] the Old Testament is a foreign land to me. [Stories from the Old Testament were known] only in as much as they affected what happened in the New Testament.[107]

The time was the 1960s (whether we mean strictly the years 1960–69 or, as many scholars of this period do, "The long sixties," ranging from around 1958 to around 1974), when great cultural changes took place in many countries. While these changes were not directly related to Catholicism and religion, they had a major impact on them. Many cultural conventions had been shaken since the end of the Second World War in 1945, but it took time for some of them to actually collapse. According to several studies,

> Religious conformity was at its height between 1945 and 1960; whilst church attendance for older age groups slipped (especially men's), the young became more than usually enthusiastic patrons of churches. . . . In [the 1950s], 58 per cent of parents claimed to teach their children to say prayers. Even if their parents were backsliding churchgoers, Christianity was hard for children to shake off. It represented the spirit of the age.[108]

Concepts about the body and sexuality were quickly changing in the 1960s. Shorter dresses for women, longer hair for men, the appearance and growing use of the contraceptive pill (allowed to be prescribed in Britain since 1961), the decriminalization of homosexuality in Britain in 1967, softening attitudes toward divorce, growing rates of premarital sex, and other changes were all part of a sexual revolution. This revolution indirectly weakened the authority of those figures and institutions—such as religious clergy—that opposed it. Politically in Britain, the different spirit of the time was also manifested in the victory in 1964 of Harold Wilson of the Labour Party, who broke thirteen years of control by the Conservative Party. Wilson

---

107. B.G., interview by author, December 16, 2014, Wallsend, REC20:17.

108. Brown and Lynch, "Cultural Perspectives," 332.

was to remain prime minister for almost six years, until the victory of Edward Heath of the Conservative Party in 1970.

One of the more dramatic changes of the 1960s was the decline of the place and role of religion in both private and public life. The decade was characterized by a clear drop in the number of those who regularly frequented religious houses of worship. This decline neither began nor ended in the 1960s, and was preceded by something many scholars noticed in the 1940s and 1950s: an actual rise in religious practices. And yet, by the early 1960s, the centrality of religion in the life of many Europeans was clearly in decline. This decline was also accompanied by the religious diversification that comes with immigration. The proliferation of ways to be religious, and ways to be Christian, had an indirect, negative impact on the status of the more traditional denominations of England. There were now more and more forces, besides religion, competing for the souls and time of both the young and the old. Amid these forces, the idea of life without religion in general, and without Catholicism in particular, became a real possibility. It should be remembered, however, that although "there has been a sharp decline in traditional Christian practices, including regular church attendance, recruitment to ordained ministry, and participation in rites of passage," Christianity nonetheless "retains influence over the cultural life of Britain, particularly in terms of language, art, music, landscape, literature and some everyday practices."[109]

Gordon clearly experienced both the decline in traditional religious practices, as well as the ongoing diversification of religious experience within the general culture.

The year 1968 was dramatic for Catholics worldwide. The council, and the years following it, seemed like a clear victory for the progressive and liberal camps of the Catholic church. Yet in the summer of that year, a major setback to the hopes and excitement of liberal Catholics took place. It happened when Pope Paul VI publicized his decision regarding contraception.

In an encyclical called *Humanae Vitae* ("Human Life"), the pope seriously and respectfully considered the various arguments in favor of the use of artificial methods for birth control, but finally ruled unequivocally against them. According to the encyclical, almost any act that is likely to prevent sexual relations from being potentially procreative is forbidden. Excepting abstinence, the only method open to Catholics interested in regulating their fertility remained the already permitted "rhythm method." The media in general, and Catholic media in particular, discussed the issue at length: "All Forms of Contraception Are Absolutely Excluded: 'No Change'

109. See Guest et al., "Christianity," 57.

Encyclical" was the headline of *The Universe* on August 2, 1968. Unsurprisingly, the editorial supported the pope's decision. However, one can easily read between the lines and see that if the position has been reversed, allowing the use of some contraceptive methods, it would have been supported with much more enthusiasm.

Countless articles revealed—sometimes explicitly, sometimes not—that tensions were high, and that objections to the document were common. Catholic centrists and progressives, many of whom had expected change and even considered that the decision to allow the use of new and efficient contraceptive methods was inevitable, were dumbstruck. Issues regarding birth control were frequently in the headlines at the time, perhaps even more so than today. The feminist revolution and the gradual integration of women into all spheres of life, especially in the developed world, enlivened the debate on women's rights to control their fertility and limit the number of children they had. The great demographic leap of the second half of the twentieth century, especially in the developing world, was also of concern, as the conventional wisdom was that it would be impossible to meet even the minimal needs of such a large population. The issue was also central to medical discourse: the birth control pill, which for the first time in history enabled women to control their fertility easily, safely, and effectively, appeared on the scene a few years prior and had already become part of the daily life of many women. The complex arguments of Paul VI, who supported the "natural" rhythm method but opposed methods involving the active prevention of conception, were unconvincing to many. Among other things, many were disturbed by the text's absolute emphasis on the physical aspect of the sexual union and its disregard for questions such as the couple's intention. The opinion that the arguments in favor of birth control included at the beginning of Paul VI's encyclical were more convincing than the arguments against it at its end was widespread among theologians. A growing feeling among Catholic laity that a supposedly celibate clergy had no right to "get into their bedrooms," dictating rules on matters of which they had no direct experience, also played a role in the controversy. The authority of the pope suffered a blow in the 1960s from which, many would say, it has never recovered.

At the time, Gordon was almost seventeen-year-old student at St Cuthbert Grammar School. He was already aware of at least some of the technicalities of human sexuality and procreation. If the publication of this document had not occurred during summer break, the topic would have certainly filled the corridors and classrooms, possibly revealing the large gaps between conservative and progressive teachers at the school, both clergy and lay. But the school year did not start until September, so the first heated debates in the press and among Catholics happened while the school was closed for the summer. And yet, this did not mean the school was shielded from them. For many years the topic continued to be the most hotly debated issue in the Catholic world, as it also came to be in the school. I asked one of my interlocutors, a classmate of Gordon's, if they had heard about the controversy while at St Cuthbert's:

> Oh yeah, oh yeah! We had many a debate in school about sexual behavior and contraception. But the conversation and the debate always had to come back to [what the] pope says. . . . [The topic] was in the papers and on television. . . . [The priests] couldn't avoid the debate, but [they] mixed in authority, "This is what you should think, this is what you should think!" At the time we had a mixture of people [at school. There was] Father Boyle who would be quite happy to talk about these issues and accept you as a growing human being. So, he would say, "Go into confession and don't worry about having impure thoughts for example, because that's natural at your age." . . . It was so nice to hear that! He kept away from the debate about contraception. Yet Father Derry, who was the opposite end, he would say, "Have nothing to do with girls, don't even think about them, etc. . . ." Then [there] was Father Tweedy who was a bit more liberal about things but still insisted that the church's authority should be obeyed on this topic. . . . They were intelligent men and we were just young developing teenagers, they would always win that debate. . . . So they equipped us in a sense to argue in a debate from one side, [but] you had to be careful not to debate too hard from the other side because you would be either ignored or you would be very quickly put down to make sure you kept in your place. . . . So I kept my head down really.[110]

There was no formal sex education at St Cuthbert's. Such discussions generally happened coincidentally, triggered generally by specific circumstances (such as press articles, TV news, or other events), and depended to a large degree on the personality of the teacher. In October 1968, Bishop Cunningham sent a questionnaire to the local clergy regarding the issue, most probably because of the uproar regarding *Humanae Vitae*. The short questionnaire was prepared by the Catholic Marriage Advisory Council and the Catechetical Centre. Before asking priests for their opinion, the text opened with the following statement: "The duty of parents to give sex education to their children has long been taught by the Church." One should know that in a Catholic context, when a document says that something "has long been

110. B.G., interview by author, December 13, 2014, Wallsend, REC13:14.

taught by the Church," it generally means that it was never taught, or at best, that it was mentioned somewhere, by someone, at some point in history, but no average Catholic would have ever heard about it. The text continued:

> More recently it has come to be accepted that schools too have an important part to play. What has not been widely given is help. Few Catholic parents are giving to their children appropriate information and nurturing Christian attitudes to sexuality. ... Few schools are consciously co-operating with the parents of their pupils to supplement home education for family life. Very few schools are integrating education for family life into their curricula.[111]

From what I was able to gather, St Cuthbert's was not among the "very few schools" that had such a curriculum. If at all, as mentioned above, discussions about the topic happened by chance.

Wallsend News had an article on the pope's encyclical on August 9, 1968, two weeks after its publication.[112] Interestingly, it consisted almost entirely of interviews with non-Catholic clergy. One can only suspect that it was hard to find a local Catholic priest that would defend the document, or, on the other hand, publicly object it. Most clergy preferred probably to simply keep quiet. It is possible that this is hinted in the words of the article,

> Many Catholic priests in Tynemouth and Wallsend feel that although they have their own personal views about the encyclical, they accept that the Pope is head of the Church and what he says Catholics should obey.

The only direct quotation from a Catholic in the article was taken from a letter by Bishop Cunningham, which had been read in all local Catholic churches several days earlier, according to the article. If the quote of the bishop's message is reliable, it is easy to see that he himself was perplexed about the encyclical, and far from enthusiastic about it. This is how the Wallsend News summarizes it:

> In the letter, the bishop pointed out that however great were their own personal problems and anxieties, the Pope had a greater burden. Every Roman Catholic should regard the Pope's appeal banning contraception as addressed to himself. . . . The Pope was aware of the distress the encyclical might cause among married people and realised with great compassion that

---

111. HND, Ad Clerum Letters, March 1966–December 1972, MR8.

112. "The Pope's Encyclical," 8.

sacrifices were involved in applying Catholic moral principles in married life.

It is obvious that due to the storm caused by encyclical, and to the fact that it was discussed openly outside Catholic circles, Bishop Cunningham felt he must say something. Whether his statement was helpful for his diocese's members that felt strongly against the encyclical, remains an open question.

The Bishops' Conference of England and Wales released a five-page statement on the controversy around *Humanae Vitae* in September of 1968. In my reading of it, it seems to be a careful and balanced document. Obviously, the bishops defend the pope and his right to issue the encyclical. They also try to justify it by saying that it was the product of much meditation and consultation. Yet, they very clearly do not applaud it, nor say that the objections to it are baseless. Bishop Cunningham sent this document to his clergy shortly after its publication.[113] A month later, he sent another letter to the local clergy, in which he spoke about the existence of priests who openly objected to the papal encyclical. From the style of the letter, it seems clear that he is borrowing entire paragraphs from another letter (if not copying it entirely) to compose his own text. In other words, though the letter is presented as Cunningham's response to a problem in his own particular diocese, the text of the letter may very well originate from Westminster. And although the letter clearly sympathizes with the priests that struggle with *Humanae Vitae*—stating that an open dialogue should not be suppressed and that it is unacceptable to compel the clergy's strict obedience, as had been the practice in the past—the text makes it clear that priests who continue their public opposition to the encyclical may not be able to continue in their pastoral work. If there hadn't been priests of this kind in the diocese of Hexham and Newcastle, it is clear such a letter would not have been sent:

> A few priests have publicly and explicitly rejected the Encyclical "Humanae Vitae". . . . Some seem to have begun to doubt that the Holy Spirit guides the whole Church and its chief pastor. . . . The open refusal of a group of priests to accept the Pope's guidance has caused dismay to their fellow priests who while being no less aware of pastoral problems give loyal obedience to the Holy Father. The opposition of these priests to the Pope's teaching had bewildered and saddened loyal members of the laity. . . . The bishops of England and Wales have no wish to inhibit reasonable discussion nor do they propose to make a return to priestly obedience. . . . [However, p]riests are required in

---

113. The document, and the letter by Cunningham that was attached to it, are found at HND, Ad Clerum Letters, March 1966–December 1972, MR8.

> preaching, teaching, in the Press, speaking on radio, television, or public platforms, to refrain from opposing the teaching of the Pope in all matters of faith and morals. If a priest is unwilling to give this undertaking the bishop will decide whether he can be allowed without scandal to continue to act in the name of the Church ....[114]

One can imagine the debate was heated. Unfortunately, I do not have more information concerning specific local priests who openly opposed the encyclical.

Two years earlier, in 1966, when Gordon was around fifteen years old, his family left Wallsend and moved to a bigger house in the nearby village of Cullercoats, near Tynemouth. It was closer to the coast, but slightly farther away from Newcastle. It is not easy to say whether this move had any effect on the religious life of the family in general, or of Gordon in particular, since so many other factors—such as age, surrounding culture, and family dynamics—were different by now. Gordon began to go to the local Catholic church, Our Lady and St Oswin's in Tynemouth:

> I liked the atmosphere, I liked the walk, by the sea and the mouth of the River Tyne.[115]

A year after graduating from the Catholic St Cuthbert's Grammar School and after one semester spent at the recently founded University of Warwick in Coventry, in Autumn 1971, Gordon enrolled at the Northern Counties Teacher Training College in Newcastle, from where he graduated in 1974. It should be noted that there was also a Catholic teacher training college in Newcastle (St Mary's), but he did not go there. The bishop that was active during most of his childhood, Bishop James Cunningham, died that July. Harold Wilson of the Labour Party became Prime Minister again, and with James (Jim) Callaghan kept the Labour Party in power until it lost to the first woman to hold the office of Prime Minister in Britain, and for almost twelve years, Margaret Thatcher of the Conservative Party. Thatcher's name still provokes strong negative reactions in the region, as I was able to personally witness multiple times, due to her being considered a major player in the region's industrial and economic decline, which is still felt today.[116]

114. A copy of the letter exists at HND, Ad Clerum Letters, March 1966–December 1972, MR8.

115. Sting, interview by author, July 23, 2017, Künzelsau, REC22:037.

116. In the musical *Billy Elliot* by Elton John and Lee Hall, which takes place in the same region, in a key song, "Merry Christmas Maggie Thatcher," Thatcher's death is explicitly wished for by the entire community. See https://links.stingandreligion.com/that.

During the same year, the first rock band that Gordon was a part of, Last Exit, was created. He then taught for two years at a Catholic elementary school in Cramlington, a short drive north from Newcastle. On the first day of May 1976 he married actress Frances Tomelty, whom he met two years earlier in a musical production, *Rock Nativity*, where she played the Virgin Mary. The wedding took place at Our Lady and St Oswin's Church, in Tynemouth: a small old Catholic church close to the spectacular waterfront and ruins of Tynemouth Priory and Castle (where King Oswin, the seventh-century successor to King Oswald mentioned earlier, was buried), a short drive from Wallsend. Being a very popular chapel, it was not obvious Gordon and Frances could marry there:

> When we went to see the Registry, we said we want to get married in that church. He said, "You can't!" I said, "Well, we go there every week!" "Oh, you can then." I could have been lying, but it was the truth. We did actually go there.[117]

The marriage was also registered in his childhood parish, St Columba's. After two generations of mixed marriages in his family, this marriage was, religiously speaking, simple: Gordon, a Catholic, married Frances, a Catholic. The couple named their first child Joseph, after Frances' father, Joseph Tomelty, a famous author and playwright. Joseph (Joe) was baptized as Catholic.

A few weeks before Gordon's and Frances' marriage (which ended a few years later with a divorce), in March of 1976, Catholics in England had a new leader: Basil Hume was elected Archbishop of Westminster. Born in Newcastle in 1923 to a Catholic mother and a Protestant father, George Haliburton Hume (who adopted the first name "Basil" when he became a monk) was raised a Catholic. Catholics living in the area under consideration in this book thus had one of their own—an avid fan of the Newcastle United Football Club and an admirer of northern saints such as Cuthbert—heading British Catholicism. Six years later, in May 1982, Pope John Paul II arrived in England. It was the first time a reigning pope visited the land. The visit happened to take place during a sensitive time, when Britain was at war with Argentina, a very Catholic country, over the Falkland Islands (or "Islas Malvinas"). The pope met with Queen Elizabeth II. He also visited Canterbury Cathedral, and met the head of the Anglican Communion, Archbishop (of Canterbury) Robert Runcie. During this historical visit, British Catholics experienced an event many of them, and definitely their ancestors, could have hardly imagined some decades earlier. The official

---

117. Sting, interview by author, July 23, 2017, Künzelsau, REC22:047.

host of the pope was, naturally, Archbishop (of Westminster) Basil Hume, who was considered by many English people, including many Anglicans, to be the most important British ecclesial figure of the time. A Northumbrian from Newcastle upon Tyne was the representative of English Catholicism in front of the bishop of Rome, the successor of those who centuries earlier were declared unwelcome in English affairs. Catholicism became, in many ways, fully respectable. Things were changing. They were also changing for Gordon. He was already called Sting, resided in London, and since March 1977 had been a member of a band formed by a drummer named Stewart Copeland: The Police. He was on his way to becoming, very soon, one of the most famous rock stars of the last quarter of the twentieth century.

Chapter 5

RELIGION AND SPIRITUALITY
IN STING'S WORK

I like being irreverent. But I also like being reverent. I think everything
has a time and place.[1]

REFERENCES TO THE BIBLE and to Catholicism in Sting's work were exam-
ined above. But what about more general allusions to religion and spirituality? These will be explored in this chapter.

The obvious first song by Sting in which faith is discussed, and in fact,
is the core of the song, is "O My God," which appeared on the cassette recording of Last Exit in 1975. The title, a common English expression that is
not generally used to actually address God, is an interesting choice. Eight
years later, in 1983, Sting reused this song in *Synchronicity*, the last, and
probably most important album of the band in which he would gain his
fame, The Police. The musical rendering in each of these two incarnations
of the song is extremely different, and the text itself is also far from identical. We will first discuss the 1975 version. Later, the newer version will be
analyzed.

"O My God" (1975) is a melodic, minimalistic, quiet song, with Sting
singing in a high pitch, reminiscent of Paul Simon's voice and style.[2] The
song opens with a strong existential statement:

1. Sting, *All This Time* CD-ROM, Part 1, "Gothic Cathedral," 11:22, https://links.
stingandreligion.com/cdr2.

2. During the "On Stage Together Tour" Paul Simon and Sting had in 2014–15, Sting
acknowledged repeatedly his debt and admiration to Paul Simon, since the beginning

149

Everyone I know is lonely,
    and God's so far away;
And my heart belongs to no one,
    so now sometimes I pray.

When analyzing a song that is written in the first person, one must be careful in determining whether the voice belongs to the songwriter-performer
or not. It is obvious that many songs that Sting has written in the first person are not autobiographical. The most famous of them is perhaps "Don't
Stand So Close to Me" (1980) about illicit relations between a teacher and
a schoolgirl, obliging Sting to explain many times that although he was a
teacher, it was at an elementary school: the song is not about something
he had experienced. It is also quite obvious that he is not one of the seven
brothers in "Love is Stronger Than Justice" (1993), nor the lone shooter in
"I Hung My Head" (1996). And yet, in this song, due to its topic, style, and
content, the possibility that this is a personal song, written in the first person for a reason, seems quite compelling.

Saying that God is distant works well with the idea of loneliness that
is so common in Sting's later work (with its most obvious manifestations
appearing in the famous "So Lonely" of 1978 and "Message in A Bottle" of
1979). Here, Sting says that people have no one, not even God, really close
to them. When Sting says, "and my heart belongs to no one," he breaks with
a popular romantic tradition, still true today, in which the listener expects
to hear that the heart "belongs" to someone special: to "daddy" as in a 1938
song by Cole Porter (a "sugar daddy," actually); to "you" as in a song by
Russ Irwin (1991); to "Jesus," as in the name of an album by Melvin Taylor
(2011), etc. This loneliness and remoteness from God leads to prayer in
Sting's lyrics.

The song continues with a line that repeats as a chorus many times:
"Take the space between us, and fill it up someway." Is this sentence, and
much of the song, directed at God, or rather at a fellow human? These two
ways of reading it seem possible. I opt though for the first one, and see this
line as the core of a prayer, and very possibly the nucleus of the song itself.
From this perspective, I understand Sting is asking God to somehow close

---

of his own career. Paul Carr seems to suggest another explanation for Sting's voice in
this recording: "As with a number of other tracks recorded by Last Exit at Impulse
[studio], Sting's vocals are double tracked—with both voices singing nearly identical
melody lines. Although this is a common production technique in order to acquire a
full vocal sound, it appears that in the Last Exit recordings, either this device is used to
cover up performance issues or the mix is a combination of an actual take and a "guide
vocal," which was accidentally included in the final mix. Whatever the reason, it results
in a slightly distant, almost unearthly sound in the vocal line" (Carr, *Sting*, 101).

the gap between them. It is a remarkably simple prayer: he does not ask for anything specific. He only wants God to make them closer. Sting seems to suggest this is in God's hands. He cannot do much. God must do it, in some unknown way. In asking for this, there is a hint of an idea that is common to practically all forms of Christianity: that closeness to God is a gift, a grace, that only God can bestow. It is not something a person can achieve alone. It seems that this prayer was written by someone that still believes but who is drifting away from that faith. It is an urgent, and rather desperate call: God, do something so that the gap between us does not become even wider. Do something before the distance between us becomes unbridgeable.

Another line appears with this request as a kind of explanation for the appeal: "I've been waiting for my brother since blessed Christmas day." The expression "blessed Christmas day" is not rare. Among other places, it appears in a poem by the nineteenth-century poet Robert Louis Stevenson, a poem that Sting adapted more than three decades later, and put (with Mary Macmaster) to music: "Christmas at Sea" (2009). But who is this "brother" Sting is waiting for, and what happened during the previous Christmas? Although Sting has an actual brother, Philip, it seems unlikely that this is who he is referring to. The "brother" is probably Jesus, whose birth is celebrated on Christmas. Later lines in the song hint at this, especially a rather blasphemous one that addresses God (the Father) directly and speaks about Jesus. We will return to this shortly.

Sting does not end his address to God with a plea for closeness. He has some accusations as well:

> Take a look around you,
>   your spirits seem so low;
> You don't speak to anybody,
>   so you can't expect to know.
> Everybody's lonesome,
>   only some of us don't care;
> If you're looking for your brother,
>   you could find him anywhere.[3]

In the last sentence of this stanza, the "you" might not be referring to God specifically, but rather might be a sort of general statement that is true for everyone: when one is looking for a brother, the brother can be found anywhere. Hence, Sting seems to be saying the following to God: Your Son, Jesus, the one some humans think of as a "brother," is not so special. There

---

3. I am not certain the word "anywhere" is a correct transcription of the lyrics. The lyrics here are based on listening to the recording. I am not aware of an official publication of them.

is no real need for him. Brothers can be found everywhere. Sting continues with his complaints:

> O my God you take the biscuit,
>   treating me this way,
> expecting me to help my neighbor
>   no matter what he say.

In British English, "taking the biscuit" means doing something that is extremely annoying or surprising or the worst of its kind. In this context though, one might wonder if it is not also a reference to the Eucharist, taken by Catholics during Mass. Following the first interpretation, God's treatment of Sting, and his commandment to be kind, is irrational. The request by Jesus (or God), to turn the other cheek to those who behave badly is also unacceptable: "Cannot turn the other cheek: it's black and bruised and torn." Sting thus refuses to act the way Jesus is alleged to have asked his disciples to act.[4] He already tried to do so and had enough of it.

Sting then expresses a rather heretical idea in the context of Christianity. If the entire Christian belief is based on the assumption that something major, and good, happened when Jesus came, Sting does not buy it anymore, and explicitly says so to God: "The world don't seem no better since your precious Son was born."

After all this, does Sting want no contact with God? No. He still yearns for it, as seen at the song's conclusions in which we find the core of the prayer that introduced his monologue. He begs God to "Take the space between us and fill it up someway." He is still waiting for God's grace.

Last Exit was, after all, mostly a local band. The first widely distributed recording of Sting, The Police's first record *Outlandos d'Amour* (1978), included no obvious religious themes or texts other than a minor "God help me please" statement in the song "Hole in My Life," or the short but possibly revealing autobiographical note, "Then we lost our faith and prayed to the TV" in "Born in the 50s." Not much religious material appeared in the following two albums. The group's fourth album, *Ghost in the Machine*, released on Sting's thirtieth birthday in 1981, was different. It has significantly more political, moral, and spiritual pronouncements than the band's previous albums. According to Sting, "apart from 'Every Little Thing She Does Is Magic' (written in 1976), all of the songs on this album were written in the west of Ireland in 1981."[5]

---

4. See Matthew 5:38–39 and Luke 6:29.

5. Sting, *Lyrics*, 53.

One reason for some of these new motifs, as well as the title of the album itself, is the impact that several books by Arthur Koestler (1905–83) had on Sting. Koestler, a productive British author of Jewish-Hungarian background (later discovered to have a rather questionable personality), was extremely interested in human psychology. He was also a strong believer in parapsychology—which both claims that certain psychological events exist that cannot be explained with traditional science, and seeks to study these supposed events.

Koestler was not the only one interested in parapsychology: the topic was extremely popular in the 1970s and early 1980s. In fact, by the 1970s, England had become one of the major centers of the interest in such supposed psychological phenomena. Research done about it both by the Soviets and the Americans led many to believe that methods such as telepathy, or "mind reading," might be useful in the Cold War. With communication abilities much more limited than what we enjoy today, it was believed by many that telepathy could provide important channels of communication across long distances and between land bases and submarines, and that whoever succeeded at harnessing it would have a tremendous advantage. It was thus not unusual for curious and smart people of the time to read about it and believe in it, since some mainstream scholars, associations, and institutions considered it to be a legitimate science and branch of psychology. This was also reflected in entertainment: one of the biggest international stars of the time was Uri Geller (b. 1946), who pretended to be a "psychic." While today parapsychology is considered by practically all scientists to be a "pseudo-science," this was not the case then.

In various places, Sting explicitly mentioned several books by Koestler that had a particularly strong impact on him. These include The Act of Creation (1964), which dedicates over 700 pages to discussing the sources of creativity of unusually gifted scientists, authors, and artists; Ghost in the Machine (1967), which considers the mind/body question, human behavior, brain structure, and more; The Roots of Coincidence (1972), which discusses the concept of "synchronicity" (a term that was coined by the psychiatrist, and for a time, collaborator with Sigmund Freud, Carl Jung, in 1952), and attempts to explain cases in which two or more seemingly unrelated events occur at the same time.[6]

---

6. See also Cambray, Synchronicity. For another way of considering coincidences of this kind in one of Milan Kundera's most famous books, see Kundera, The Unbearable, 52: "It is wrong, then, to chide the novel for being fascinated by mysterious coincidences . . . but it is right to chide man for being blind to such coincidences in his daily life. For he thereby deprives his life of a dimension of beauty."

In an interview, three years after the album came out, Sting described the impact of Koestler's *Ghost in the Machine* in this way:

> Through the book, I became more spiritual in a very scientific way. . . . Rereading it, it spoke to me, and in a logical way it ended my lazy grip on logic. . . . Prior to that, I was very much a robot. . . . The idea of a hard, mechanistic universe is ludicrous. Therefore, we are not machines either.[7]

Decades later, in his preface to the lyrics of "Spirits in the Material World" (which opened the album *Ghost in the Machine*) Sting explained what "spiritual" means for him:

> I thought that while political progress is clearly important in resolving conflict around the world, there are spiritual (as opposed to religious) aspects of our recovery that also need to be addressed. I suppose by "spiritual" I mean the ability to see the bigger picture, to be able to step outside the narrow box of our conditioning and access those higher modes of thinking that Koestler talked about.[8]

The song's refrain, "We are spirits in the material world," makes it clear that Sting is not a materialist in the philosophical sense. He insists we are not machines.

Another song from the same album, "Secret Journey," has obvious mystical ideas, but they apparently emerge from a different source. In his book of lyrics, Sting prefaces it with this:

> I was intrigued by G. I. Gurdjieff's *Meetings with Remarkable Men*, his account of the travels and discoveries of an intrepid group of spiritual adventurers. I was looking for some spiritual guidance for my own life and, after a few false leads, finally began to listen to the discrete language of my own heart.[9]

In my meeting with him in 2017, the only word he said when I mentioned this song was still "Gurdjieff."

George Ivanovich Gurdjieff (1866–1949) was a Greek-Armenian spiritual teacher who gained much fame outside of his native land. One of the main themes of his *Meetings with Remarkable Men* is that many of us live our lives as machines, unconscious of inner abilities and spiritual truths,

---

7. Sting, interview by Timothy White, *Penthouse*, January 1984. See also Campion, *Walking on the Moon*, 178–82.

8. Sting, *Lyrics*, 55.

9. Sting, *Lyrics*, 70.

and obviously should not. The book, written in Russian, was published in English in 1963. The similarities between Koestler and Gurdjieff are obvious.

When he wrote "Secret Journey," Sting was living a very unusual life, having already become an extremely successful international rock star. At the time, he was residing in Ireland. Harboring rather obvious issues already with the God he was raised to believe in (as we saw in "O My God"), the fact that he was looking for some new spiritual direction is hardly surprising. In the song, he describes a (probably imaginary) meeting with a blind "holy man," and mentions again his own sense of loneliness: "Upon a secret journey I met a holy man; His blindness was his wisdom, I'm such a lonely man." The holy man promises that he will "see light in the darkness," understand the "sense of it," and finally, find love. Sting says that he pondered for days about the man's words, and finally adds something that he heard from the man: "When you've made your secret journey, you will be a holy man." For Sting, becoming a "holy man" thus seems to involve a certain quest of a mystical nature. This seems closer to Asian traditions regarding holiness, rather than to the Catholic traditions about saints that Sting was raised on. At thirty years old, Sting was clearly already moving toward new spiritual horizons.

It should be noted that among his peers in the musical scene, Sting was not unusual in pursuing such a quest and in using it in his work. The Police was very much related to what was called "Progressive Rock," a type of rock that was strong in Britain at the time, and that was characterized mostly by two elements that were obvious in the case of The Police and its members: having talented musicians that actually knew how to play and had significant training in multiple musical styles (unlike the typical "Punk" bands), and having song lyrics that generally made sense and at times tried to convey sophisticated ideas. Many of the lyricists of such groups, who were also often their lead singers, looked for inspiration in similar places. As Edward Macan put it,

> The spiritual impulse that lay at the root of all progressive rock's most representative lyrics is the belief that Western society's spiritual sterility is increasing in direct proportion to its technological prowess. On the one hand, this belief stimulated the hippies' interest in Eastern spirituality, mysticism, mythology, fantasy literature, and other models of more organic, "natural" mode of society; it also drew them to texts that attacked the spiritual poverty of modern industrial society.[10]

10. Macan, *Rocking the Classics*, 73.

Two years later, in 1983, The Police released their fifth (and last) album, *Synchronicity*. The choice of the album's title was obviously Sting's: at various times, the two other members of the group, and especially Stewart Copeland, made it clear that even after many years, they still do not buy into the concept nor understand what Sting wanted to express with it. Both the title and some of the songs in the album were inspired by Koestler's *The Roots of Coincidence*, and during various concerts with the band, Sting would declare, "There is no such thing as coincidence" before singing the second song of the album, "Walking in Your Footsteps." In that song, Sting speaks to a dinosaur, hinting that being liked by God does not offer much assurance:

> Hey Mr. Dinosaur,
>   you really couldn't ask for more.
> You were God's favorite creature,
>   but you didn't have a future.

Whether Sting was just playing with rhyme, or actually trying to say something substantial about God, is impossible to know.

The next song in the same album is "O My God," a song that we have already mentioned and that is much more significant for our study. The version in *Synchronicity* (1983) is quite different from its 1975 predecessor, recorded with Last Exit. It is no longer a quiet tune: Sting shouts the words, and the band's members provide a rich musical background. In concerts, female singers added their voice to the piece. Sting recognizes that this song has deep religious layers. In his official book of lyrics (which unfortunately does not include his songs prior to The Police and thus presents only the 1983 version), he prefaces it with this:

> I'm told the word religion comes from the Latin *ligare*, to connect. So I assume religion means to reconnect, and yet more often than not, religions seem to separate us from one another. I've chosen to live my life without the "certainties" of faith, but I do maintain a great reverence for the mystery and wonder of our existence, and my agnosticism is a tolerant cousin to my curiosity.[11]

Here, as in many other places, Sting speaks of his "agnosticism," or simply says that he is agnostic. We will return to this question and these statements in the final chapter of this book.

---

11. Sting, *Lyrics*, 80. The mentioned etymology is indeed one of several ancient etymologies. It should be noted that Sting, like many of his generation who received a good education, has a solid knowledge of Latin.

The 1983 version begins with practically the same stanza as the version of 1975. Later, however, it becomes quite different. For example, the complaint in the earlier version concerning God's expectations of Sting regarding his relations with other humans, is changed to refer instead to his relationship with God: "Expecting me to treat you well, no matter what you say" replaces the verse we saw in the earlier version.[12] The sentence about Christmas and Sting's "brother" was removed, and replaced with "I've been waiting since the day that I was born." The claim that the world is not better since the birth of God's Son was also dropped. And yet, it is hard to say whether the version of 1983 is more "orthodox," or actually less, than the 1975 version. It includes two new parts. The first one seems to criticize God for allowing economic injustice:

> [The] fat man in his garden,
>   [the] thin man at his gate.
> My God you must be sleeping:
>   Wake up, it's much too late.

A fat man, possibly a symbol of wealth and the good life, has a garden; a thin and possibly poor man can only reach the garden's gate. And God is doing nothing about it. This text unmistakably hints at, and objects to, ideas found in a well-known British hymn, published in 1848 by Cecil Frances Alexander, and in which the third verse is this:

> The rich man in his castle,
> The poor man at his gate,
> God made them high and lowly,
> And ordered their estate.[13]

Sting's text also hints at a New Testament story found in the Gospel of Luke, chapter 16:

> There was a rich man who used to dress in purple and fine linen and feast magnificently every day. And at his gate there lay a poor man called Lazarus, covered with sores, who longed to fill himself with the scraps that fell from the rich man's table . . . .

In another famous biblical story from the Old Testament, Elijah mocks his opponents, who believe in another god, when their god does not seem to act:

---

12. See p. 152.

13. I would like to warmly thank Robin Parry for calling my attention to this text and to a few other references elsewhere in this book.

> [Perhaps] he is preoccupied or he is busy, or he has gone on a
> journey; perhaps he is asleep and will wake up.[14]

Sting's claim is a bit different. As he cannot accept the possibility that the
God he is supposed to believe in is indifferent to injustice, he tries to tell
himself, in order to avoid some kind of cognitive dissonance, that God must
be temporarily sleeping. He most probably does not believe such a thing,
but for now, he cannot come up with a better explanation.

The 1983 version ends officially (even if the section was not always included in concerts) with a long quote from an earlier and famous song from
the album *Ghost in the Machine*, "Every Little Thing She Does Is Magic"
(1981):

> Do I have to tell the story
>   of a thousand rainy days since we first met?
> It's a big enough umbrella,
>   but it's always me that ends up getting wet.

According to Sting,[15] that text was written in 1976, before The Police was
created. Regarding the inclusion of this paragraph in "O My God," Sting
says,

> This song started something of a tradition with me, where I
> would quote lines from previous songs in the coda. The effect
> seemed to be disarming and humorous and perhaps uncon-
> sciously pointing out that all of these songs are one song re-
> ally—modular, mutable, and not too serious.[16]

Sting does not refer, however, to the possible meaning of this inclusion here.
In its original context, it was a complaint about him always getting less pro-
tection in interactions with a woman he adores. Here, he is possibly claiming that God (with whom Sting has had relations already for "a thousand
rainy days") remains protected, while he is left to his own devices.

The album's sixth track, "Synchronicity II," describes banal and rather
depressing situations from daily, working-class life, while hinting that
"many miles away," something very different, and very magical, happens in
a certain Scottish lake. The reference to Loch Ness is obvious.

In another song in the same album, "King of Pain," we encounter a
word that later becomes very common in Sting's lyrics, and which we cannot

14. See 1 Kings 18:27 (JB).

15. Sting, *Lyrics*, 56.

16. Sting, *Lyrics*, 80. Sting would quote the same paragraph again a decade later, in
"Seven Days" (1993). See also Stojilkov, "A Poet Who Sings," 197–98.

ignore considering the topic of this study: "soul." While this is not the first time this term is used in Sting's corpus, it is possibly the first significant instance. In fact, souls, perhaps more associated for many with "spirituality" than with "religion" (whatever these two terms mean), are extremely frequent visitors in Sting's lyrics. In some songs they appear sporadically: "Your voice of hell has filled my soul with fear" ("Carrion Prince," 1975), "The river song will sing my soul to sleep" ("Savage Beast," 1975), "In this theatre that I call my soul" ("So Lonely," 1978), "Heal my soul, O Lithium sunset" ("Lithium Sunset," 1996), "I'm the devil in your soul" ("Brand New Day," 1999), "The priest has said my soul's salvation is in the balance of the angels" ("When We Dance," 2001), "your memory feeds my soul" ("Whenever I Say Your Name," 2003), "To face up to the truth of his soul" ("I Love Her but She Loves Someone Else," 2013), "Many a soul on the Queen's highway" ("Heading South on the Great North Road," 2016), "It seemed like she'd found the secret key to my soul" ("Sad Trombone," 2018) are some examples. In his memoir, Sting described a feeling he had while using the hallucinogenic brew Ayahuasca for the first time: "I am suspended from a roof of souls, a sky-arching dome of seraphic hosts."[17] In its architectural nature, "roof of souls" reminds of two other expressions found in his lyrics: "A tower of souls" ("A Thousand Years," 1999), and "Net of souls" ("Show Some Respect," 2013). Perhaps his inclusion of a late-nineteenth-century folk song, "Soul Cake" (a name given to cakes traditionally eaten on All Souls Day), on his album *If on a Winter's Night . . .* (2009) should be added to the list.

In other songs, souls are definitely the center of the story; "The Soul Cages" (1991: the title of a song, and an entire album), "Let Your Soul Be Your Pilot" (1996), and "Language of Birds" (2013), are such cases. If we consider "spirits" as similar to souls, then they are also central in "Spirits in the Material World" (1981). Souls also play a rather central role in "King of Pain" (1983), the song we explore here.

One possible reason for Sting's use of the term is his complex relation to death, having lost both his parents at relatively young ages. In fact, death appears frequently in his songs.[18] If he believes in the eternity of souls, it is possible they appear in his lyrics as a way to counterbalance death, as something possibly eternal that not even death can kill.[19]

17. Sting, *Broken Music*, 13.

18. See also Sting, *Broken Music*, 17–18. An interesting book about death in popular music does not mention Sting, nor many other "mainstream" rockers or rock bands, other than a quick reference to one of The Police's songs, "I Can't Stand Losing You" (1978), with its reference to suicide. See Partridge, *Mortality and Music*, 110.

19. See also "Language of Birds" (2013).

The *Catholic Encyclopedia*, which gives us a window into pre-Vatican II Catholic thought, defines soul as "the ultimate internal principle by which we think, feel, and will, and by which our bodies are animated."[20] The *Penny Catechism* used during Sting's childhood does not seem to provide much information about what a soul is, but it is almost certain that teachers had to explain the issue orally. The *Baltimore Catechism*, which was used at the time in the United States, was perhaps not used by Gordon's teachers or parents, but it is very likely that in the United Kingdom, similar ideas were also shared with Catholic children:

> Q: What is man?
> A: Man is a creature composed of body and soul, and made to the image and likeness of God.
> Q: Is this likeness to God in the body or in the soul?
> A: This likeness to God is chiefly in the soul.
> Q: How is the soul like God?
> A: The soul is like God because it is a spirit having understanding and free will, and is destined to live forever.[21]

What Sting was told about the nature of "souls" during his childhood was probably similar to the definition given above. What the term meant for him later in life is an issue we will return to towards the end of this book.

In some cases, the imagery Sting uses with regard to souls is Christian, as in his statement that "my soul's salvation is in the balance of the angels" ("When We Dance," 2001), gesturing to a common motif in Christian art of the archangel Michael weighing souls in balance.[22] Other soul metaphors he uses come from other sources. His mention, in various songs, of the idea of souls trapped in a cage, seems to be inspired by stories about the souls of sailors drowned at sea, which are trapped on the seabed in "Davy Jones' Locker." In one interview, he said this on the matter:

> "The Soul Cages" is an old British folk tale I remembered from being a child. . . . [It] is about the souls of the dead being kept under the sea by an old fisherman. . . . If you want to free the souls of the dead, you have to go under the sea yourself and drink with him. If you drink him under the table, the souls will go free. If he drinks you under the table, he keeps you forever in a lobster cage . . . .[23]

---

20. Maher and Bolland, "Soul."
21. *A Catechism*, Questions 48–50.
22. See examples in https://links.stingandreligion.com/miso.
23. See http://links.stingandreligion.com/soca. See also Sting, *Lyrics*, 156.

This maritime folklore is recorded in various works of literature; Sting may have learned about it from a book he was apparently extremely fond of in his childhood, *Treasure Island* by the Scottish Robert Louis Stevenson.[24] He might also have heard that according to some Irish (Celtic?) traditions, some of the points of access for souls to the otherworld are through doors concealed on the bed of the sea.[25]

In the song we explore here, "King of Pain" (1983), following a list of many objects and images, most of which seem to hint to something that went wrong, Sting says "that's my soul up there." Thus it seems that his soul is in a "little black spot on the sun," in a "black hat caught in a high tree top," in a "flag-pole rag," in a "fossil that's trapped in a high cliff wall," in a "dead salmon frozen in a waterfall," in a "blue whale beached by a springtime's ebb," in a "butterfly trapped in a spider's web," in a "red fox torn by a hunts-man's pack," and in a "black-winged gull with a broken back." Some of the expressions can be seen as surrealistic. According to Aaron West, literary surrealism was an important element in the aesthetic of the "Progressive Rock" trend that had influenced Sting and The Police.[26] Interpreting these objects, which are, or contain, Sting's soul, is thus rather complex and prob-ably highly subjective. And yet, other than the first three, which are perhaps a bit less clear, all of the other images are of animals of various kinds that died or that are dying in an unpleasant way. Sting thus perhaps equates his condition with theirs, and also breaks a certain barrier that exists in many Western cultures between a human soul and an animal soul. Sting's soul is there, with, or in, these animals.[27]

In his first solo album, *The Dream of the Blue Turtles* of 1985, Sting included one song that is deeply spiritual, "Love Is the Seventh Wave." Sci-entists have their ways of explaining ours and the world's existence. Philoso-phers may have other explanations. Theologians are likely to understand it in terms of God and creation. For Sting, love explains it all.

Another song in the same album, "Consider Me Gone," contains a line that has little to do with religion, although it uses (and in a way, secularizes) two important religious terms: "To search for perfection, is all very well, but to look for heaven, is to live here in hell."

24. Sting, *Broken Music*, 32. See for example in chapter 20, where Captain Smol-lett warns the sailors, "and I'll see you all to Davy Jones." Gordon received a copy of the book from his parental grandmother Agnes Sumner (née Wright), who played an important role in his childhood.

25. See for example in Hutton, *The Pagan Religions*, 184.

26. West, *Sting*, 6.

27. On the concept of soul in the Bible, religious texts, literature, and popular cul-ture, see Nava, *In Search of Soul*. See also Stojilkov, "A Poet Who Sings," 208–9.

Sting's second solo studio album, . . . *Nothing Like the Sun* of 1987, includes the song "History Will Teach Us Nothing." It is a song that could be considered to be in the tradition of what biblical scholars call "Wisdom Literature": a list of ideas and instructions from a reputedly wise person, seemingly based on what that person has learned from experience and history. The song's overarching topic is the importance of peaceful solutions to conflicts, the usefulness of reason, and the need to protect human rights. Considering that religions played a central role in human history, it is not surprising Sting has something to say about them. In fact, he has two things to say. First, he claims,

> If God is dead, and an actor plays his part,
> his words of fear will find their way to a place in your heart.

The idea that God is "dead" became common in Western thinking due mostly, it seems, to Friedrich Nietzsche (1844–1900), who famously declared it in several places in his work.[28] Here Sting is indirectly claiming that in order to be afraid of God, God does not even have to be real. An actor who "plays his part" can be just as successful. It is likely that this statement is directed towards many believers: it is quite possible, Sting tells them, that what they believe to be God's words, are not. What they fear might be nothing more than the words of a human who pretends to deliver God's message.

Following this statement about God, Sting immediately has something to say about faith, or perhaps religion itself: "Without the voice of reason, every faith is its own curse." Sting is not opposed to faith in general. He cautions though that "the voice of reason" is what can keep faith from becoming a curse—not an unusual statement, one should note, among Catholic thinkers of past and present.

Sting was clearly thinking about religion and its place at the time. As I suggested earlier, one may identify in his next album, *The Soul Cages* of 1991, even stronger opposition to elements of the Catholic context in which he grew up.[29] The first two songs in the album, mentioned in previous chapters, seem to be related to his father's death. The opening track, "Island of Souls," depicts a child named Billy, who seems to be a codename, or pseudonym, for Sting himself. It does not include any religious content, but its title, and its final line, where the boy is said to wish to take his dead father and "sail to the island of souls," bring us again to the question of the meaning of souls

---

28. The expression first appeared in his *The Gay Science*, 125, and later in his *Thus Spoke Zarathustra*.

29. See p. 75.

for Sting.[30] The idea of an "Island of Souls" has also, like "Soul Cages," strong mythological roots. When referring to the way this song was integrated into *The Last Ship*—the album and musical he created more than two decades later—Sting wrote me the following:

> The Island of souls could be a cultural shadow of the old Norse myth of High Brazil, a mythical island in the middle of the Atlantic. I suppose I was trying to recreate a syncretic myth for the community of the play, nominally Christian, but with a memory of the old religion, hence the burial at sea. . . .[31]

"Hy Brasil" has been described like this in a dictionary of Celtic mythology:

> Mysterious island, an earthly paradise, once thought to lie at the same latitude as Ireland but far out to sea. The island Hy Brasil appears, under many different names, on medieval maps. . . . In *The Celtic Twilight* (1893), W. B. Yeats reports speaking to fishermen who claimed to have sailed out as far as "Hy Brazil"; they describe an island without labour, care, or cynical laughter where one can enjoy the conversation of Cúchulainn and his heroes.[32]

Traditions about islands of souls have existed in many cultures. Among the Greeks, they were known as the "Fortunate Isles." The Irish myth about "The Voyage of Bran," and traditions about the Irish St Brendan, might be also related.[33] Boats were also an important symbol for Celts, including possibly boats that take the dead to the other side (similar to what one finds in Roman mythology). It should be remembered that the Roman belief that the dead are taken beyond the river Styx, by Charon, was widespread during their time, and probably also common among Romans in Britain. Very regularly the dead were buried with a coin in their mouth, so that they could pay for travel. Sometimes they were also given boots for the same reason.[34]

The religion of the Romans who lived around Hadrian's Wall, close to Sting's birthplace of Wallsend, is explicitly discussed in another song from the same album, "All This Time." Sting gives a fictional teacher the opportunity to say the last word about these ancient Romans: they worshipped gods of stone, and their empire crumbled. Whether the two facts are related or

---

30. See also Gable, *The Words and Music*, 57.

31. Sting, email exchange with author, February 8, 2015.

32. MacKillop, "Hy Brasil." See also in Eco, *The Book of Legendary*, 145–81.

33. See also Walsh Pasulka, *Heaven Can Wait*, 24.

34. See Hutton, *The Pagan Religions*, 190–91 and 236.

not is left for the listener to decide.[35] In other songs in the album, religious motifs appear momentarily. Thus, in "Why Should I Cry for You," Sting says that "dark angels follow me, over a godless sea." "The Wild Wild Sea," seems to speak of a dream in which the narrator's father appears. The narrator says, among other things, "if a prayer is spoken please offer it for me."

In a later album, *Mercury Falling* of 1996, the idea of a prayer, which appeared in previous albums and is discussed above, is mentioned again in two songs: "I Hung My Head" and "You Still Touch Me." The soul, a motif we explored earlier, is the main player in "Let Your Soul Be Your Pilot" on the same album.[36]

In 1999, just before the end of the second millennium CE, Sting released his album *Brand New Day*. The album contains only limited references to religion: a quick reference to souls in "A Thousand Years," and to "empty skies" and "Eden" in "Desert Rose." It should be noted though that the opening track of the album, "A Thousand Years," can easily be understood as a spiritual quest, directed not toward the love of a human, but towards some transcendent reality. The title song that closes the album, "Brand New Day," does not contain many religious ideas, other than the statement "You're the church and I'm the preacher." The outstanding and surprising music video that was created for it by Jan Houllevigue, however, brings religious themes to the fore, despite their absence from the song's lyrics. Houllevigue specializes in both music videos and commercials; "Brand New Day" is a mixture of both. Sting appears as a fusion of Moses and Jesus. He preaches to believers who watch him, he transforms an unshaved, miserable person into a happy man in white, and he seems to walk on water while everybody else is on dry land. Suddenly, it seems like his message is a new detergent. The messiah falls into the water, and everybody leaves. As he said many years earlier, "Sometimes it's hard to tell the game shows from TV evangelists."[37] Sting closed the millennium, with Moses, Jesus, a song that spoke about a "Brand New Day," and with a video that mocked various types of religious preachers.

35. See above, pp. 79–81.

36. According to Aaron West, Sting wrote this song in response to the experience of having a friend suffering from AIDS (and if I understand correctly, dying from it). The song does not say whether the soul remains after death, but it is considered to be a good "pilot" towards the end of life. West says that Sting gave this friend *The Tibetan Book of Living and Dying* by Sogyal Rinpoche. I imagine that if this is the case, Sting himself found this book, and the spiritual ideas in it, inspiring. See West, *Sting and the Police*, 53.

37. Liner notes to . . . *Nothing Like the Sun* (1987).

In 2003, Sting released a studio album, *Sacred Love*. The album's title summarizes in perhaps the most efficient way possible what is arguably the core threads in Sting's entire oeuvre: love is what counts, and love is sacred. According to subsequent interviews, Sting began working on this album the morning after September 11, 2001, and some parts of the album are a reaction to the attacks on the US that day (attacks in which Sting lost a friend), and the wars that followed in Iraq and Afghanistan. As a whole, this album includes some of Sting's most sophisticated (and lengthy) lyrics, a sad reminder that traumas often open new sources of creativity. Unfortunately for those who are interested in the album's lyrics, many of the words are difficult to decipher due to the album's very fast and rhythmic music. Almost each and every song from this impressive album deserves a lengthy analysis, but because this chapter focuses only on texts that deal with religion and spirituality, only a few of its powerful and intriguing songs will be studied here.

In "Send Your Love," the second track in the album, there is a long and intensive paragraph, sung very quickly, that defines what religion is and is not, according to Sting:

> There's no religion but sex and music,
>   there's no religion but sound and dancing;
> There's no religion but line and color,
>   there's no religion but sacred trance;
> There's no religion but the endless ocean,
>   there's no religion but the moon and stars;
> There's no religion but time and motion,
>   there's no religion, just tribal scars;
> There's no religion but the joys of rhythm,
>   there's no religion but the rites of Spring;
> There's no religion in the path of hate,
>   no prayer but the one I sing;
> There's no religion but sex and music,
>   there's no religion that's right or winning;
> There's no religion in the path of hatred,
>   ain't no prayer but the one I'm singing.

As discussed earlier in this chapter, Sting likes to refer to a common etymology for the word "religion," based on the Latin *ligare*, "to connect." This etymological tie seems to be at work in Sting's description of religion: "sex and music," "sound and dancing," "line and color" are all religion, or in other words, things that connect people. On the other hand, "there is no religion," i.e., connection, "in the path of hate."[38]

---

38. See Sting explicitly giving a rather similar interpretation of this song in McLean,

The next song in the same album, "Whenever I Say Your Name" (performed with Mary J. Blige), can definitely be understood as religious, even if a secular interpretation is also possible. In that, it strongly reminds one of "A Thousand Years" from 1999, mentioned above. The obvious question is to whose name does the title refer. God's name? Is this song a prayer? Or is it a lover's name? Each and every line in the song can be read as referring to God, but some stanzas give stronger hints than others that it should be read this way. The second line, "Whatever bread's in my mouth, whatever the sweetest wine that I taste," may refer to Sting's enjoyment of his large Italian estate's produce, however it seems that anyone who knows anything about communion in many Christian traditions, including Catholicism, might reasonably wonder whether Sting is speaking of or alluding to sacramental bread and wine. Statements such as "Whenever I kneel to pray," "Whenever I say your name, I'm already praying," "Whatever it was that I believed before," have also a religious connotation that is hard to dismiss.

Sting has acknowledged the two ways, spiritual and romantic, in which this song can be interpreted, and has remarked several times that the two are not mutually exclusive. He is alleged to have said that he specifically wrote this song with Mary J. Blige and religious concepts in mind:

> I was totally blown away by her passionate, open singing, . . .
> raw emotion. . . . I had decided . . . that I'd love to write a song
> for her one day, and I came up with this idea of "Whenever I Say
> Your Name." . . . It's very romantic. It also has a kind of religious
> component, . . . she's very churchy in the way she sings.[39]

Jim Gable, who had worked on many projects with Sting, directed the music video that documented the duet. The video is impressive, and at various moments displays the most obvious symbol of Christianity, the religion that both singers grew up in: the cross. One cross is made by framing the camera on part of a door, another by focusing on a tattoo on Blige's arm.[40] Additionally, it is clear throughout the song, and in Blige's songs in general, what Sting probably meant by the term "churchy singing."

The same year *Sacred Love* was released, Sting published a memoir: *Broken Music*. If "Dead Man's Rope" (discussed in a previous chapter)[41] seems to be related to it, another song in the album, "The Book of My Life,"

"The Man."

39. This quote seems to be reliable, although I have not been able to authenticate it. See http://links.stingandreligion.com/blig.

40. See http://links.stingandreligion.com/when, 0:31, 2:13, 2:17 and 3:35.

41. See p. 90.

is probably even more so. Talking about chapters in his own life, Sting says the following:

> There's a chapter on God,
>   that I don't understand.
> There's a promise of Heaven and Hell,
>   but I'm damned if I see.

Other parts of the song also hint at existential questions. One line is particularly enigmatic: "all these pages are burning, all that's left is you." Is this "you" a human? Or maybe a divinity? Sting does not tell us.

The album's title song, "Sacred Love," has countless religious motifs. It describes a thirst for spiritual answers. After asking in despair, "Have I been down on my knees for long enough?" it says to whomever it addresses, "You're my religion, you're my church, you're the holy grail at the end of my search." As the song progresses, Sting uses metaphors from the beginning of two biblical books whose connection to one another has long been acknowledged: the New Testament's Gospel according to John, and the much older Old Testament's Book of Genesis. To these metaphors, he adds images from the other Gospels: darkness and earthquake at the death of Jesus on the cross.[42] All of this is included in a reflection on the Christian concept of the incarnation of the divine in the flesh, and the Spirit as a feminine being, something obvious in Semitic languages, but not necessarily in English:

> The spirit moves on the water,[43]
>   she takes the shape of this heavenly daughter;
> She's rising up like a river in flood,[44]
>   the word got made into flesh and blood;[45]
> The sky grew dark, and the earth she shook,
>   just like a prophecy in the Holy Book.

Sting then, in two separate places, repeats three of the so-called "Ten Commandments": "Thou shalt not covet, thou shalt not steal," and "Thou shalt not steal, thou shalt not kill." He adds to them two commandments (or observations) of his own, about love: "Thou shalt not doubt that this love is real" and "But if you don't love her, your best friend will." He then prays again:

> So I got down on my knees and I prayed to the skies,

42. See Matthew 27:45–51; Mark 15:33; Luke 23:44–45.
43. See Genesis 1:2.
44. See Isaiah 59:19.
45. See John 1:14.

when I looked up could I trust my eyes?
All the saints and angels and the stars up above,
   they all bowed down to the flower of creation.
Every man, every woman, every race, every nation,
   it all comes down to this sacred love.

If in many common Christian images, all bow to Christ, here, they all bow to Love. Sting finishes the song with a lengthy reflection on faith, the Bible, and relationships, a quote we have already cited above:

I've been thinking 'bout religion,
I've been thinking 'bout the things that we believe;
I've been thinking 'bout the Bible,
I've been thinking 'bout Adam and Eve;
I've been thinking 'bout the garden,
I've been thinking 'bout the tree of knowledge, and the tree of life;
I've been thinking 'bout forbidden fruit,
I've been thinking 'bout a man and his wife;
I been thinking 'bout, thinking 'bout, sacred love, sacred love.

Sting's album *The Last Ship* of 2013 includes, as discussed earlier, many biblical and Catholic references. There are also some references that are more generally about faith, religion, and spirituality. In the song "Language of Birds"[46]—parts of which were included in the musical *The Last Ship* as a piece called "Underground River"—Sting speaks again about souls. "So to Speak," another song from the album and musical, deals with serious illness, and approaching death. In its content, it has clear ties to an older song by Sting, "Let Your Soul Be Your Pilot" (1996). "So to Speak" ends in the musical with words of similar meaning: "Follow your heart." It is impossible to ignore the fact that both of Sting's parents died of cancer at a relatively young age, and possibly went through painful treatments trying to fight the disease. In the musical (American version), the main part of the song is sung by Father O'Brien, who reveals to Meg, a young woman, that he is in the terminal stage of cancer. In the song, he expresses two core convictions, which can be found throughout Sting's body of work: that "our mission" in life "is love and compassion and grace" and that it is not "eternal life we should seek" but rather "an eternal love." It is interesting that Sting put this statement (along with the idea that it is not always appropriate to prolong life by means of radical medical treatment) in the mouth of a priest. By

---

46. From the liner notes in this album it is not clear if the producer Rob Mathes was involved in both the music and the lyrics of this song. Regardless, the text is very typical of Sting's work.

doing so, this statement is not simply the idea of one who is sick and suffering, but a theological opinion. It can be read as a rather heretical statement: it is not "eternal life," meaning, in a Christian worldview, "life in Christ," that one should seek, but rather eternal love between fellow humans, a love that remains even after death, in the memory of those left behind. It can also, of course, be read as a more religiously conventional worldview: one should seek both eternity with the Divine, and "eternal love" with fellow humans.

In 2016, Sting released his album *57th & 9th*. Its first song, "I Can't Stop Thinking about You," can be understood as speaking about God. Lines such as "The fact remains until we find you, our lives are incomplete,"[47] or the opening lines of the refrain "I can't stop thinking about you, I can't stop wanting you this way, I can't face living without you, that's why I am searching night and day," can easily be interpreted as referring to the Divine— similar to U2's 1987 hit, "I Still Haven't Found What I'm Looking For." The fact that the song elsewhere mentions the sound of church bells, further suggests the feasibility of a Christian reading. The closing line of the refrain, "I don't care if you exist," can be possibly read as an actual, healthy doubt of a seeker, as some kind of agnostic statement, or as a strong disinterested in the question of God's actual existence.

The title itself of another song in the same album, "Inshallah" (a word in Arabic that means, as many know, "If God wills" or "God willing") and the refrain "Inshallah, Inshallah, if it be your will, it shall come to pass," are likewise obvious religious statements, even if the word is also used by Arabic-speaking secular people and in secular contexts. The song is about refugees on boats, seeking a safer land. Although there are millions of Arabic-speaking Christians, I am almost sure Sting is hinting at a Muslim prayer. In fact, several months after the release of the album, Sting was invited to re-open the famous Parisian club *Le Bataclan*, a year after a horrendous attack by Islamist militants took place in it during a concert, killing dozens of attendees. By singing it at the reopening, Sting may have wanted to emphasize that just as religion (including Islam) can bring hatred and death, so religion (including Islam) can also bring hope.

The last song in the album, "The Empty Chair," contains some statements that can easily be understood as spiritual, using common religious metaphors. The first stanza is probably the strongest in this respect:

> If I should close my eyes, that my soul can see,
> and there's a place at the table that you saved for me,

47. Compare for example with one of the first statements in Augustine of Hippo's (354–430) famous book *Confessions*: "You [God] have made us for yourself, and our hearts are restless, until they can find rest in you."

so many thousand miles over land and sea,
I hope to dare, that you hear my prayer,
and somehow I'll be there.

The song was written in memory of, and for a documentary about, the journalist James ("Jim") Foley, who was kidnapped in 2012 in Syria and executed two years later by the terrorist organization *Daesh* (a.k.a. "The Islamic State").

In Sting's album of 2018, *44/876*, created in collaboration with the reggae singer Shaggy, there are several brief hints at the question of faith. For example, the song "Just One Lifetime" claims that

Just one lifetime,
And there's only one,
yes there's only one.
Just one life to live,
assuming that we'll make it,
we've no choice but to take it.

Even if for many westerners this is a rather obvious statement, this is not the case for those believing in reincarnation of the soul. Sting (and Shaggy) say it clearly: No, We have just one round.[48]

In another song, "Crooked Tree," Sting plays with a sentence by the German philosopher Immanuel Kant (1724–1804), who said that "From such crooked wood as man is made of, nothing perfectly straight can be built."[49] Kant possibly based his words on the Indo-European (including Germanic and Nordic) creation myths in which humans were created from trees or lumber.[50] The sentence was made famous in particular by the British philosopher Isaiah Berlin (1909–97) in his book of 1959 (with many subsequent editions), *The Crooked Timber of Humanity: Chapters in the History of Ideas*. It is not impossible that Sting came to know this text by Kant through Berlin's book. Sting created an actual story from Kant's saying:

"The day that I was born," she said, "the Good Lord woke from slumber;
Looking 'round his timber yard, He found He had no lumber;
Apart from some old twisted branch, in shadows left to lurk;
He pulled it out into the light and set about his work."
She told me that the world should not expect too much of me,
when the Good Lord carved my crooked soul, out of a crooked tree.

---

48. See later, pp. 190–91, statements by Sting about the idea of reincarnation.

49. Kant, "Idea." On Sting's use of classic works see also Solomon, "Sting in the Tradition," 33, and Stojilkov, "A Poet Who Sings," 197–98.

50. See Hultgård, "The Askr and Embla."

Another song, "16 Fathoms," seems to be strongly related to Sting's own explanation of "Soul Cages," about souls trapped under the sea. The song apparently speaks about a drowned person who prays to God, only to discover that, although God appears, no rescue is coming:

> 16 fathoms down, where my soul is bound . . .
> I pray to God this darkness pass,
> I pray that I won't drown. . .
> Of course, God come to find me,
>   in the place where the ship went down.
> The prophecy will bind me,
>   and that's where I'll be drowned.

Are religion, spirituality, and God things that can lead to salvation, or inversely, lead to spiritual shipwreck, in Sting's eyes? And what type of religious and spiritual experiences has he had since becoming an adult, not being a student anymore in Catholic institutions? How has he seen religion and spirituality in recent decades? Where does he stand on the question of faith? The following concluding chapter will discuss these questions and others.

Chapter 6

STING AND RELIGION

> I think to have faith in nothing at all is to be, to run pretty close to madness. I think insanity is very close behind if you are totally nihilistic about everything. I mean there is a certain sort of latter twentieth century existentialist who believes in nothing, just a dark figure in a raincoat, which is kind of a romantic image which we've adopted in the cinema [and] other places. But I don't want to be that person. I don't think that's terribly helpful. You got to believe in something.[1]

IN THIS BOOK I have argued that Sting's religious background, especially his childhood and teenage years in a Catholic parish and in Catholic schools, had a major impact on his artistic output; it is indeed something that Sting has himself proudly admitted many times. The book thus contributes, hopefully, to the discussion both of what this religious background looked like, and where religious elements appear in his work.

At the same time, I did not try to find, other than in a very few cases, straight lines connecting a certain teaching or event to which Sting was exposed as a young person, to a specific segment in a song. Education is one thing, creativity is another. They are surely connected, but in extremely complex ways, which one can rarely reconstruct.

Of course, many factors other than his Catholic education played a part in shaping Sting's worldview and art. In many books, articles, and

1. Sting, *All This Time* CD-ROM, Part 1, "Gothic Cathedral," 13:41, https://links.stingandreligion.com/cdr7.

interviews, several aspects of his childhood town are cited as being crucial to understanding the mindset of the adult Sting: the relative poverty
of many of its inhabitants (although his family was in a slightly better economic situation than many of his friends),[2] its remoteness from the capi-
tal, a certain North Eastern and "Geordie" mentality, and the centrality of
shipbuilding (and mining) to its economy. Particularities of his family life
and upbringing—such as his mother's musical talent as a pianist and a collector of records, his father's singing in parties and hard work as a milkman,
an affair that his mother had with an assistant to his father ("suddenly we
[were] like a doomed family in a falling airplane," Sting wrote about it in
his memoir),[3] the divorce of his parents, the quietness and introversion of
his father, the relatively early death of both parents, the people, including
spouses, Sting has been with, and more—have surely had a strong impact
on his personality as well. Possibly more than anything that would explain
his outlook and work are, nevertheless, the traits he may have been born
with and/or individually developed: his personality, looks, musical talent,
creativity, attention to detail, willingness to work hard, professionalism, and
intellect. Being born into, and writing and performing in, the only international language of our time surely also helped. Luck was also, and Sting
admits this often, extremely important in his rise to fame.

Studying Sting's religious background can surely teach us much about
many people like him, even if they are significantly less famous. It can tell
us something about people who were raised in a religious environment in
general, and those raised in a Catholic one in particular. It can help us to
understand even more profoundly the millions who were raised in Catholic
environments, similar to the one studied here, during the third quarter of
the twentieth century: Catholic (and ex-Catholic) early baby boomers.

Scholars of religions generally see mainstream Catholicism as a non-
radical group. It is not a "sect" by any common definition of the word. It is
not a group that is obsessively engaged in the question of who is in and who
is out. In reality, it does not have a very strict hold on the discipline of its
members. Thus, this story is hopefully useful beyond telling the story of one
person or one community. Much of what is described is not exceptionally
surprising, shocking, or unusual, even for total outsiders. The community's
children go to school; in the good schools, the students get a good and wide
education; they know people from other traditions, and they are not told
to systematically disrespect them; they see movement between religious

---

2. See Sting, *Broken Music*, 57. This was also what some of his childhood friends
told me.

3. Sting, *Broken Music*, 66–67.

denominations among some members; they see debates inside their own group. Perhaps all this makes the story, after all, not entirely foreign to many of us.

Obviously, raising children as Catholics, and sending them to Catholic schools, does not guarantee producing Catholic grownups; a saying common already at the time when Gordon attended his Catholic schools declared that "the best way to prevent your children from being Catholic is to send them to a Catholic school." Even if meant to be ironic, this statement no doubt reflects the reality that a Catholic (or more generally, religious) background does not guarantee the production of a Catholic (or religious) adult.

Among Sting's classmates whom I know, or know of, there is a wide range of engagement (or non-engagement) with Catholicism. The saying above is thus, not surprisingly of course, not of a scientific nature. But in his case, well, yes. The young Gordon went to Catholic schools, and the older Sting does not consider himself Catholic. Is he a "Cultural Catholic"? Or a "Lapsed Catholic"?

According to Catholic doctrine, the answer to the question "Who is Catholic?" is clear: a Catholic is someone, like Gordon, who was baptized in the Catholic church, or someone, like probably his mother, who was validly baptized in another Christian church but who has joined the Catholic church at a later phase of her or his life.[4] As long as that person has not officially and explicitly declared himself or herself as quitting the Catholic church, or as long as the church has not excommunicated him or her (either explicitly or as a consequence of certain actions he or she has taken), this person, as far as the church is concerned, is Catholic. According to these rules, more than half of the Christians in the world and about one-sixth of humanity—more than 1.2 billion women and men—are Catholics.

Not surprisingly, many scholars of religious studies, including the author of this book, cannot easily accept this theological-doctrinal definition, especially because the levels of involvement of many of these people in the life of the church and their identification with it are quite diverse. Should someone whose last visit to a church was when she or he was baptized as an infant, and who perhaps defines himself or herself as "without religion" (or a "none" in today's parlance), but did not ask their name to be removed from their parish register, nor committed a "formal act of defection," be considered a Catholic, from a sociological point of view, just because of his or her baptism? Can we really say that he or she is as "Catholic" as (to use an

4. Some of the material here is taken, with slight changes, from my earlier book, Marienberg, *Catholicism Today*.

extreme example) the pope is, because both were baptized in the Catholic church? Obviously, the answer is no: we should not put all those that are formally Catholic in the same basket. So how can we distinguish between them?

One important objective factor that many think can help us is attendance at Mass, the central ritual of Catholicism. Various statistics show that in many countries today (including those that are considered in popular imagination to be very Catholic, like Italy, Poland, or Brazil), only about 10 to 20 percent of those who define themselves as Catholics consistently attend Mass on a weekly basis. This seems to be also the reality in England. True, in some countries the situation is different. Thus, for example, in France it is estimated that only about 5 percent of Catholics attend Mass regularly, while in Nigeria, we are told that about 90 percent do so. In the United States, the number seems to be around 25 percent. And yet the bottom line is that in Europe, North America, and many other places, only a small minority of those who are considered Catholics by the church, or even by themselves, attend services on a weekly basis.

Those who attend Mass regularly should probably be included in our sociologically defined basket entitled "Catholics." What should we do with the other 80 to 90 percent? Should we say that they are not Catholics? Certainly not. Some of them do not attend because of various personal circumstances: if they could, they maybe would. Others avoid participating in the public ritual life of the church because they disagree with general issues in the universal church, or with issues affecting their local parish or diocese. They do not leave the church, but they express their disagreement with different issues by staying away. Those of them who actually care about the church and hope for a change might see themselves as a "Faithful Opposition." They might feel that their parish, or diocese, or the entire church, is too conservative, or too liberal, or not in line with their own agenda in another way. With another type of universal or local leadership, maybe they would attend. And yet there are those who do not attend simply because they do not see themselves as Catholics, do not care much or at all about the Catholic aspect of their identity, do not feel a need to attend services, or are just bored by them. For some, this lack of attendance is a sign of their growing detachment with the church. For others, the situation is more complicated. How should we treat those who indeed rarely enter a church, but who proudly identify themselves as Catholics? And what about those who call themselves "cultural," "lapsed," "surviving," or "recovering" Catholics? Sociologists of Catholicism will continue to wrestle with these questions, and the church itself will continue to do the same. The only thing we can do is to keep in mind the formal definition mentioned above, while remembering that in real life the answers to these questions are rather complex.

I am not sure where to put Sting in all of this, and I am not sure even that he could give a clear answer. Many factors have played a role in bringing him to where he is today on questions of religion, faith, and spirituality. Some of the coming pages will be devoted to these factors and questions. This examination will not be conducted here for the sake of voyeurism, or some kind of pop-psychological superficial analysis. It will be made in order to understand some of the reasons that can affect one's decisions and feelings regarding one's childhood religion.

Among the factors that Sting believes played a role in his informal defection from Catholicism, he mentioned a few times the fact that he grew up in a "mixed-marriage" household:

> [In my childhood] I was conditioned to accept that God is a Catholic, and that non-Catholics were somehow outside of the pale, but I was in an interesting position because my mother was Anglican, and I always would question this thing. I could not accept it, because now in hindsight I realise it's nonsense. I feel now as if this conundrum opened a door for me that would have been closed otherwise. So I suppose that's when me and the church started to separate.[5]

It is of course reasonable to imagine that many other factors also contributed to this "separation" from the church. If we are to believe another recollection of his, written, obviously, decades after the memories were made, it was at St Cuthbert's Grammar School, and at least partly due the corporal punishment used there, that Gordon lost his "belief in the Holy Church." Describing the painful details of one such excruciating, humiliating, and rage-causing "six of the best" sessions, he wrote in his memoir that,

> Any idea that I would become an unquestioning and uncritical follower of the church's wisdom flew out the office window as the final swipe found its target at the seat of my resentment.[6]

When I asked him again in 2017 if indeed the corporal punishment he suffered in school contributed to his losing his faith, he replied with no hesitation, "Absolutely."

Some of his classmates confirmed that Gordon moved away from church life in his later teenage years. When I asked him why he still

---

5. Sting, interview by author, July 23, 2017, Künzelsau, REC22:008.

6. Sting, *Broken Music*, 95.

continued to go to church in his early twenties (in other words, in the early 1970s), at least occasionally, according to some of his own statements, he said this:

> I went to church regularly up until [the] end of the late 1960s. . . . It was all that conditioning and programming that meant giving it up took a while. I didn't revolt against the church all in one day *[laughing]*. . . . I think [I continued to go to services] from inertia, from the sense of . . . habit. But did I believe in the church? No.[7]

Inertia, or the tendency to continue doing things to which one has been habituated from an earlier age, even if they do not fully make sense in the present, is surely something that has an effect on the religious practices of many. Sting gives an example of such behavior in his 2003 memoir, when he describes his life just before The Police's breakthrough. The year was 1978; he was already having his first child:

> In my anxiety about the future, I've taken to praying. Whatever my doubts were as a child, I'd maintained a belief in this tenuous personal lifeline to the spiritual realm, having faith that when the chips were down I'd be forgiven and welcomed back into the fold as if my religious conundrums had been understood and allowed for. So whenever I wake up in the middle of the night and start to recite the rosary, I am comforted.[8] Five decades of the rosary adds up to fifty *Hail Marys*, and although with repetition the words become meaningless, they begin to work like a soothing mantra for an anxious mind fraught with worries. . . . I'm now praying on a nightly basis for no more than that God or the Goddess will help keep us safe.[9]

In various places Sting uses the word "certainties" to describe something that was claimed to exist in his childhood religion, and which pushed him out of it. Among other things, one can imagine that the Q&A style of the catechetical religious instruction he received was, in his mind, and not unjustly, a manifestation of a religion that believes it offers "certainties."[10] And being certain, for Sting, can be extremely dangerous:

> I don't regret my Catholic upbringing, but I really don't like certainty in spiritual matters. I find that very dangerous. You

7. Sting, interview by author, July 23, 2017, Künzelsau, REC22:017, 095.

8. On the Rosary, see above, pp. 31 and 128–29.

9. Sting, *Broken Music*, 329–30.

10. See on this above, p. 156.

end up with massacres and you end up with 9/11. Certainty is
wrong. Uncertainty is a much more sensible position.[11]

Is he still "religious?" Does he believe in "God?" Sting has at various
times and places given answers to these questions, answers that at first
glance might seem contradictory, but which I think reflect, after all, a rather
coherent and more or less constant worldview.

In a video interview done in the Newcastle area near the sea, possibly
around 1987 or 1988, the journalist said that "religion gets a beating on
quite a few songs [in the album . . . *Nothing Like the Sun* of 1987]." Sting
laughed, and gave a rather long and thoughtful answer:

> I don't think religion gets a beating. I think the form of religion
> gets a beating. In other words, I think God's salesmen can have
> their eyes taken out of them, that doesn't mean to say that I'm
> anti-religious, or anti-God, or anything. I'm actually question-
> ing the idea of the rituals that are served up to us, and in many
> ways I think they're inadequate for what we need. I think they
> need to be reassessed, maybe revamped or linked closer to real
> symbols of continuity, like the ocean, like rivers, like the earth.
> . . . The old religions were about that, they were based in exis-
> tence, that you can touch, and then in a certain point in history
> religion became about a God who was outside of existence, that
> side of reality, existence beyond the world. I think as soon as
> they did that, then they could set about destroying it, because
> if God isn't in the tree let just chop the tree down. If God's not
> in the river then we can pollute the river. If God's not in the sea
> then we pollute the sea. It's almost as if we're trying to find God
> by destroying the world, and I think that's crazy, and wrong. So
> I think we need to get back to basic issues. We're talking about
> God or spiritualism. I do believe in spiritualism, sense of spirit,
> but not in the form that it's served up.[12]

In another interview in 2003, if the quotes are accurate, Sting spoke in
no uncertain terms about his belief in God. The interviewer, Craig McLean
from *The Independent*, asked him if he would call himself religious. According to the interviewer, Sting thought for a second, and then said this slowly:

> I believe in God. . . . But I don't think I could describe God in
> any coherent way. It's an unembraceable concept. I don't think
> God looks like me. . . . I think a lot of people do think God
> looks like them. I'm sure bin Laden thinks God looks like him,

11. Day, "Interview: The Thing."
12. See http://links.stingandreligion.com/ncin.

that He's a Muslim. Presbyterians or Catholics might see Him as Presbyterian or Catholic. But He can't be any of those things. The concept is vastly above our intelligence.[13]

Several years later, in 2010, in an interview with Charlie Rose, when asked what he was looking for in life, Sting said this:

> I enjoy the mystery. I would never say I am an atheist. Let's say I am agnostic, and agnostic means "I don't know." And I embrace that "not knowing."[14]

A major study done in 2017 in fifteen West European countries found that only a very small percentage of Europeans describe themselves as agnostics. Among the "non-religious" (often referred to as "nones"), many more describe themselves as atheists or "nothing in particular." According to the median numbers, which happened to be those found in Britain, 8 percent of the population described themselves as "atheists," 13 percent as "nothing in particular," and only 2 percent as "agnostics."[15] "Agnostic" thus seems to not be a title many people in contemporary Western Europe choose to describe themselves with: whether this is the case in the United States, I do not know. Sting adopts this term regularly.

In another place, Sting provided a certain philosophical logic that might bring one, if followed, to the suspicion that there is something above humanity:

> I believe that there are level of consciousness. . . . If everything on the planet is . . . [with] some kind of hierarchy of consciousness, and we seem to be at the top of the tree in that regard, the animals slightly below us, plants slightly below that, and rocks below that. But if there is this hierarchy why should we be the top? Maybe there's something above us, something transcendent. I have no proof either way. But I think it's important to keep asking those questions. I think it's wrong to say "Well that's it, we are the sum total of everything."[16]

We have already addressed the high frequency of the appearance of the word "soul" in Sting's output.[17] When I asked him if I am right in my

---

13. McLean, "The Man."

14. Sting, interview by Charlie Rose, 18:40.

15. "Being Christian," 39.

16. Sting, *All This Time* CD-ROM, Part 1, "Gothic Cathedral," 2:20, https://links.stingandreligion.com/cdr0.

17. See above, pp. 158–61.

impression that the term plays a very significant part in his work, he fully agreed. I then asked what a soul is for him:

> Who knows what a soul is. I'm unable to tell you. But I don't think anyone else can either. I think God, and the concept of soul, are works of the human imagination. That doesn't mean to say that they are not significant. You know, New York City is a work of the imagination. The human imagination is incredibly powerful. So we have to be careful what we imagine. . . . I don't think I'm just flesh and blood. I think there's something that connects me to you, connects me to everyone I meet, everyone I perform to tonight, there is a connecting tissue, a connecting entity, that I am very aware of. I think music helps me to visualize it, people connected to a note, a long note, a chord, an emotion. . . . That's soul. I don't think science quite understands what that is yet. Maybe one day we will know. I like the mystery of it. . . . [People are] imagining the soul of [the departed] into existence. This is the power of magic. Sometimes I have dreams of my parents and I converse with them, or of friends I've lost. But I am creating it. This whole universe is here somewhere *[laughing, pointing to his head]*. The human mind is limitless, totally limitless . . . .[18]

The current online version of *Oxford Dictionary* defines soul as "The spiritual or immaterial part of a human being or animal, regarded as immortal." It is not impossible that the younger Sting read a short essay from 1953 by the British philosopher Bertrand Russell (1872–1970), in which he describes what it is to be an agnostic—a title that Sting uses at times to refer to himself, as we have seen. The essay is made up of questions and answers. To the question, "Does an agnostic deny that man has a soul?" Russell answers thus:

> This question has no precise meaning unless we are given a definition of the word "soul." I suppose what is meant is, roughly, something nonmaterial which persists throughout a person's life and even, for those who believe in immortality, throughout all future time. If this is what is meant, an agnostic is not likely to believe that man has a soul. But I must hasten to add that this does not mean that an agnostic must be a materialist. Many agnostics (including myself) are quite as doubtful of the body as they are of the soul, but this is a long story taking one

18. Sting, interview by author, July 23, 2017, Künzelsau, REC22:026, 030, 101.

into difficult metaphysics. Mind and matter alike, I should say, are only convenient symbols in discourse, not actually existing things.[19]

Sting's answer above seems to be, although phrased differently (and orally), rather similar. An internet search also showed that many thinking people who consider themselves agnostics do believe in the existence of something they call the "soul." Some consider it to exist only while the body does, and some believe that its existence continues after death. Regarding this issue then, Sting's thinking on the matter does not seem to be at odds with a declaration of agnosticism.

So is he indeed an agnostic, or is he a believer? Or perhaps he is SBNR, "Spiritual but Not Religious"?[20] Or maybe he is SBNA, "Spiritual but Not Affiliated?" If the word "spiritual" in these expressions means a kind of secular spirituality, which is only or mostly about the inner life of an individual, not about her or his connection to something transcendental, Sting is definitely not there. But if the word also includes those who are seeking or who are willing to assume the possible existence of a transcendental reality, perhaps Sting falls into these categories, which sociologists tell us now are large and growing. For some, a part of being "Spiritual but Not Religious" has to do with a lack of desire to be part of a community, or even an explicit desire not to be part of a community. I asked Sting if he is looking for communal life whenever he happens to be in a church. No, he answered.

> [For me being in a church building] is less about community, and more about a spiritual connection to God, rather than a ritual of community. That might be contradictory, but I can find God in a forest. I always found it hard to be a member of any community. I've always been remote.[21]

There are definitely various elements in what Sting says about religion and spirituality that can be seen as quite clear signs of his being "Spiritual but Not Religious." But as I did not see any mention of his using the term to define himself, nor ever heard him say it, I will not insist that this title fits him. It is quite possible that people with similar views but of younger generations would have adopted it more easily.

---

19. Russell, *The Basic Writings*, 560.

20. On this term and those who use it, see for example Fuller, *Spiritual, but Not Religious*; Thomas, "Spiritual but Not Religious"; Huss, "Spirituality"; Kenneson, "What's in a Name."

21. Sting, interview by author, July 23, 2017, Künzelsau, REC22:007.

It is not surprising that with a wide view of spirituality, Sting not only left behind the title of Catholic, but also the title of "Christian": "I would not consider myself a Christian any longer. My beliefs are much wider than that," he apparently said when interviewed in India in 2005.[22]

In an interview published in 2011, Sting said things similar to some of those quoted above, again using the term "agnostic," immediately before speaking about God. Again, the "certainties" of religious faith bother him in particular, it seems:

> I'm essentially agnostic. I don't have a problem with God. I have a problem with religion. I've chosen to live my life without the certainties of religious faith. I think they're dangerous.[23]

After reading and hearing all this, I needed some answers, some clarifications. "You are definitely not an atheist," I said to him when we talked in 2017. "What do you think about atheists?" He paused for a second, and replied:

> I find [living without God] very courageous. To live without a certainty of religious dogma. To live with that, it's courageous. To a certain extent, I do that. . . . I prefer to live without the certainties of religious dogma. But atheism too can become dogmatic; my mind is open.

I wanted more precision, so I insisted:

> The fact that you generally declare yourself to be agnostic—considering that, for many, being agnostic means not caring about the question of God's existence—seems to me rather problematic, seeing how often, during our discussion, you actually mention the word God.

"Well," Sting said,

> I cannot describe it, him, her, because you can't. So [the word God is] just a shorthand. I believe in something greater than our understanding. . . . In the terms that organised religion is presented, you have to believe in their God, and this God is a jealous God, for example, and he doesn't want you to wear skirts that are higher than this. This all seems ridiculous to me, or that God is Presbyterian or God is a Jew, or God is a Muslim. . . . It has to be beyond these narrow tribal concepts. . . . [God] is only a shorthand, because there is no other word for it. There's

22. Sting, interview by Malvika Nanda.

23. Luscombe, "10 Questions for Sting."

no other word that is common to all of us, so we say God. It's a
code for a mystery. Something that is certainly beyond my understanding, beyond my grasp. Because science is telling me "we
don't know everything," whether it's quantum physics or what's
inside black holes. We have a reasonable grasp of what is in the
middle of all this, but it's hard to make sense of the extremes,
either in the quantum world or in the cosmic world. That's God
to me. The mystery of it. The humility that it demands from
me when I think "Wow, I am part of this, and it's vast, so vast."
Well that's God to me. So when I say "God" I am happily in
this universe, in this cosmos, it's so inexplicable. I love that. We
are in a great mystery story. I wouldn't be happy knowing that
it was just a simulated digital game, with finite edge to it. For
me it's much bigger. I do get spiritual vertigo. It makes me feel
uncomfortable. The dimension of eternity. It's always made me
feel uncomfortable but I'm fascinated by it . . . .

He then explicitly mentioned his Catholic upbringing:

In the catechism it says "In whose image did God make you?"
and the answer there is "God made me in his own image." Well,
I believe the opposite is true. That we make God in our own
image. So if you are small-minded, bigoted, cruel, jealous, that is
the God you will create. Whereas if you are more open-minded,
gracious, kind, then that's the God you make. So we have to be
very careful what it is we imagine. I believe in the power of that.
I trust that if "God" exists, he, she, or it is hopefully kind, and
merciful, and generous, and not small-minded. Because that's
what I at least aspire to. . . . When I look at cosmology, I look at
the universe, and how enormous it is, and what's beyond that,
the concept of multi-universes and eternity, how can I possibly
say that I know for sure what created this, what made this? Did
anything make it? I don't know. I'm not prepared to say anything.
I'm in awe of it, I love and embrace the mystery of it. Can I say
I love God? It's [an] extraordinary concept, an extraterrestrial
super-intelligence, but is it a man in the heavens with a flowing
beard? Who just happens to be a Catholic or a Presbyterian?
Well, I don't imagine so.[24]

The concept of "mystery" is rather obvious in Sting's thinking. There
are things that exist but that we do not, and cannot, and maybe should not,
understand. One should remember that to say that there are impenetrable

24. Sting, interview by author, July 23, 2017, Künzelsau, REC22:101, 008, 069, 026,
029.

mysteries in the divine or the transcendent is not something that is unheard of in Catholicism, or indeed in many other "organized religions." Quite the contrary is true. Not a few religious thinkers in the past have claimed that the theology of God's radical otherness gives a place to significant agnosticism concerning the nature and being of God. In Catholicism, the Trinity, for example, is considered a mystery that cannot be fully grasped. Similarly, in the late nineteenth century the Vatican Council (later called "The First Council of the Vatican") promulgated the centrality of the idea that divine revelation cannot fully be understood in a clear way, declaring that one who says the following is in such great error that she or he should be excommunicated:

> That in divine revelation there are contained no true mysteries
> properly so-called, but that all the dogmas of the faith can be
> understood and demonstrated by properly trained reason from
> natural principles.[25]

Claiming thus that everything about the divine can be rationally understood is a heresy. But Sting goes significantly beyond that catholically legitimate (and obligatory) doubt, questioning much more. He does not know if there is a divine entity at all, and he does not always use the terms that Catholicism, and Christianity in general, would use to describe that entity. And yet, if agnosticism lies somewhere between a strong and unbreakable faith in the existence of something transcendent, and a certainty that nothing of this kind exists, one gets the feeling that Sting is not exactly in the middle. He has his doubts, he does not know how to describe a transcendent entity, but he seems to be closer to having faith than to being without it. I fully agree with Michael Tylor Ross, who wrote that, "Ironically . . . Sting is not necessarily as heretical as he might think."[26]

In the real world, religious and spiritual beliefs and convictions, as well as participation in related practices (or lack of participation), are not only related to one's positions on deep theological questions, but also to reality: to family history, family conditions in the present, personal experiences, experiences in times of crisis, questions of convenience, and more. All of these, from the perspective of religious studies, are of no less importance and merit than intellectual positions. This book has shown what brought Gordon/Sting into Catholicism: a father (and possibly also a mother), a grandmother, a parish, a community, three schools. We have also explored some issues that he says brought him out of Catholicism. There are

25. Vatican I, Third session (1870), Canons, 4, 1. See also McHugh, "Mystery."
26. Ross, "Sacred Love," 88.

unquestionably more factors that have made him change, even if never formally, his loyalty. In his memoir of 2003, Sting speaks about an Anglican priest who daily visited his father's dairy:

> I like the vicar, I like his friendly smile, I like the white hair beneath his black hat, I even like his silly joke. He seems to be the prophet of a gentler religion than that of the Irish zealots who are beginning to terrorize me at the Catholic church two streets away.[27]

It should be remembered that this passage was written many years after Sting had indeed come to appreciate some aspects of the Church of England, which was partly due to becoming the partner, and later spouse, of a member of that church, so we cannot be sure if he does not describe here, at least in part, Sting's thoughts and not Gordon's. Regardless, it seems reasonable to suspect that the fact that Catholicism was not the original religion of his mother, the physical proximity of his family's apartment and shop to a local Anglican church, and the complicated relationship he had with his father, nourished, above or under the surface, a certain hesitation with regard to Catholicism on the one hand, and a connection to Anglicanism on the other hand. Later events in his life brought that possible connection and appreciation to the foreground.

As mentioned before, Sting was married in 1976 to actress Frances Tomelty in a Catholic church. It was a marriage between two Catholics. It was registered in that church as well as in his childhood parish, Our Lady and St Columba's in Wallsend. Children were born from it. By all external, public standards it was, according to Catholic teaching, a valid and sacramental union.

According to Catholic doctrine, a sacramental and consummated marriage ends only with the death of the husband or wife.[28] This rule of the church does not mean, however, that couples must continue to live together under all circumstances. The church recognizes that sometimes this is impossible or undesirable, and in such situations partners may justly decide to separate for practical purposes. The church recognizes such "separation from bed and board" as legitimate. When in such circumstances a civil divorce proceeding can assist in the distribution of the couple's joint

27. Sting, *Broken Music*, 44.

28. The Catholic position on divorce does not come out of nowhere. The New Testament denounces divorce in various passages. See Matthew 5:31–32 and Mark 10:12, as well as Matthew 19:1–12 and 1 Corinthians 7:10–11. In reality, even if some might consider these texts clear, many Christian interpreters through history found them to be, for various reasons, not as clear-cut as one might think.

property and in the arrangement of custody over children (if there are any), the church generally, in most countries, does not oppose it. Nevertheless, as far as the church is concerned, a spiritual, sacramental bond continues to link the couple, even if they have broken up for all intents and purposes. This link is only dissolved upon the death of one of the partners, and so long as it remains, both are forbidden to marry another person. In other words, Catholics can divorce, and in many parts of the world they do divorce at rates similar to the rest of the population. Sting and Tomelty indeed were divorced several years after their marriage.

Divorce aside, Catholics whose previous marriages were valid, sacramental, and consummated are not allowed to remarry under church law so long as their ex-partners are alive. In reality, many divorced Catholics remarry without church involvement. Sting did just that, when he married (the Anglican, something we will return to soon) Trudie Styler in 1992.

The story of their decision to get married, after having already been a couple for a decade and having had children together, is well-known to Sting's fans, but here it is again, in Sting's words, when I asked him about the religious aspects of it:

> My son Jake asked us [if he and his sister Mickey were bastards], because he had heard the word at school. [Then Trudie said,] "No you're not a bastard, your father is!" She was joking. But they said, "Look, we'd feel better if you got married." The children were at Salisbury Cathedral School, a very conservative Anglican school, I imagine they were teased there about their famous parents. So we said, "Well, okay, we'll do it for you." And in the end it was fun. I liked the priest. [He is] very easy-going and sweet,[29] and he said "I can't give you a proper marriage," but I said, "a blessing is enough." It is a High Anglican church, it's almost the same [as Catholicism regarding remarriage]. The ceremony was enough for me.[30]

The reason that the Anglican priest said he could not celebrate a "proper marriage," and that, in Sting's words, the church was "almost the same" as Catholic churches, is worth explaining. The Catholic church is aware of the reality that many of its members divorce and remarry, and its law includes several loopholes enabling a measure of flexibility. Today, these loopholes are much larger than they were before the Second Vatican Council. One of them is through an appeal by at least one of the spouses asking

---

29. Based on Sting's memoir (p. 437), the name of this vicar was John Reynolds.

30. Sting, interview by author, July 23, 2017, Künzelsau, REC22:007. See a picture from the event at https://links.stingandreligion.com/wedd.

the local ecclesiastical court to declare the contested marriage null (saying it was impeded in principle from the beginning), or to dissolve it (saying for example the marriage was not fully sacramental, even if valid). Following the reforms associated with the Second Vatican Council, the procedure became much simpler and more accessible. This change, together with the rising divorce rate, has made annulment a practical option for some, especially in certain western countries. Most people who desire an annulment or dissolution of their marriage today do so for one of two reasons. The first is the case of couples that have separated in a civil proceeding, and at least one of whom is seeking the church's recognition of the separation. Usually the petitioner is interested in marrying another person and in being declared eligible for marriage according to church law. Another common situation is that of people who have already married others without ecclesiastical authorization, and would now like to declare their previous marriages null. In such cases, the purpose is a certain legitimization of the current marriage, as well as permission to receive the Eucharist at Mass. Since in the church's eyes a person in this situation is, de facto, cohabiting with someone who is not his or her lawful spouse, his or her new life is considered a form of adultery— even if many would avoid explicit use of the term. As one guilty of a grave, public, and ongoing sin, he or she is prohibited from receiving the body and blood of Christ.[31]

Those who may wonder why not all Catholics who remarry request a process of annulment of their previous marriage should remember that it can be complicated, and many do not want to do it for very good reasons. Primarily, there is a problem of moral principle: many are reluctant to pronounce a marriage, even one that has come to an end, as null and void. Would it be right to announce that what both partners and society believed to be a "real" marriage, in fact, was not? In many cases, such marriages have produced children. Though the Catholic church insists that the annulment of a marriage does not impinge in any way upon the children, many fear that it does. The legalistic nitpicking over a marriage that has in practice ended, often following a long secular procedure filled with its own challenges, is also emotionally difficult for many. The expense involved, and even more so the issue of access to legal information and legal culture also act as a barrier for many Catholics. In addition, not all petitions are of course answered in the affirmative by the ecclesiastical courts. In its current form, this process does not answer the needs of many.

The prohibition on the partaking of the Eucharist is a great detriment to the religious lives of many remarried Catholic divorcés. Many of them

---

31. The prohibition is codified in the Catholic *Code of Canon Law*, canon 915.

feel that remarrying after the failure of their previous marriage was the right thing to do, spiritually and morally speaking, and that it is far removed from adultery. Some may also argue that their decision has rehabilitated not only them but also their children: Sting's testimony above is a perfect example of exactly that. The fact that the church regards them as sinners and therefore denies them its most important sacrament pains many Catholics greatly. It also draws the fury of many church members who sympathize. On the other hand, many conservative-leaning church members believe that despite the pain, this ruling is just. Whoever defies a grave prohibition publicly and continually, should not expect to be received by the church with open arms. In reality, many priests and bishops grant the Eucharist to those who ask for it, even if they know them to be remarried divorcés. Others may refuse it.

In 2016, Pope Francis published an "exhortation," entitled *Amoris Laetitia* ("The Joy of Love"). Conservative Catholics insist this is not the case, but a reasonable reading of it suggests that Pope Francis is against an absolute prohibition on remarried Catholics to receive communion, and for encouraging both clergy and lay people to find ways to allow some of these Catholics to take communion. In this, he went against clear declarations of his predecessor's, Pope Benedict XVI, who said that the subject was not up for debate, and that communion should not be offered to remarried Catholics unless their previous marriage was officially declared invalid. Nevertheless, because of the conservative fight against such an interpretation of the text, and Pope Francis's avoidance of releasing a binding and absolute clarification on the matter, the issue is still not resolved.

Sting's and Styler's marriage took place, as said above, in 1992. At the time, like the Catholic church, the Church of England would normally not allow remarriage, a fact that of course explains the Anglican priest's words. Some of the rules were relaxed in 2002 to allow re-marriage of divorcees,[32] but in the case of Sting and Styler, many Anglican priests would have probably refused to celebrate their marriage even with the new rules, because of two clauses in them. First, the rules ask for caution if the new couple's relationship caused the initial divorce, something that, at least from a superficial point of view, it did. In addition, special caution is required if the new marriage is likely to provoke "hostile public comment or scandal," something it would have probably caused simply because of the couple's fame. A "blessing" was thus something the priest was fine with doing, and for many uninitiated observers its difference from a full marriage ritual would not be obvious anyway. In addition, the Church of England was able to afford Sting

32. See "Marriage in Church After Divorce" (GS 1449), The General Synod of the Church of England, The Archbishops' Council 2002, https://links.stingandreligion. com/mcad.

and Styler something that the Catholic church would not: a full participation for both of them in its rituals.

When Sting's first two children were born, Sting was still relatively young, and probably still felt in some way connected to the Catholic church. His wife was also Catholic. Having their children baptized in the Catholic church was thus not a surprising act. But what about his other four children with Styler? Yes, they were baptized, Sting told me, but in the Church of England.[33] This decision is rather understandable. Not only is it the church of Styler, the mother of these children, but also there would not be there an issue with communion. The Church of England practices an "open communion," which means that any baptized person (and for some, any person) can receive the consecrated bread and wine, the ritual at the center of the church's life. The Catholic church, except in extreme cases, is a "closed communion" church, in which only members (and conservatives would add, only members "in good standing") can partake of it. Thus, Styler would not be allowed to partake since she is not Catholic, and Sting would be prohibited from partaking since he was cohabiting with her, while still sacramentally married to Tomelty. In a way, his second union brought him to the church his mother had to leave.

I asked Sting if he would take communion in the Catholic church today, if, for whatever reason, he happened to find himself in a Catholic service. This made him also speak of communion in the Church of England:

> I have taken communion in the Anglican church because it is open to me. But ancient theological arguments about transubstantiation do not interest me.[34] I was at the pope's Mass at Madison Square garden [=Pope Francis, 2015], at the big Mass, and I didn't take communion. I didn't feel like it, or perhaps I'm still conditioned by the church's dogma [that I should not]. But I do like the pope. . . . My wife loves him too. There is something very engaging about him. I enjoyed being there. But I'd still go in the Anglican church because of its welcome. Occasionally Trudie and I would go.[35]

33. Sting, interview by author, July 23, 2017, Künzelsau, REC22:026.

34. "Transubstantiation" is a famous Catholic dogma declaring that even though the taste, smell, appearance, and chemical composition of the bread and wine used in the Mass have not changed, their essence is no longer that of bread and wine but rather of the Body and Blood of Christ: Christ is *really present* in these elements. Many Protestant groups disagree, and consider the idea that Christ is found in those bread and wine as symbolic. There are also those who hold a position which is somewhere in between these two extremes.

35. Sting, interview by author, July 23, 2017, Künzelsau, REC22:018, 033.

In an interview Sting gave to a rather conservative Catholic reporter about a year later, he is reported to have said "I'd probably seek out the sacraments at the end of my life."[36] This statement is interesting, but not surprising. As we have seen, Sting does not have strong theological disagreements with core concepts of Catholicism. In addition, not only does he seem to appreciate rituals, but he also seems to have a particular interest in the ritual that, during his childhood, was called "Extreme Unction"—and in thinking of death.

Sting's admiration for Pope Francis has by now a rather concrete outcome:

> I have been asked [by the Vatican] to write a piece of music for [a show about] the Sistine Chapel. I didn't want to write something brand new. I like Pope Francis saying that God is mercy. So I found the old Latin hymn *Dies Irae*, the "Day of Wrath."[37] I looked at a translation, and a lot of the verses are awful. . . . Selectively dispatching people to hell. I have created a new musical setting, with an eighty-piece choir. I took out the verses which I thought were offensive, and I end with *Deus misericordia*, "God is Mercy," which is one of Pope Francis's maxims.[38]

Later, in a video message, he said this:

> I was immersed and well-schooled in the music of the church as a child, and this [project on the *Dies Irae* for the show in Rome] was an opportunity to reacquaint myself with the sacred music that had such a powerful influence on my life and work as a musician.[39]

Starting 2018, this piece is a part of an audiovisual show about the Sistine Chapel, playing in Rome.

During his career Sting was exposed, or made an effort to expose himself, to religious and spiritual traditions and notions that were definitely not discussed in the "Penny Catechism" of his childhood. In a few places, for example, he spoke about the idea of reincarnation of the soul in a new body. He told me that despite some admiration and appreciation for some aspects of such beliefs, he has never succeeded in relating to them:

36. Pentin, "Sting."

37. During Sting's childhood, this hymn was used on All Souls' Day, funeral Masses, and requiem Masses.

38. Sting, interview by author, July 23, 2017, Künzelsau, REC22:033. See also "Vatican collaborates with Sting."

39. See https://links.stingandreligion.com/dies, March 12, 2018.

A Buddhist would say you'd be in a *bardo* for forty-nine days and then you'll have another life. Intellectually though I find this difficult, but it's a beautiful poetic idea. It's hard for me to imagine another life. I don't particularly want another life. This one is pretty good *[laughing].*[40]

Earlier, in 2000, he said this:

I'd like to believe in reincarnation. I'd like to subscribe in the idea that we can karmically come back as something better, something more evolved, and the world is more evolved. But culturally and intellectually I find it difficult to accept. I look at my children, and I see myself reincarnated in them. And I hope to see my grandchildren have the same blueprint. . . . My philosophy is that we might as well live as if reincarnation is true. It's a nice idea.[41]

A year later, he expressed the same viewpoint in a slightly different way:

I have never really subscribed to the idea of reincarnation logically or intellectually, but as a poetic idea, I find it very appealing. That you will come back, or part of you will come back, and you will be rewarded or punished for whatever you have done in this life. Maybe [it's] complete nonsense, but to live that way would do you no harm at all. So if you live your life thinking "well, I'd like to come back as a higher being or someone better than myself at this moment then I have to work for that. If I am a bad guy then I'd become a cockroach or something." No offense to cockroaches.[42]

There are at least two acts or activities—if one may use the term—in which Sting is openly engaged and that can have a religious connotation (but are not required to, especially when practiced outside of the places where they originated). The first is the occasional consumption of Ayahuasca, a drink with hallucinogenic powers, used mostly in South America. Sting opens his memoir of 2003 with the description of the first time he, together with his wife Trudie, encountered this substance in Brazil. There, he speaks about it in clear religious, even "Catholic," terms: the event took place in a "church," and it was a "sacrament":

The church, while nominally Christian, is the home of a syncretic religious group that uses as its core sacrament an ancient

40. Sting, interview by author, July 23, 2017, Künzelsau, REC22:101.

41. Sting, *All This Time* CD-ROM.

42. Sting, ". . . *All This Time*," DVD, 32:30.

medicine derived from plant materials known as ayahuasca
. . . .[43]

He was not shy of talking about it again in 2017 (and allowing this to be published):

> I have taken Ayahuasca on numerous occasions. It seems to put you in eternity. In fact, you feel like you've died, your life passing in front of you. And it's terrifying, and then after the terror you feel this incredible sense of belonging in the universe and its love and support and a radiance, mortal fear and then this feeling of elevation. And that's why I describe this as a medicine, not a drug. It seems like a genuine religious experience. It's a sacrament. The shaman gives you a cup of vile tasting green liquid, you drink it, and within an hour you are in a trance state that feels close to death. Often throwing up, crying, you purge. I am very open about it. Ultimately, I have found it to be a very positive experience. The psychedelic experience as a whole is one that has helped to open up my head. . . . The main chemical [in Ayahuasca] that creates the visions is called DMT [N,N-Dimethyltryptamine]. We have it in our spinal fluid, all of us. And we get a dose of it when we're born, or when we die, or suffering trauma. For me it feels like an opportunity to rehearse for death. Allowing us to navigate this terrifying realm, where the mind enters the possibility of the eternal.[44]

In another place, Sting is seen saying that, after taking Ayahuasca, he

> realized for the first time, this is the only genuine religious experience I have ever had. It is communion. Direct access to the Godhead, whatever you think that is, I have no idea what it is. There is definitely a higher intelligence at work in you during this experience.[45]

In his memoir, he also expressed his lack of religious experiences other than when taking Ayahuasca:

> I have never had a genuine religious experience. I have paid lip service to the idea, certainly, but a devastating, ego-destroying, ontological epiphany I simply have not had. More devout souls than I may have visited this realm through prayer, meditation, fasting, or from undergoing a near-death experience. Religious

---

43. Sting, *Broken Music*, 1–2.

44. Sting, interview by author, July 23, 2017, Künzelsau, REC22:073, 101.

45. Amorim, *2102: Time for Change*, 33.

literature is full of such visionary claims, and while I've no reason to doubt their veracity, I would venture to say that such experiences are rare. For every St Teresa, Ezekiel, or William Blake, there are millions like me with no direct experience of the transcendent, of the eternal, of the fathomless mystery at the root of all religious thought. But the ayahuasca has brought me close to something, something fearful and profound and deadly serious.[46]

"So Ayahuasca inspires you religiously more than, let's say, a Catholic communion," I said. "You moved in a certain direction in the search of religious experience?" "Yeah," he answered:

And I prefer to call [Ayahuasca] a medicine and not a drug. A drug gives you an instant reward. You feel euphoric for a little while and then comes the hangover. A medicine asks you to pay first, psychologically. You are forced to come to terms with your fears, asked to atone for your misdemeanors, and after this are you rewarded. A feeling of well-being that can last for days or weeks. Your visual acuity is higher. You feel more connected to nature, to everything around you. . . . I've read recently that there is some serious research treating the terminally ill with plant substances like psilocybin. It is said that people are imbued with sense of acceptance, of heart opening, connection with the world that otherwise the death experience is diminishing. It sounds to me like a fruitful line of research.[47]

The second practice that seems to be worth mentioning—and in this case, Sting says in various places it is part of his daily morning routine—is yoga. Sting has practiced yoga, of various types, since the early 1990s. "I have been doing yoga for about five years," he said in 1995:

Ashtanga Yoga, which is fairly physical, and really about breathing. . . . It is essentially a religious practice. . . . An aide to meditation. You put your mind I suppose in an alpha state, through exhaustion in my case [laughing]. With the breathing you enter a different space and then you can sit and meditate in the

---

46. Sting, *Broken Music*, 18. See also his words elsewhere in the same book: "Since a genuine religious experience had . . . eluded me, I always felt like something of an imposter in the house of the faithful. I didn't quite belong." (*Broken Music*, 47–48).

47. Sting, interview by author, July 23, 2017, Künzelsau, REC22:105. Sting's claim that serious research is done about medical uses for Ayahuasca is correct. For one among many other examples, see http://links.stingandreligion.com/aya1.

lotus position. Meditation is really thinking about nothing. Just breathing and being I suppose. It's very relaxing.[48]

Another type of yoga that has become associated with Sting in the mind of many, due to a statement that was probably said without much thought, is tantric yoga. Even if his oft-quoted claim that tantric yoga enriches his sexuality was imperfectly formulated at best, as his wife, Trudie Styler, claimed various times, many elements in his spiritual quest indeed correspond to it. One of his yoga teachers, Ganga White, explains it in this way, in a book prefaced by Sting:

> Tantra differs from traditional yoga which tends to center around ascetic and renunciative practices and beliefs, in that Tantra seeks spiritual development through the mundane. The Tantric path cultivates awakening in daily life through the feminine, goddess worship, sexuality, and even limited intoxication.[49]

Sting himself explains, in the foreword to the same book, what yoga means to him:

> I don't spend a lot of intellectual energy thinking about yoga, or trying to articulate the processes it awakens, because, for one, I don't have to teach it, and, two, it's become an intrinsic part of my whole life, permeating it to such an extent that I don't really know where it begins or ends.

Quoting White's saying, based indeed on the very etymology of the word "yoga," that "part of yoga practice is to connect," Sting continues, saying yoga's aim is

> to connect flexibility and strength, balance, concentration, sexuality, consciousness, and spirituality, so that what may have begun solely as a physical practice can evolve into an integrated and holistic approach to all aspects of one's life. . . . To be conscious of this, as we breathe, turns the physical practice into a devotional one, connecting us via resonant vibration to the cosmos. . . . [Y]oga helps us resonate more efficiently with the universe.[50]

It seems rather clear that Sting adopted an attitude that some, but certainly not all, western practitioners of yoga have. Beginning with yoga as a type of

48. Sting, *All This Time CD-ROM*, Part 4, "Yoga," 0:45, https://links.stingandreligion.com/cdr8.

49. White, *Yoga Beyond Belief*, 16–17.

50. Sting, "The Yogi."

physical activity (thus the great success in the West of Hatha yoga, probably the most physical type of yoga), they are drawn later also to some of its spiritual layers. It does not become a "religion," whatever the term might mean, to them, but they draw elements from it and integrate them in other spiritual ideas they might already have.[51] Another important point to notice in Sting's switching between different branches of yoga through time, as well as his support of Ganga White's school, is that he did not become a strong believer in any specific type of yoga orthodoxy, but rather picks and chooses whatever suits him physically and spiritually at any given time.

In some places, and perhaps this is related to his interest in yoga, Sting is quoted as expressing strong feelings toward Hinduism. For example, one journalist quoted him as saying, "In a sense I am more of a Hindu [than a Christian]. . . . I like the Hindu religion more than anything else at the moment."[52] In another place, he talked about the special experience The Police had in 1980 in a concert in Mumbai (then still called Bombay), a concert that is said to be the first major rock concert to ever take place in India. Whether he would agree today with his own statement I do not know, but the thirty-year-old Sting, in the midst of his time with his successful band, was clearly undertaking an exercise in "comparative religion" after experiencing something of India:

> In India, people are dying on the street, living in cardboard boxes, but you don't see the kind of hopeless despair you'd see in any British city or in a lot of American cities. What they say is, life is cheap. And in a way, it is, although it's a horrifying thing to agree with. Life and death—It's their religion, and they have a way of coping with it. We don't.[53]

I asked him if he could talk more about his experience with India and Hinduism. Even though almost four decades had passed since that interview, and I did not mention it, the motif of death came up again:

> I spent some time in India, walking pilgrim routes, I've walked to the source of the Yemuna, and the Ganga, washed myself in the waters of the glacier, and slept by the roadside with people close to dying who want to die at the source of the river. Of course no one knows who I am. The concept of pilgrimage is one

51. See on this, for example, Syman, *The Subtle Body*.
52. Sting, Interview with Malvika Nanda.
53. Henke, "The Police."

that's important to me. I'd rather be a pilgrim than a tourist. So I would often seek out experiences that were uncomfortable.[54]

In fact, while talking with him I realized, when I asked him about a silver bracelet, with a text engraved on it, that he regularly wears, that it is a Hindu artifact. "It is a mantra by Ravi Shankar," he said.

> [It is] something good, very positive. It was given to me, I wear it every day. It's insurance, you never know. I like what Christopher Hitchens said. He was a famous atheist, he was dying, and they said, "Well, how would you feel if after you're dead you meet God?" And he said, "I like surprises!" I like surprises too, and I am looking forward to them![55]

Rituals that are related to death seem to attract Sting. If this is related to the loss of both his parents in the same year, and his inability to mourn them in a traditional way due to his fame, I do not know, although the following paragraph from his memoir of 2003 might suggest such a possibility:

> My father has died only a few days before [a tour in South America in 1987], and his death comes only months after my mother has passed away. For complex reasons I have attended neither funeral, nor will I seek any consolation from the church. But just as the recently bereaved can be drawn to the solace of religion, psychoanalysis, self-reflection, and even séances, despite my agnosticism, I too am in need of some kind of reassuring experience or ritual that will help me to accept that perhaps there is something beyond the tragedy of death, some greater meaning that I can conjure for myself.[56]

The spiritual dimensions of pilgrimage also interest him, and it seems that in his mind they are related to his special fondness for the image of a labyrinth. In the booklet that accompanies his album *Songs from the Labyrinth* (2006), Sting says that:

> The labyrinth based on the design on the floor of Chartres Cathedral [which appears on a lute that Sting received as a gift from his guitarist Dominic Miller] had become something of an obsession of mine in recent years, so much that I'd had one constructed as an earthwork in my garden in England.[57]

---

54. Sting, interview by author, July 23, 2017, Künzelsau, REC22:075.

55. Sting, interview by author, July 23, 2017, Künzelsau, REC22:123.

56. Sting, *Broken Music*, 9.

57. See the labyrinth in his garden at http://links.stingandreligion.com/laby.

He even has an image of that famous labyrinth from Chartres tattooed on his back. When I met him, he spoke about the labyrinth in his garden, which is located in an area teeming with prehistoric monuments, both large and small, some of which were probably built for spiritual reasons. "I live two miles from Stonehenge. It drew me there":[58]

> I walk my labyrinth whenever I'm home in Lake House. For me it is a meditation tool, a very old tool, the turning right, left, right, left, right, left, the binary rhythm of walking, and just meditating, it's probably a meditation on death, you get to the end and there is no other way, and if you walk with other people sometimes you get close to each other or far away. . . . It's an extraordinary mathematical structure, and at the end of twenty minutes of walking, if I have an issue that troubles me, I feel a little clearer, it helps me think, it helps me see a path.[59]

In some places Sting mentions tarot cards. In a CD-ROM he released in 1995, the player needs to collect tarot cards, and then Sting "interprets" them. And yet Sting says explicitly in those videos that he sees the cards as an ancient and fun tool for introspection without any transcendental power or meaning. Sting told me about other types of spiritual experiences, which he takes more seriously:

> I was inducted into a peyote cult in Mexico, in the mountains, me and three other initiates were blindfolded, and taken up a mountain in the middle of Mexico, a very high mountain, and we had to hold each other's shoulders, and before we went they stuffed our mouths with peyote, with crystals of strychnine sprouting from [the] top of the mushroom. Not exactly appetis-ing! and so as you're climbing you enter this profoundly altered state, and when reached the top they sprayed us with deer's blood, eagle feathers, and all kind of stuff, tequila, it was insane. . . . I spent the whole night freezing on the mountain, very high. It was the time of Halley's comet [1985/1986]. I'd seen it in Los Angeles where it was but a dull, fuzzy thing in the sky, but in that mountain, in the rarified air, it looked like a fiery dragon. I could understand why people were fearful of this comet, why it was so incredible. I spent the night shivering around the fire, and the next morning I somehow became separated from the party, I was wandering in the desert alone, no water. After a few

58. Sting, interview by author, July 23, 2017, Künzelsau, REC22:108.

59. Sting, interview by author, July 23, 2017, Künzelsau, REC22:055. The music video of the song, "Let Your Soul Be Your Pilot" (1996) takes place in its entirety in a labyrinth: see http://links.stingandreligion.com/lysb.

hours I found where I was supposed to be, but it was a challenging experience, and of course I'm thinking why the hell am I
doing this? I am a millionaire rock star, I could be lounging in
a nightclub sipping vodka cocktails. Why am I doing this? I'm
intrigued by this kind of experience, awakening something in
me that's lacking in modern life. I have a desire to re-enchant my
life, I need to be re-enchanted. So I've explored methods that I
imagine can do that. Methods that go back thousands of years.
Tribal religions and beliefs have been mocked and devalued and
yet there is often profound knowledge there.[60]

Sting is asked often by journalists if he is religious. Perhaps one of his
most refined answers to this tricky, and possibly superficial question, was
given in a Commencement Speech he gave in 1994:

If ever I'm asked if I'm religious I always reply, "Yes, I'm a devout
musician." Music puts me in touch with something beyond the
intellect, something otherworldly, something sacred.[61]

He was later asked to elaborate on that answer. This is what he said in 2011:

It's not a frivolous answer. . . . Music is something that gives my
life value and spiritual solace.[62]

Do you have sacraments in this religion, I asked him in 2017? "Absolutely!"
he replied. "Of course! Performing is a ritualised celebration, an offering to
God perhaps. It's a Mass! Sharing things, singing together, praising God, if
you like."[63] In another place, describing a case when he had been electro-
cuted on stage while playing through a storm, he said a similar thing: "Since
that incident I've come to consider singing as a form of prayer."[64]

In this book I believe that I have demonstrated, among other things,
through one detailed example, that one's rejection of the religion in which
one was raised is often neither complete nor final. The narrative we have dis-
cerned when examining Gordon's/Sting's relationship to religion is one that
may correspond, without major differences, to the personal stories of many.
Having been raised in a religious environment, some, often during their
teens or early twenties, begin to doubt some aspects of it, frequently both
because of theological questions and negative experiences of various kinds.

60. Sting, interview by author, July 23, 2017, Künzelsau, REC22:075.

61. Sting, "The Mystery and Religion."

62. Luscombe, "10 Questions for Sting."

63. Sting, interview by author, July 23, 2017, Künzelsau, REC22:068.

64. Sting, Broken Music, 226.

A period of rejection comes, followed at times by exposure to other religious/spiritual traditions and concepts, or to fully secular thinking. As the person matures, it is possible that more intellectual and theological mines in the childhood tradition are exposed. Encounters with other people, family, professions, and other factors, continue to shape feelings of affiliation with or rejection of the tradition of one's youth. At times a certain longing for positive aspects of this tradition, and acknowledgment of good memories of it develops. With time, some aspects of the tradition may become attractive again, while also obviously shaped by new ideas, insights, experiences, and encounters. Slowly a synthesis of all these factors may be achieved. This synthesis might remain relatively stable and become one's mature worldview, and it might go through various adjustments as time, and more life events, both good and bad, occur.

Bruce Springsteen, who is two years older than Sting, and also grew up Catholic, says this in his memoir:

> On my eighth-grade graduation day, I walked away from [Catholicism], finished, telling myself, "Never again." I was free, free, free at last . . . and I believed it . . . for quite a while. However, as I grew older, there were certain things about the way I thought, reacted, behaved. I came to ruefully and bemusedly understand that once you're a Catholic, you're always a Catholic. So I stopped kidding myself. I don't often participate in my religion but I know somewhere . . . deep inside . . . I'm still on the team.[65]

Would Sting agree? In 1987 he went through a rather dramatic moment. One of the biggest shows of his career was about to begin in Rio de Janeiro. The risk of bad weather, an uncontrollably large crowd, and technical difficulties merged, and made the moments before the concert's opening tense. Sting, obviously and understandably stressed, made a quick, almost invisible sign of the cross above his heart, just before going up on stage.[66] Was this an instinct, or did Sting, like many who were raised religious, prefer to not take a risk, just in case—as he would wonder some years later in his 1993 song "Saint Augustine in Hell"—somebody, after all, is up there?

---

65. Springsteen, *Born to Run*, 17
66. See https://links.stingandreligion.com/crss.

BIBLIOGRAPHY

This bibliography includes only works that are explicitly mentioned in foot-notes. Many other works were also of great use, although they are not cited here, for reasons of brevity.

Acta Apostolicae Sedis 38. Rome: Vatican City, 1946.

Amorim, Joao G., dir. *2102: Time for Change*. New York: Mangu.tv, 2010. DVD.

Behind the Music. VH1. September 26, 1999, https://links.stingandreligion.com/betm.

"Being Christian in Western Europe." Pew Research Center. May 29, 2018, https://links.stingandreligion.com/pew8.

Berryman, James. *Sting and I: The Totally Hilarious Story of Life as Sting's Best Mate*. London: Blake, 2005.

Bolt, W. V. *800 Years of Service: A Brief History of the Wallsend Churches*. n.l.: n.p., 2001.

Bond, Helen K. *Pontius Pilate in History and Interpretation*. Cambridge: Cambridge University Press, 2004.

Bowman, Marion. "Drawn to Glastonbury." In *Pilgrimage in Popular Culture*, edited by Ian Reader et al., 29–62. Basingstoke, UK: Macmillan, 1993.

Brown, Callum, and Gordon Lynch. "Cultural Perspectives." In *Religion and Change in Modern Britain*, edited by Linda Woodhead et al., 329–51. London: Routledge, 2012.

Brown, Richard, and Peter Brannen. "Social Relations and Social Perspectives amongst Shipbuilding Workers—A Preliminary Statement." *Sociology* 4.1 (1970) 71–84 (Part I); *Sociology* 4.2 (1970) 197–211 (Part II).

Browne, Sarah. "The Last Ship from Broadway to Newcastle: A Feminist Political Musical for the Brexit Era." *Studies in Musical Theatre* 12.3 (2018) 377–85.

Calhoun, Scott, ed. *U2 and the Religious Impulse: Take Me Higher*. London: Bloomsbury Academic, 2019.

Cambray, Joseph. *Synchronicity: Nature and Psyche in an Interconnected Universe*. College Station, TX: Texas A&M University Press, 2009.

Campbell, Lorne. *The Last Ship*. Unpublished musical book/libretto, 2018.

Campion, Chris. *Walking on the Moon: The Untold Story of the Police and the Rise of New Wave Rock*. Hoboken, NJ: John Wiley & Sons, 2010.

Carr, Paul. *Sting: From Northern Skies to Fields of Gold*. Reverb. London: Reaktion, 2017.

Cascone, Gina. *Pagan Babies and Other Catholic Memories*. New York: Washington Square, 1992.

A Catechism of Christian Doctrine, Prepared and Enjoined by Order of the Third Council of Baltimore. New York: Benziger Brothers, 1885.

"Catholic Priest to Retire." *Wallsend News,* June 9, 1961.

"Catholic Schools Are Commended." *Wallsend News,* June 15, 1956

"Churches Unite for a Week of Prayers." *Wallsend News,* District News by Churchman, January 15, 1965.

Coad, F. Roy. *A History of the Brethren Movement: Its Origins, Its Worldwide Development, and Its Significance for the Present Day.* Exeter, UK: Paternoster, 1968.

Coffey, Tony. *Answers to Questions Catholics Are Asking.* Eugene, OR: Harvest House, 2006.

Common, Jack. *Kiddar's Luck.* London: Turnstile, 1951.

"Consecration Ceremony Watched by 500 People." *Wallsend News,* July 18, 1958.

Conway, Martin. *Catholic Politics in Europe, 1918–1945.* London: Routledge, 1997.

Conway, Mary Agnes. "An Investigation into the History of Roman Catholic Education on Tyneside, with Particular References to the Parish of Our Lady and St. Aidan's, Willington Quai." M.A. diss., The University of Newcastle, 1995.

Cornwell, John. *Seminary Boy.* New York: Doubleday, 2006.

Coupland, Simon. "The Vikings on the Continent in Myth and History." *History* 88.2 (2003) 186–203.

Coy, Patrick, ed. *A Revolution of the Heart: Essays on the Catholic Worker.* Philadelphia: Temple University Press, 1988.

Day, Elizabeth. "Interview: The Thing about Sting . . ." *The Guardian,* September 24, 2011.

de Bhaldraithe, Eoin. "Mixed Marriages and Irish Politics: The Effect of 'Ne Temere.'" *Studies: An Irish Quarterly Review* 77 (1988) 284–99.

Drinkwater, F. H. *Catechism Stories: A Teachers' Aid-Book in Five Parts with References to the Revised Baltimore Catechism No. 2,* Westminster, MD: Newman, 1949.

Duffy, Eamon F. *The Stripping of the Altars: Traditional Religion in England, 1400–1580.* 1992. Reprint, New Haven: Yale University Press, 2005.

Eco, Umberto. *The Book of Legendary Lands.* New York: Rizzoli Ex Libris, 2013.

Engelhardt Herringer, Carol. "The Virgin Mary." In *Making and Remaking Saints in Nineteenth-Century Britain,* edited by Gareth Atkins, 44–59. Manchester: Manchester University Press, 2016.

Field, Robert. "L. Oppenheimer LTD and the Mosaics of Eric Newton." In Tile and Architectural Ceramic Society's Conference on Church Ceramics. Ironbridge, UK: October 7, 2006, https://links.stingandreligion.com/mosa.

Field-Bibb, Jacqueline. "Women and Ministry: The Presbyterian Church of England." *The Heythrop Journal* 31 (1990) 150–64.

"Five Services for Unity of Churches." *Wallsend News,* District New by Churchman, January 12, 1962.

Fuller, Robert C. *Spiritual, but Not Religious: Understanding Unchurched America.* New York: Oxford University Press, 2001.

Fulton, John. "Young Adult Catholics in England." In *Young Catholics at the New Millennium: The Religion and Morality of Young Adults in Western Countries,* edited by John Fulton et al., 137–59. Dublin: University College Dublin Press, 2000.

Gable, Christopher. *The Words and Music of Sting.* Westport, CT: Praeger, 2008.

Garbarini, Vic. "Invisible Son: Death, Rebirth, and This Business of Music—Sting on the Ties That Bind." *Spin* 3.7 (1987) 46–51 & 68–70.

Gilbert, Alan D. *The Making of Post-Christian Britain: A History of the Secularization of Modern Society*. London: Longman, 1980.

Gilmour, Michael J. "The Bible and Popular Music." In *The Bloomsbury Handbook of Religion and Popular Culture*, edited by Christopher Partridge et al., 67–76. London: Bloomsbury, 2017.

———. *Gods and Guitars: Seeking the Sacred in Post-1960s Popular Music*. Waco, TX: Baylor University Press, 2009.

Gilroy, Lyn, and Bernadette Lawson. "The Catholic Women's League: A Short History of Hexham and Newcastle Branch." *Northern Catholic History* 39 (1998) 63–69.

Gordon, Mary. "My First Communion." *The Furrow* 58.6 (2007) 331–42.

Greeley, Andrew M. *The Catholic Imagination*. Berkeley: University of California Press, 2000.

———. "The Catholic Imagination of Bruce Springsteen." *America Magazine*, February 6, 1988.

Guest, Mathew, et al. "Christianity: Loss of Monopoly," In *Religion and Change in Modern Britain*, edited by Linda Woodhead et al., 57–84. London: Routledge, 2012.

Harris, Alana. "Thérèse de Lisieux." In *Making and Remaking Saints in Nineteenth-Century Britain*, edited by Gareth Atkins, 262–78. Manchester: Manchester University Press, 2016.

Hart, Charles. *The Early Story of St Cuthbert's Grammar School Newcastle upon Tyne*. London: Burns Oates & Washbourne, 1941.

Hawkes, Jane. "The Rothbury Cross: An Iconographic Bricolage." *Gesta* 35.1 (1996) 77–94.

Heenan, John C. *My Lord and My God: A Book for First Communion Year*. London: Burns & Oates, 1957.

———. *Our Faith*. London: T. Nelson and Sons, 1956.

Heimann, Mary. *Catholic Devotion in Victorian England*. Oxford: Clarendon, 1995.

———. "Devotional Stereotypes in English Catholicism, 1850–1914." In *Catholicism in Britain and France Since 1789*, edited by Frank Tallett et al., 13–25. London: Hambledon, 1996.

Henke, James. "The Police: Policing the World." *Rolling Stone*, February 19, 1981.

Hornsby-Smith, Michael P. "The Catholic Church and Education in Britain: From the 'Intransigence' of 'Closed' Catholicism to the Accommodation Strategy of 'Open' Catholicism." In *Catholicism in Britain and France Since 1789*, edited by Frank Tallett et al., 43–65. London: Hambledon, 1996.

Hultgård, Anders. "The Askr and Embla Myth in a Comparative Perspective." In *Old Norse Religion in Long-term Perspectives*, edited by Anders Andrén et al., 58–62. Lund: Nordic Academic, 2006.

"Hundreds Take Part in Week of Prayer." *Wallsend News*, District News by Churchman, January 26, 1968.

Huss, Boaz. "Spirituality: The Emergence of a New Cultural Category and Its Challenge to the Religious and the Secular." *Journal of Contemporary Religion* 29.1 (2014) 47–60.

Hutton, Ronald. *The Pagan Religions of the Ancient British Isles: Their Nature and Legacy*. Oxford: Blackwell, 1991.

Jones, Norman. *The English Reformation: Religion and Cultural Adaptation*. Oxford: Wiley-Blackwell, 2002.

Kant, Immanuel. "Idea for a Universal History from a Cosmopolitan Point of View (1784)." In *Kant: On History*, edited by Lewis White Beck, 11–26. Indianapolis: Bobbs-Merrill, 1963.

Kenneson, Philip D. "What's in a Name? A Brief Introduction to the 'Spiritual but Not Religious.'" *Liturgy* 30.3 (2015) 3–13.

Key of Heaven: A Manual of Devotions and Instructions, for the Use of Catholics. Baltimore: John Murphy, 1901.

Knowles, W. H. *The Church of the Holy Cross, Wallsend, Northumberland*. Newcastle upon Tyne, UK: Andrew Reid & Co., 1910.

Krasniewicz, Louise. "Growing Up Catholic and American: The Oral Tradition of Catholic School Students." *New York Folklore* 12.3–4 (1986) 51–67.

Kulish, Nicholas. "Homeless in Poland, Preparing an Odyssey at Sea." *New York Times*, August 1, 2009. https://links.stingandreligion.com/nto9.

Kundera, Milan. *The Unbearable Lightness of Being*. New York: Harper Perennial Modern Classics, 2005.

"*Liber Confirmatorum*." Unpublished. Wallsend, UK: St. Columba's Parish.

Logan, John, and Brian Yorkey. *The Last Ship: Book by John Logan and Brian Yorkey; Music and Lyrics by Sting*. Unpublished musical book/libretto, August 26, 2013.

Lucie-Smith, Alexander. "Why Are so Many Priests Alcoholics?" *Union of Catholic Asian News*, August 25, 2014, https://links.stingandreligion.com/alco.

Luscombe, Belinda. "10 Questions for Sting." *Time*, November 21, 2011.

Macan, Edward. *Rocking the Classics: English Progressive Rock and the Counterculture*. New York: Oxford University Press, 1997.

Macartney, Sydney, dir. *A Love Divided*. London: BBC, 1999.

Mackay, Charles. *Memoirs of Extraordinary Popular Delusions and the Madness of Crowds*. London: Richard Bentley, 1841.

MacKillop, James. "Hy Brasil." In *A Dictionary of Celtic Mythology*, edited by James MacKillop. Oxford: Oxford University Press, 2004.

Macpherson, Ben. "Heritage, Home and Heredity: Performing English Cultural Identity in *The Last Ship*." *Studies in Musical Theatre* 10.2 (2016) 227–41.

Maher, Michael, and Joseph Bolland. "Soul." In *The Catholic Encyclopedia* 14. New York: Appleton, 1912.

Marienberg, Evyatar. "Bible, Religion, and Catholicism in Sting's Album and Musical *The Last Ship*." *Studies in Musical Theatre* 12.3 (2018) 319–35.

———. *Catholicism Today: An Introduction to the Contemporary Catholic Church*. New York: Routledge, 2015.

———. "Death, Resurrection, Sacraments, and Myths: Religion around Sting." In *Cultural Icons and Cultural Leadership*, edited by Peter Iver Kaufman et al., 167–85. Northampton, UK: Edward Elgar, 2017.

———. "O My God: Religion in Sting's Early Lyrics." *Journal of Religion and Popular Culture* 31.3 (2019) 223–35.

Marmion, J. P. "The Penny Catechism: A Long Lasting Text." *Paradigm* 26 (1998) http://links.stingandreligion.com/pctx.

Martindale, C. C. *Bernadette of Lourdes*. London: Catholic Truth Society, 1958.

"Mass Facing People Best: Liturgy Head." *The Universe*, November 12, 1965.

Massa, Mark. "The times they were a'changing: Mark Massa on the Catholic '60s." *US Catholic*, May 2011, http://links.stingandreligion.com/ma60.

McCartney, Derek. "'How Many 'Papists' in Borough'? Asked Bishop—'Only Two' Was Reply." *Wallsend News*, May 25, 1956.

McGrail, Peter. *First Communion: Ritual, Church and Popular Religious Identity.* London: Routledge, 2016.

McHugh, John. "Mystery." In *The Catholic Encyclopedia* 10. New York: Robert Appleton Company, 1911, https://links.stingandreligion.com/myst.

McLean, Craig. "The Man Who Would Be Sting." *The Independent*, October 4, 2003, http://links.stingandreligion.com/in03.

McLeod, Hugh. *The Religious Crisis of the 1960s*, New York: Oxford University Press, 2007.

Metzger, Bruce M. *A Textual Commentary on the Greek New Testament.* 2nd ed. Stuttgart: United Bible Societies, 1994.

Nava, Alejandro. *In Search of Soul: Hip-Hop, Literature, and Religion.* Oakland, CA: University of California Press, 2017.

Nixon, Philip. *St Cuthbert of Durham.* Stroud, UK: Amberley, 2012.

Norman, Edward. *Roman Catholicism in England from the Elizabethan Settlement to the Second Vatican Council.* Oxford: Oxford University Press, 1986.

Northern Catholic Calendar. Durham: Diocese of Hexham and Newcastle, 1975.

Opie, Iona, and Peter Opie. *The Lore and Language of Schoolchildren.* 1959. Reprint, New York: New York Review Books Classics, 2001.

Our Lady and Saint Columba Centenary, 1885–1985. Wallsend, UK: n.p., 1985.

"Packed Church at Induction: Miss Gordon Is New Minister." *Wallsend News*, November 23, 1956.

Partridge, Christopher. *Mortality and Music: Popular Music and the Awareness of Death.* London: Bloomsbury, 2015.

Pasulka, Diana Walsh. *Heaven Can Wait: Purgatory in Catholic Devotional and Popular Culture.* New York: Oxford University Press, 2014.

Pentin, Edward. "Sting: 'The Church's Music and Liturgy Fed This Artistic Soul.'" *National Catholic Register*, August 8, 2018.

Peters, Edward N. *The 1917 Pio-Benedictine Code of Canon Law.* San Francisco: Ignatius, 2001.

"Plans for Pilgrimage to Isle of St. Columba." *Wallsend News*, District News by Churchman, October 19, 1962.

"The Pope's Encyclical." *Wallsend News*, District News by Churchman, August 9, 1968.

"Possibilities in Shipbuilding Never so Good." *Wallsend News*, December 21, 1956.

Power, Edmund. "St. Cuthbert and St. Wilfrid." In *Benedict's Disciples*, edited by David Hugh Farmer, 52–68. Leominster, UK: Gracewing, 1980.

"Priest Speaks in Anglican Church." *The Universe*, April 6, 1962.

Purdue, A. W. *Newcastle: The Biography.* Stroud, UK: Amberley, 2012.

Ross, Michael Tylor. "Sacred Love: The (Eco)Theology of Sting." In *Music, Theology, and Justice,* edited by Michael O'Connor et al., 73–93. Lanham, MD: Lexington, 2017.

Rothman, Joshua. "The Church of U2." *New Yorker*, September 16, 2014.

Ruff, Mark Edward. *The Wayward Flock: Catholic Youth in Postwar Germany, 1945–1965.* Chapel Hill, NC: University of North Carolina Press, 2005.

Russell, Bertrand. *The Basic Writings of Bertrand Russell.* London: Routledge, 2009.

Rynne, Xavier. *Vatican Council II.* 1968. Reprint, Maryknoll, NY: Orbis, 1999.

"The Sacred Liturgy: From the Hierarchy of England and Wales to the Clergy, Secular and Religious, throughout Those Countries." Unpublished. Rome: October 20, 1964.

Schaff, Philip, and Henry Wace, eds. *Nicene and Post-Nicene Fathers, Second Series*, 12. Buffalo, NY: Christian Literature, 1895.

Schultz, Carrie T. "Do This in Memory of Me: American Catholicism and First Communion Customs in the Era of 'Quam Singulari.'" *American Catholic Studies* 115.2 (2004) 45–66.

Scorer, Richard. *Betrayed: the English Catholic Church and the Sex Abuse Crisis*. London: Biteback, 2014.

"Service." *Wallsend News*, The Week's Church Notes, September 20, 1968.

A Simple Prayer Book. 1957. Reprint, London: The Catholic Truth Society, 1965.

Smith, Jeff. "The Making of a Diocese 1851–1882." In *Newcastle Upon Tyne: A Modern History*, edited by Robert Colls et al., 93–112. Bognor Regis, UK: Phillimore, 2001.

Smith, W. Vincent. *Catholic Tyneside from the Beginning of the Reformation to the Restoration of the Hierarchy 1534–1850*. Newcastle on Tyne, UK: Catholic Truth Society, 1930.

Solomon, Jon. "Sting in the Tradition of the Lyric Poet." *Popular Music and Society* 17.3 (1993) 33–41.

Springsteen, Bruce. *Born to Run*. New York: Simon & Schuster, 2016.

"St. Columba's Church Demolished—Gap on Carville Road Landscape." *Wallsend News*, Church Notes, May 18, 1956.

"Step towards Unity through a Supper." *Newcastle Journal*, April 16, 1966.

Sting. *All This Time*. CD-ROM. 1995.

———. . . . *All This Time*. Directed by Jim Gable. DVD. Universal Island, 2001.

———. *Broken Music: A Memoir*. New York: Dial, 2003.

———. Interview by Charlie Rose. *Charlie Rose*. Season 18, Episode 229, December 10, 2010, http://links.stingandreligion.com/cr10.

———. Interview by Malvika Nanda. *Hindustan Times*, 2005.

———. *Lyrics*. New York: Dial, 2007.

———. "The Mystery and Religion of Music." Boston: Commencement Address at Berklee College, 1994, https://links.stingandreligion.com/comm (a partial recording).

———. *Ten Summoner's Tales. Interview Disc*. New York: A&M Records, 1993.

———. "The Yogi and the Shower Singer." Forward to Ganga White. *Yoga beyond Belief: Insights to Awaken and Deepen Your Practice*, xiv–xv. Berkeley: North Atlantic, 2007.

Stojilkov, Andrea. "Sting: A Poet Who Sings, a Singer Who Reads." In *Symphony and Song: The Intersection of Words and Music*, edited by Victor Kennedy et al., 194–217. Newcastle upon Tyne: Cambridge Scholars, 2016.

Summers, Andy. *One Train Later: A Memoir*. New York: St. Martin, 2006.

"Sunday School Is Not a School of Manners, Says Vicar of St. Luke's." *Wallsend News*, Church Notes, August 31, 1956.

Syman, Stefanie. *The Subtle Body: The Story of Yoga in America*. New York: Farrar, Straus and Giroux, 2010.

"Teams to Meet at Mass." *Wallsend News*, Church Notes, December 13, 1968.

Teresa. *The Life of St. Teresa of Jesus: The Autobiography of St. Teresa of Avila*. Translated and edited by E. Allison Peers. Garden City, NY: Image, 1960.

Thomas, Charles. *Christianity in Roman Britain to AD 500.* Berkeley: University of California Press, 1981.

Thomas, of Celano. *The First Life of Saint Francis of Assisi.* Translated by Christopher Stace. London: SPCK, 2000.

Thomas, Owen C. "Spiritual but Not Religious: The Influence of the Current Romantic Movement." *Anglican Theological Review* 88.3 (2006) 397–415.

"Try Churches of Other Sects When on Holiday—Says Rev. Basham in Magazine." *Wallsend News*, Church Notes, August 17, 1956.

"Vatican Collaborates with Sting and Olympics Producers to Share Sistine Chapel with the World." *The Telegraph*, October 13, 2017.

"The Vocations Exhibition." *The Tablet*, July 11, 1953.

"Wallsend Will Have a Traditional Good Friday." *Wallsend News*, Church Notes, March 20, 1959.

Ward, Conor K. *Priests and People: A Study in the Sociology of Religion.* Liverpool: Liverpool University Press, 1961.

West, Aaron J. *Sting and The Police: Walking in Their Footsteps.* London: Rowman & Littlefield, 2015.

Whetstone, David. "Sting Talks to *The Journal* about His New Album and Stage Show." *The Journal*, September 20, 2013.

White, Ganga. *Yoga beyond Belief: Insights to Awaken and Deepen Your Practice.* Berkeley: North Atlantic, 2007.

Wills, Gary. *Bare Ruined Choirs: Doubt, Prophecy, and Radical Religion.* New York: Doubleday, 1972.

Winchester, Tom. "Sexualizing Saint Teresa of Avila." *Degree Critical* (Fall 2017) https://links.stingandreligion.com/avil.

Wolffe, John. "Change and Continuity in British Anti-Catholicism, 1829–1982." In *Catholicism in Britain and France Since 1789*, edited by Frank Tallett et al., 67–84. London: Hambledon, 1996.

Yadin-Israel, Azzan. *The Grace of God and the Grace of Man: The Theologies of Bruce Springsteen.* Highland Park: Lingua, 2016.

PERMISSIONS

SONGS BY STING MENTIONED OR QUOTED IN THIS VOLUME:

"Carrion Prince (O Ye of Little Faith/Hope)" (1975). Music and Lyrics by Sting. Copyright © 1975 G.M. Sumner. Copyright Renewed. All Rights Administered by Sony/ATV Music Publishing LLC, 424 Church Street, Suite 1200, Nashville, TN 37219. International Copyright Secured. All Rights Reserved. Reprinted by Permission of Hal Leonard LLC.

"Don't You Look at Me" (1975). Music and Lyrics by Sting. Copyright © G.M. Sumner. International Copyright Secured. All Rights Reserved. Reprinted by Permission of Hal Leonard LLC.

"O My God" (1975). Music and Lyrics by Sting. © 1983 G.M. Sumner. Administered by EMI Music Publishing Limited. All Rights Reserved. International Copyright Secured. Used by Permission. Reprinted by Permission of Hal Leonard LLC.

"Savage Beast" (1975). Music and Lyrics by Sting. Copyright © 1975 G.M. Sumner. Copyright Renewed. All Rights Administered by Sony/ATV Music Publishing LLC, 424 Church Street, Suite 1200, Nashville, TN 37219. International Copyright Secured. All Rights Reserved. Reprinted by Permission of Hal Leonard LLC.

"Visions of the Night" (1977). Music and Lyrics by Sting. © 1980 G.M. Sumner. Administered by EMI Music Publishing Limited. All Rights Reserved. International Copyright Secured. Used by Permission. Reprinted by Permission of Hal Leonard LLC.

"Born in the 50's" (1978). Music and Lyrics by Sting. © 1978 G.M. Sumner. Administered by EMI Music Publishing Limited. All Rights Reserved. International Copyright Secured. Used by Permission. Reprinted by Permission of Hal Leonard LLC.

"Hole in My Life" (1978). Music and Lyrics by Sting. © 1978 G.M. Sumner. Administered by EMI Music Publishing Limited. All Rights Reserved. International Copyright Secured. Used by Permission. Reprinted by Permission of Hal Leonard LLC.

"Secret Journey" (1978). Music and Lyrics by Sting. © 1981 G.M. Sumner. Administered by EMI Music Publishing Limited. All Rights Reserved. International Copyright Secured. Used by Permission. Reprinted by Permission of Hal Leonard LLC.

"So Lonely" (1978). Music and Lyrics by Sting. Copyright © 1978 G.M. Sumner. All Rights Administered by Sony/ATV Music Publishing LLC, 424 Church Street, Suite

Printed in Great Britain
by Amazon